The authors' manual : a complete and practical guide to all branches of literary work

Percy Russell

THE AUTHORS' MANUAL

THE

AUTHORS' MANUAL

A COMPLETE AND PRACTICAL GUIDE TO ALL
BRANCHES OF LITERARY WORK

BY

PERCY RUSSELL

AUTHOR OF "KING ALFRED," "AFTER THIS LIFE," "A JOURNEY TO
LAKE TAUPO, AND AUSTRALIAN TALES AND SKETCHES,"
"BUDDHA'S JEWEL," ETC.

FIFTH EDITION

LONDON

DIGBY & LONG, Publishers

18 BOUVERIE STREET, FLEET STREET, E.C.

PII
145
R8
'SS

THIS BOOK

IS

INSCRIBED LOVINGLY

TO MY WIFE,

WHO HAS INSPIRED AND SWEETENED

THE LABOURS OF MANY YEARS.

PART I.

THE NEWSPAPER AND PERIODICAL.

I. INTRODUCTORY.

AMONG the most marked features of the Victorian age are the development of the Press, the comparatively liberal education of the masses, and the increasing organisation of all forms of technological training. Technics, indeed, are quite a Nineteenth Century invention, as applied to the mass, and are, probably, the natural outcome of competitive examinations, and especially of the general introduction of what is called a scientific base to all, or almost all, regular vocations. The spread of national education, conjointly with the development of the newspaper and periodical to a position of unparalleled power and influence, has enormously multiplied readers, and the demand for writers in the many departments of literary work, is constantly increasing, and is likely to increase still.

Time was when comparatively few contemporary writers were ample to serve the national literary requirements ; and beyond these, outsiders could not hope for recognition unless through a death-made vacancy, or thanks to the possession of that very rare gift absolute genius, in which case, indeed, the recognition was commonly barren enough of any means for sustaining the physical existence of the gifted soul's gross environments; and, as in the instance of poor Samuel Butler, the author of *Hudibras*, it was too often

found that by the posthumous monument the writer's fate
was

in emblem shown,
He asked for bread, and he received a stone!

At all events, few lived by their pen, even in a miserable way, while many starved outright, and the rest generally kept body and soul together by soliciting help from
the patrons of the literature of the day, so that Johnson's well-known warning—

You know what ills the author's life assail,
Toil, envy, want, the patron and the jail,

is not in the least degree an exaggeration of "iron times"
that were absolutely fatal to writers who tried to make
crutches of their pens.

It could not well be otherwise; when we consider how
things were before the era of cheap printing and of universal popular education began.

Publishers could be counted on the fingers; booksellers
were few, and as late as even 1731, comparatively speaking,
in the history of the newspaper press, the total number of
periodicals then printed in this country was only 40; Scotland did not possess a single daily journal, and America,
now *the* special happy land of newspapers, had but *two*.

Readers were in proportion, and thus it came about that
practically hardly any writer could live by his pen alone.
Take an example—Chatterton.   His was by no means a
genius unappreciated by the few magazine editors of his
day, for editors, both then and now, were, and ever are, on
the look-out for ability, and especially for *original* power:
Chatterton's articles were accepted after his establishmer
in London, and some paid for in advance until he blocke
himself out of further paid work by his own success, an l
then came destitution, culminating in that ever memorab'e
tragedy.   In one word, gifted as he was with extraordinaiy

enius and a wonderful versatility, the limited periodical press of that day was inadequate to maintain him as a free-lance contributor. Now, all this has undergone a magical transformation. Publishers are now to be found in all the great cities of the United Kingdom, and in London they are legion. Booksellers and bookstalls are more numerous by far than probably all the important shops in the kingdom in the days of Chatterton, and the newspaper press has multiplied a thousand-fold, to say nothing of the hosts of periodicals of all kinds, and the enormously increased outlets for almost all forms of literary productiveness. In a word, letters—to use the old fashioned term—in their Protean forms, embracing, as they now do, every department of human activity, have come to by, at last, quite a recognised profession, industry, or business, and—outside the charmed region of the higher imagination, of which we shall speak at length in another place—the more the man of letters is one of business, too, the greater, and the more certain, will be his reward.

Half a century ago, there were only about a dozen daily papers in the United Kingdom. In 1889, the newspapers alone of the British Isles were, in round numbers, 2400, London engrossing about 500. This mighty change is due to several causes, among which the principal are the development of the electric telegraph, the marvellous improvements in, and cheapening of, printing, and the entire abolition of all the old taxes on knowledge. Then another cause exists, and is ever active in the extraordinary diffusion of education, and of the means for self-education, which are a thousand-fold beyond anything known prior to the great Victorian era.

It needs but a very simple sum in multiplication to find out roughly what must be the numbers of those employed to write the enormous mass of matter required to fill all the news-sheets of the day, and then have we not besides

trade journals and periodicals for over a hundred vocations?
Many of these are of considerable literary merit, and some
of the improved technical and industrial journals of the day
are, to the full, as ably written and edited as most books in
the reference class. Every year the standard of excellence
is rising in that portion of the press devoted to the productive work of the nation.

Then we have periodical literature, which is increasing
apace, and may be put down roughly at about a thousand
publications for the United Kingdom, of which the Metropolis
has over 650. These are of all kinds and prices, ranging
from one half-penny up to as much as six shillings each
copy, and even these do not exhaust the exceedingly
numerous channels outside newspapers waiting to be filled
with literary work, for there are annuals of many kinds, and
a number of miscellaneous publications, all of which involve
much practical literary work, and furnish pretty regular
employment to many writers.

Even now we have not quite exhausted our possible
avenues for literary work. The local press is everywhere
rapidly advancing into a position of new power, and of ever
increasing literary excellence. Papers that never used to indulge in "leaders" have them now, and other "features,"
while a mammoth press in the United States (about 15,000
strong), and in the Australasian and other British colonies,
offer fields for action to those who have properly qualified
themselves for distinction by industry and ability, and who
may finally emerge from the rank and file of anonymous
journalism. Everywhere the strong tendency of the day is
to multiply newspapers, and the newspaper, and after it the
periodical, constitute universal reading. More than this,
both newspaper and periodical are attaining to more influence and authority among us, and are more or less making
the contemporary world of men and women what we find
them   Another noticeable sign of the times is the increas-

ing disposition to bring the newspaper and the periodical sheets more and more to the level of the normal book. During the past decade, this process of elevating the literary standard of the best newspapers has been very conspicuous, and now scarcely a day passes but we can point to descriptive passages in ordinary newspaper reports, to paragraphs in leaders, and to writing generally, which is quite on a plane with good bookwork, and is, now and then, of very great excellence, indeed.

Then, as we all know, many of our great and most successful writers—men who now belong to literature—have graduated on the newspaper press.

The host of writers employed in producing the periodical reading matter of the nation is now much more considerable than many people imagine. Let it not be supposed for one moment that there is any extraordinary difficulty in obtaining admission to the ranks thereof. No barriers exist in the way of large fees as in the case of solicitors, or of severe examinations and prescribed courses of study. The one passport to getting work on the newspaper or the periodical press is MERIT. It is the possession of the requisite knowledge of how things are done that have to be done, the possession of real adaptability to circumstances, and especially the power of bringing all one's mental faculties to bear on a given subject exactly when wanted, and in exactly the manner required. There is no other profession in the world so liberal as this, or one requiring so little of the candidate for admission to its ranks, if only he give signs of possessing true literary ability. Such a one beginning at the lowest rung of the ladder may climb to the topmost eminence, and ultimately find, as many have done, that the newspaper press is indeed one of the great avenues in England to fame, wealth, and power.

But slight, comparatively speaking, as are the requirements demanded of every candidate for admission to a place

in the rank and file of the great army of journalists, these
requirements are in themselves absolutely essential, and
nothing can be more absurd than for any one to base his
ideas of entering the literary profession on Anthony Trollope's
famous remark about paper, pen, and ink being all that
were required by anyone embarking in this calling The
great novelist was but jesting, for he, of all men, knew well
what kind of preparatory training and of initial knowledge
was essential, and anyone who presumes to act on his oft-
quoted advice is almost certain to find that he is not wanted,
and had better turn to any trade rather than to that of
literature.

Thus much by way of introduction. We will now assume in
the succeeding chapters the case of an aspirant for literary
employment in journalism, who seeks to know how best to
equip himself for actual and practical work. The object of
the following pages is to impart, as far as is possible, only
what is absolutely essential to success in obtaining initial
work. All the rest must obviously depend on individual
effort, on individual industry, ability, and on the possession
of those moral qualities which are necessary aids to success
in any walk in life.

What may be conveniently called the technics of journalism may and can be imparted through the medium of a book,
and much which is the fruit of accumulated experiences
extending over many years, can be compressed into brief
advice. Thus an enormous amount of time and trouble
can be saved the aspirant, and he can be placed on
the threshold of the work he seeks in a state of pre-
paredness, and of capability, too, for much that is before
him.

This, then, is the object of the present work, and more
than this, of course, no book or teacher, school or college,
can accomplish.

II.—LITERARY TECHNICS.

A knowledge of the practical technics of every recognised calling in life, is essential for success therein. The earlier this knowledge can be acquired the better, and in most cases the difference between entering on work, well equipped with all that can be known respecting that work, minus actual experience, and having to pick up that knowledge as you go, must be great, indeed, and may well be a serious hindrance to advancement. Everywhere around us we find all the unmistakable signs of greater demands on candidates for *practical* work. Schools and colleges now train boys and men for special callings in special ways, and symptoms are not wanting that—as already is the case in some of the joint-stock banks—even the better class of clerkships will be barred to some by the necessity for passing first a more or less competitive examination. The times we live in are essentially practical, and even genius, unaided by commanding influence, is in these days almost certain to be thrust aside in the rush and press of life, unless it condescends to equip itself with some knowledge of the technics of the calling that it has taken up. Painters for example, have in these days to go through long courses of detail study and to learn very much that does not seem to the outsider exactly art, but only those who are thoroughly well grounded in what may be called the *Technique* of painting, can reasonably hope for success. The world in its work-a-day aspect is no respecter of genius, and genius untrained may surprise us by spasms of greatness, but will generally be found incapable of sustained exertion in the right direction.

Obviously, there is much that the aspirant for literary work may acquire with advantage before venturing to approach editors, publishers and others who keep the doors of the world of letters, and the more the tyro knows in *limine* the better evidently must be his prospect of obtaining early employment and of securing what is so important—a good start in his career.

No doubt there are books that teach composition and deal largely with the literary life, but what is wanted to aid the beginner is to put him in the way of being able to do what is sure to be wanted of him at first and showing him how to do it well. It is practical not theoretical work that is required of the young journalist, yet many attempt to enter the newspaper office who have not the least notion of the work before them and resemble the typical case of a would-be *Times* reporter, who having taken a long speech and being told to reduce it by one-half, asked innocently "*which* half?" and was promptly sent back to his native village.

In one word, there is very much knowledge that can be imparted by means of a book which can, if applied in the right way, save the young journalist enormous trouble and spare him from much painful disappointment and most materially help him onward.

One special advantage in attempting to impart Literary Technics through a book, is the complete parallelism that exists between the advice given and the things to be done. In a technical handbook on say chemistry, it may be well objected that the laboratory cannot be really explained properly on paper, but here the very illustrations given are exactly similar to the very work that the student will be called on to do!

Only those behind the literary scenes know how much the technical inaptitude, combined with the obstinacy, arising out of ignorance of the routine of practical literary work, has cost even great writers. I know an instance of an exceedingly able writer, a man of university training and a graduate too, who sacrificed a good post because he *would* not reduce his articles to a proper length, and he checked his career considerably because he imagined that papers should be accommodating as to space to their writers, and not the writers to the papers. Then again the writer who starts work knowing pretty well what is likely to be required of him, understanding the ways of the editorial room and of the printing office, knowing how matter is composed, read, and in what way proofs are to be corrected, and how that matter is "made up" into the newspaper, the periodical and the book, must necessarily be at a very great initial advantage, and is infinitely more likely to obtain work and also to move upward than the ordinary embryo writer.

I have seen many a young worker miss his chance of promotion to work of a higher character, simply because some trifling technical disability stood in his way. Thus the editor of a certain magazine of good standing being called abroad passed over several excellent writers who might very ably have filled his place, to install a young man who knew how to "make up" a paper, how to manipulate contributors' "copy," to calculate quantities, to fill up gaps as they might arise, &c.; all these being purely technical matters, but a knowledge of them enabled the young man in question to satisfactorily edit the magazine, and thus proved a great turning point in his literary career. It is perilous for any one, however gifted by natural ability, to rely on *that* alone or to imagine that—

The steep where Fame's proud temple shines afar—

can be stormed by genius untrained and crude as to its out-pourings. Perhaps one in a million may thus succeed, but, as a rule, a writer in these days will find it necessary to learn much that is purely outside the actual business of composition. In like manner a painter must know how to prepare and mix his colours.

The object here is to convey in a simple form a clear knowledge of what may be called the indispensable part of literary technics, and to show to the literary novice how professional work of all kinds, from the humble paragraph to the leader, and from the essay to the book, is really done. This includes the whole range of actual literary work and also a consideration of the kind of *working* knowledge essential to the professional writer, and how that knowledge can best be obtained, what books should be read, and how, in one word, the greatest possible literary effects may be produced with a minimum expenditure of time, that being the great requirement of nineteenth century days, and especially of the " new journalism". Among other points, the functions of the sub-editor will be found fully and practically set forth, and as many have risen from the sub-editorial rung of the literary ladder to authorship, a fully detailed account of the duties and work involved in that executive post is here given, as also an account of reporting, in all its many phases, reviewing, dramatic art, and sporting criticism, war correspondence, general descriptive work (for which the demand constantly increases), financial and trade journalism, and in one word, the whole art and mystery of practical journalism, together with all essential facts belonging to the business side of journalism and authorship.

In these days too, women—thanks to the higher class education of the day—engage in literary work of the periodical kind; thus Miss Frances Power Cobbe, the writer of many very able books, has been on the staff of the London *Echo*, and probably many women will now embark in current literature, and for these a course of technics such as is given in this volume must prove helpful.

We have no desire to make writers, nor even to stimulate those who have not a decided bias towards literature to engage therein. Those however, who have once discovered that they *can* write, will not accept the dictum that silence is golden. They will be articulate, and the purpose of this manual is to supply such with the ready means for quickly getting into practical work, and thus fully testing the real worth of their natural gifts.

The Second Part of the manual is devoted to the production of the Book, and embraces, therefore, a full account of Literature in its principal phases.

III.—PARAGRAPH WRITING.

The humble paragraph is the base, the unit, the initial of all newspaper work. Originally the early news-sheets consisted of nothing else, and probably the tyro will be first required to write paragraphs, and anyway, an ability to do this to any extent at the shortest notice, and on the barest hints, or to reduce a column to a paragraph, is essential.

There are technics of literature as of all other human operations, and, at the outset, let it be remembered that, however eloquent and original a writer may fancy himself to be in his style, or, for the matter of that, may really be, for practical work he will be found of little use unless he stoop to technical details, and acquire the art of writing exactly what is wanted for the occasion and neither more nor less. How many at the very outset of their journalistic career have come to grief, humiliating and signal, and have been saved from dismissal and disgrace by a kindly old journalist who, with a few dashes of his practised pen, has put awkward, slovenly, hopeless "copy," as it is called by the printers, straight; and, if not he, occasionally the good angel may be found in the much-suffering printer's reader—that functionary who does so much to improve style and obtains so little recognition from anyone except those who come into contact with him, and can recognise his sterling worth and almost invariable modesty. Let it be borne in mind that in these times much writing has to be done which is not ill-paid and is in constant demand, but which is generally scorned by men who think they have literary genius, but which work, faithfully and honestly executed, wins anyway the bread and cheese reward of literature, and may even lead in the end to far higher work.

One golden rule to be observed at all stages of the literary life is be honest and do your best. You who may have started work in private with poem, play, or novel must not suppose that a humble paragraph or headed article, the next stage thereto, need not be carefully written and that style is of little consequence. How much writing of this kind is marred or spoiled by bad arrangement, tautology, inelegant phraseology, and an absence of force !

Take a very simple illustration   Let us assume that a blue book giving statistics of factory accidents is given you to convert into a paragraph.   First, you are expected to reproduce *all* the essential points in the fewest possible and most elucidatory words.   How should this be done?   First ascertain the principal results, as shown in the summary figures, and having thus in a manner mastered the facts, it is your business to reproduce them in a readable manner.   All forms of practical literature come to this in the end.   Suppose the killed and wounded are numerous, and smart headlines are affected by the journal you are writing for, you might head the paragraph "Life and Limb Tax on Manufactures," and then you would begin by stating that *so* many persons had been killed and maimed during such a period, next you would analyse the different *kinds* of accidents, and point out [citing the figures] where the *principal* dangers lay. By cultivating an orderly method of performing tasks of this kind it will be found that the work will, in a manner, clothe itself with fitting words, and the *habit* once acquired of dealing clearly with subjects of this type, becomes at last a second nature. This is the secret of the succinct summaries of news that most of the morning papers now give, generally models of perspicuity, in which each word goes straight to the mark, which is to inform the reader in the easiest and most rapid way possible as to the salient items of news in that particular issue.

I am not here considering brilliant and eloquent writing, but that which is eminently practical and plain, meant to be "understanded of the people," and which should, therefore, be wholly clear of all ambiguity, tautology, or inaccuracy of any kind. The great aim of every writer should be to employ only such words as can be readily understood by his readers, and, as far as possible, special rather than general terms should be used. Professor Campbell happily illustrates this point by the following example. In the splendid song of Moses, prompted by the miraculous passage of the Israelites through the Red Sea, the inspired writer exclaims (Exodus, chap. xv., ver. 10)—

> Thou didst blow with Thy wind, the sea covered them,
> They sank as *lead* in the mighty waters.

This is very much more effective than—

> They *fell* as *metal* in the mighty waters.

The idea is just the same, but the use of *special*, in place of *general*, terms, makes all the difference in the effect produced. This point will be even more accentuated if we substitute for the Divine words—

> " Consider the lilies, how they grow,"

obviously a clear statement made in *specific* terms, the following version, couched in *general* terms only—

> Consider the flowers, how they gradually increase in size.

This example may appear forced, but very much amateur writing is of this kind, and hence is altogether ineffective. It is said that a member of the House of Commons once asked a witness appearing before a Parliamentary Committee—"Will you have the goodness to state, for the information of the Committee, what is the ordinary beverage of the industrial population in your locality?" What the honourable gentleman should have asked was—"What do working men in your part of the country usually drink?" These are points as to style which are really of importance to the young writer who is usually prone to drop into vague and redundant expressions, as in the case of one who wrote —"The night, now far advanced, was brilliantly bright with radiance of astral and lunar effulgence," instead of saying, "The night was far gone, and the moon and stars were shining brightly". Paragraphists are very much given to this sort of florid writing, which borders closely on nonsense, and long persisted in, ruins the style of the writer. A daily London journal, wanting to tell us that miners live, on an average, 27 years, did it thus—"The miners' average tenure of life is a brief twenty-seven summers". Another writer, in the same journal, told us of a miners' procession he was describing, that "two helmets, towering over their heads, betokened that the eye of the Law was upon them". This, of course, borders on the ludicrous, but it indicates how easily a craze for fine writing may lead the writer into absurdity. It may be retorted here that these instances occurring in published work indicate that a certain degree of slovenly writing *is* tolerated within the sacred precincts of the realms of journalism. True, but the writers did not *enter* through *such credentials*, and such work, so far as it goes, does *not help them on*, but rather *keeps them back*, and editors, sub-editors, press-readers, and managers are all more or less aware of the increasing need there is for culti-vating a pure, perspicuous style; and in the ever-increasing competition of rival publications, this is likely to be more and more a desideratum. Often these may appear but little things, but let the young writer rely on this, that the more he writes in a plain, forcible, intelligible way, the more likely by far is he to be advanced, and to have a better class of work given him.

Articles—really enlarged paragraphs—are now required

on a variety of persons, places, and things, and the young writer, when he has to provide these, should refer, if in doubt or ignorance, to an encyclopædia, and even if he thinks he knows the subjects well, such reference is wise. It will frequently prove suggestive, and likewise, when instructed to visit some place, or, perhaps, to describe some new invention, it is well to look up any references within reach that may bear on the subject. This will, if habitually done, impart the habits of taking up the *allusive* side of subjects, and the writer who does this will not only acquire great facility of composition, but he will learn to illuminate and illustrate what he writes by just those hints and references to cognate matters that constitute such a charm in descriptive work.

It is highly important for the writer who would be successful to have a wide and good vocabulary. Poverty of language is a fatal obstacle to the career of any aspirant for literary work, and on the other hand, attempts at out-of-the-way archaic expressions are exceedingly objectionable. Generally prefer plain, simple English words to those of classical or foreign origin, but then this must greatly depend on *what* you are writing about. If, for example, the subject was Science, "the impenetrability of matter" would be fitting, but "a mother's love" is infinitely better as a phrase than "maternal attachment," and in like manner "happiness" is better than "felicity". One of the best models for a plain forcible English style is Cobbett, who is almost wholly Anglo-Saxon and always to the purpose in every word he writes. At the same time, the best writer will necessarily use each form in its proper and fitting place if he has at command ALL the resources of his language, and has learned how to use these to the best advantage.

Language, be it borne in mind, is more than a mere matter of grammar or rhetoric; it has its moral side and its undying relation to our spiritual nature. It has been well said that the vastness of the power inherent in language should make us feel the responsibility of cultivating and guarding it from degradation and corruption. How degradation of language and the lowering of the tone of morality go together is well known, and has been repeatedly illustrated in history. Thus the language was vitiated in the days of Charles the Second, when the debased and wicked disowned the common language of the land and indulged in a far-fetched vocabulary of their own. It has ever been so, and words which serve the good and pure, are to the base and sensual exceedingly obnoxious. as such words are associated with goodness. Hence it has been well said that a man should love and venerate his native tongue as the first of his benefactors, as the awakener and stirrer of all his thoughts, the frame and mould of his spiritual being . . the mirror in which he sees his own nature . . . as the image in which the wisdom of God has chosen to reveal Himself. Thus is it that most truly, accuracy of style is akin to veracity of mind, and language is, indeed, a part of every man's character. Thus, too, was it that the poet felt, who declared—

> We must be free or die, who speak the tongue
> That Shakespeare spoke

If this be so, how careful should the writer be in the initial stages of his vocation, to cultivate a good and pure style, and to avoid, above all things, the great fault of employing *words* without *thoughts* or *feelings* to correspond with them. Then, too, there is the fault of employing words of force out of all proportion to the occasion. A thing simply pleasing is called " delightful," " exquisite," or " perfectly charming," or something a little unpleasant or unsightly, is written of as " dreadful," " horrible," or " awful ". All this is the very immorality of speech, and leads directly to impotence and futility, for when the occasion *does* arise for the use of strong words, the writer finds he has exhausted his vocabulary and descends into what may be called the feeble, forcible style as a result. These are all important considerations and should be laid to heart by the young writer. Except when there is good reason for employing foreign or Latin words, it is decidedly best to keep to idiomatic Saxon English. Thus it is only that a clear and powerful style may be gradually formed, and then as the writer advances, his range will widen and he will find himself, little by little, drawing on the vast stores of the 40,000 words of which the language consists, and whereof quite 23,000 are of Saxon origin.

It often happens, too, that the young writer is embarrassed by the fact, owing to the copiousness of our language, that several words will often present themselves which, to the hasty and superficial, appear equally good and appropriate, although in reality there is a great difference among them. To explain this more clearly, I will take an illustration from Shakespeare, emphatically *the* master of English composition. The words *apt* and *fit* seem to have little difference between them, but *apt* has an *active* and *fit* a *passive* significance, and so in *Hamlet* the poisoner says "hands *apt*, drugs *fit*," and Wordsworth, in a beautiful passage, speaks of our hearts as

> More *apt* to sympathise
> With heaven, our souls more *fit* for future glory.

It is on these nice shades that the difference between good and bad writing generally depends, and the young writer, by awakening his perceptions early to such points, will certainly form a *habit* in his composition, which practice will quicken into an instinct to guide him aright in even the most rapid composition.

I need hardly say that *slang* in all forms should be

avoided Of course, it is different in certain classes of descriptive work, where it may be even necessary, but do not "work up" slang into *ordinary* composition, and avoid especially the silly and slovenly practice of clipping words into what seem smart brevities, but which are in reality more often silly inanities.

I affirm that right, pure and thorough thought lies at the bottom of all good writing, and verbal levity will never lead to great work.

To acquire a knowledge of the right use of words read the best poetry—there you will assuredly find the best words in the right places; while a work like Roget's *Thesaurus*, if repeatedly consulted, should greatly increase and improve the stock and choice of the young writer's words. The subject of Books, what to read and how to read, will be found fully dealt with under other sections.

IV.—REPORTING.

Reporting and paragraph-writing lie at the very base of practical journalism. Too often shorthand, not always of a very advanced character, is the principal equipment of the young candidate for reportorial employment. Shorthand, however, is now quite a *sine qua non*, although until recently a few police court reporters still managed to do their work well with the aid of abbreviated longhand. Shorthand cannot be learned too early, and *pari passu* with it must be carefully cultivated a clear-headed way of attending to what is reported and a ready and graphic style of writing out the "notes" into good, intelligible English. Many imagine that to follow a speaker pretty closely and to find (as is not always the case) the shorthand fairly legible afterwards, is to be a capable reporter, but such a qualification alone would not keep its possessor long engaged on a daily or even a weekly journal where the duties of the reporter are really multifarious, and unless the reporter be steady, strong, honest, active, good-tempered, and quick of hearing, as well as of apprehension, he will very quickly earn and receive his dismissal. No successful reporter can possibly be slow and stupid. In the first place, swift decision and sound judgment are constantly being called into requisition. Very often with rapid speakers he will have to summarise in short-hand as he goes, always a difficult but often a necessary thing with speakers of rapid articulation, and then, be it remembered, that in the reporting style of any shorthand a large number of the words are simply *indicated*, not actually written.

Public company reporting is, in some respects perhaps, the easiest of all, and with the vast increase of joint-stock undertakings and the multiplying of class organs, there is ever more and more of this work to do. Usually the reporter finds his seat at the board table opposite the chairman and directors, with the shareholders behind him. This is the most favourable of all positions. The chairman's speech invariably has to be given either entire or so as to preserve all the substance, and this done, the rest is not so difficult. Reporters of the "raw" type will find, in general, much consideration shown them, if they preserve their presence of mind and courteously ask for necessary information that they have failed to obtain. When, for example, a shareholder in the body of the building is "up," the reporter may slip a piece of paper across the table to the secretary, inquiring the name of the speaker, and he will receive back the pencilled information, or, perhaps, "we don't know," in which case the reporter must in writing out say simply "a shareholder said so and so," or "urged this or that". Let the reporter, as I said above, be honest and beware of writing out a single word that he is not *sure was uttered*. The golden rule for the reporter is to err, if err he must, by *omission*, never by *commission*. There must be no clever guesses, or dashes at the meaning   What he cannot read of his notes he must leave alone, for if *ever* he ventures to *guess*, although he may for a time escape detection, he will most certainly, sooner or later, write something which will get into print and be the infallible cause of his utter confusion and probable ruin as a reporter.

Much reporting has to be done under extraordinary difficulties.   Sometimes the reporter is in a crowded room, where either no provision has been made for his accommodation, or where he is elbowed by the audience, and where he has to follow a speaker amid an uproar enough to distract his thoughts of itself, while his pencil goes staggering about, and he, perhaps, loses the thread of the discourse altogether ; or, as frequently happens, an excited and nervous speaker has been delivering himself of fragmentary sentences to the horror of the reporter, not one of which is properly composed or even grammatical, although, to the ear at the time, they may *sound* very eloquent, indeed !

This is very hard, no doubt, but it often occurs, and the young reporter may have to go to a bank meeting in the morning, a philanthropic society's gathering in the afternoon, and to a public dinner in the evening, and, possibly, be expected to get all his "copy" out before midnight !

The verbal snares, the awful pitfalls that lie in the way of the young reporter, are legion. Indistinct speaking, defective hearing on his part, some sudden confusion of ideas, and generally a thousand and one sources of error, more or less serious, beset the way   Still all these can be overcome, and once the beginner is able to "take" a legible "note," and reproduce it in plain English, he will find all comparatively smooth   Much cleverness and adaptability are imperative   As a rule, not a tithe of what is said can be reproduced for publication. There would not be room. I remember a meeting of the Peninsular and Oriental Steam Navigation Company, which lasted for several hours, and had all the speeches delivered thereat been reported verbatim, they would have almost filled a whole newspaper. The older and experienced reporters will generally be seen at protracted meetings writing out the earlier portion of their notes, and yet intently watchful, and ever ready, directly some prolix speaker says aught of importance, to commit it to their notes. Sometimes a speech of twenty minutes' duration must go into the space of ten lines, or even less, so that the reporter who cannot *summarise* and *condense*, and, in a word, when required, give the pith of what is said, in a sentence, is simply useless, in a reporting sense, and cannot reasonably expect to succeed. The great point in summarising is to keep strictly to what the speaker *really said*, and, as far as possible, to use only his words.

Law-reporting is not, as a rule, so difficult, for the proceedings are usually conducted with great deliberation, and the judge has to take his notes generally in longhand.

The highest work in the profession is that of Parliamentary reporting, which is carried out by a staff of some six, seven, or eight men—one of whom is the chief. All the London morning journals and a few others have each their staff, who are told off for the gallery. Each reporter has what is called a "turn" of varying duration from five to even thirty minutes, and, after his turn, he immediately repairs to the reporters' room to write out his notes. In these days, vast improvements have occurred in Parliamentary reporting, which once was a very trying form of work, but is now to those, properly qualified, the most attractive form of reporting, but for the drawback of the late hours entailed. As each man after his "turn" retires to the writing-room, his relief is taking notes, and thus the work goes on uninterruptedly, so that part of the debates are in print before they are concluded. Every Parliamentary reporter must be absolutely an expert shorthand writer, but he must

3

have a large amount of general information too, a good working knowledge of history, of politics, of political economy,
rudimental any way, of languages, to some extent, and
much more, for he cannot possibly write out his matter properly if he is totally in the dark as to what it is all about,
and, very curiously, although quite naturally, it is always the
case that what is not understood is likely to be imperfectly
heard, while it is what he does *not* understand that the
reporter needs to take down with perfect accuracy As a
rule, Parliamentary reporters have had previously much experience, and have proved themselves to be possessed of the
proper qualifications The pay is about six guineas a week.
The *status* is good, and those who excel may qualify for
the higher function of a summary writer, or may become
sub editors, or even editors. Some men remain in the
gallery until old age compels retirement. There are, by the
way, two kinds of Parliamentary reporters—those engaged
for the year, and those for the session only. The former
are employed in other work during the intervals, and especially in reporting members who, during the recess, address
their constituents, or, in many other ways, which as often do
not involve taking speeches down at all—a welcome relief and
a grateful change—for the gallery work, at its best, is hard.

The Parliamentary reporter is usually and rightly held to
have reached the top of the profession, while below him
stands the general reporter, who may be, and often is, his
equal, but who is practically the all-round man of the newspaper, invaluable to weeklies, and especially to journals when
the finances do not admit of engaging a complete staff.
On the provincial journal the general reporter is frequently
the all-providing genius, and if smart, may easily rise to be
editor, and thence advance rapidly ; and a man who keeps
an untarnished and honourable record behind him of good
work honestly and faithfully done, may reasonably expect
to graduate constantly upwards.

The importance of paragraphing may be inferred from the fact that a great portion of the ordinary newspaper consists of paragraphs, great and small. These range from a line or two to what is really a fair sized article, and involve every kind of newspaper writing, for some paragraphs are really good examples of original work. Many are supplied by writers outside the salaried staff, and these casual contributors are termed "liners". Formerly they were known as "penny-a-liners," but now the rate of pay is three half-pence a line and in some cases two pence, and although this somewhat humble department of journalistic labour is held in slight esteem by the ambitious literary aspirant, much money may be made by doing this kind of work, although the tendency now is for journals to have larger staffs and this, of course, leaves less space to be filled from outside To do this kind of work a man must be out and about and have his eyes and ears always open.

Here, as in all kinds of literary work, *style* tells, combined with accuracy, for unfortunately some liners will draw on imagination for facts, and often thus for a temporary gain destroy their reputation and eventually reduce, if not close up, the sources open to their pens It was "lining" that originally led to a fustian style of composition wherein a spade became "an agricultural implement," fire "the devouring element," and the like, and although much of this sort of thing has now grown obsolete, much remains to be desired in the way of paragraph composition. To take a case in point· some years ago a crack-brained starveling fired a revolver in the way of the royal carriage at Windsor and was promptly arrested, no harm being done, and probably none was intended. Such an incident might and should have been dismissed in a couple of lines, but a popular London paper chose to encourage the descriptive liners to "work up" the trumpery incident, and one reporter fastening on the wearing apparel of the culprit, told

his readers that " the principal part of his attire consisted
of an overcoat reaching down to his knees   Once upon
a time the cloth had been a dark blue colour, but is
now, by constant wear, not only deprived of the nap
it once possessed, but of any distinct and distinguish-
able colour. . . .   Its seams were threadbare, the binding
ragged, and the button-holes frayed to a degree.   This
garment he wore — hiding whatever under-vestment he
possessed—closely buttoned around the body, but displaying
the unwashed collar which encircled his neck, or the aged
scarf—once black—which half hid the nervous twitchings of
his throat."   There was much made of this twaddle, and
another writer attacked the subject of the bullet which he
actually declared " by the noise it made appeared to travel
slowly," and much more of the same stuff appeared, while an
" expert " in gunnery, according to one journal, went down
to trace the exact course of the missile which it was gravely
and dogmatically pronounced must have gone behind or
before the body of the carriage (!)   In addition to this,
the miserable wretch who had thus attracted universal
attention to himself, was announced in large type to be a
regicide, and thus a matter that deserved only a brief
paragraph, was whipped up into an intolerable quantity of
verbal froth.   Let the young journalist avoid all work of
this kind which leads neither to honour nor profit, and
eventually only provokes well merited ridicule.   The Press
of late has evinced a lamentable disposition to " pile the
agony" as the phrase runs on every occasion, and as newspapers are universally read, a vicious stimulus is given to
the morbid minded among the lower and imperfectly
educated classes   The late Lord Lytton, a shrewd
observer of the times, wrote years ago on this very subject
words of warning.   "It may be observed," he said, " that
there are certain years in which in a civilised country some
particular crime comes into vogue.   It flares its season and

then burns out. . . . Almost every year there is one crime
peculiar to it ; a sort of annual which overruns the country,
but does not bloom again. Unquestionably the Press has
a great deal to do with these epidemics. Let a newspaper
once give an account of some out of the way atrocity that
has the charm of being novel, and certain depraved minds
fasten on it like leeches. They brood over and revolve it ;
the idea grows up a horrid phantasmagorian monomania,
and all of a sudden the one seed sown in a hundred places
by the leaden type, springs up into foul flowering. But if the
first reported abnormal crime has been attended with
impunity, how much more does the imitative faculty cling
to it !"

Truly these words suggest strongly that the writing in a
thousand newspapers on the earlier Whitechapel atrocities
may have urged the murderer on to perpetrate those
additional undiscovered murders which remain a blot on
and a reproach to our civilization.

But enough of this. A hint is sufficient, and there is ample
room for the reporter who will sedulously avoid all vicious
appeals to the many-headed, and who will write of things
utterly abominable in such a manner as to deprive them of
everything that can fascinate even the depraved, and thus
present vice and crime before his readers in all their naked
repulsiveness, entirely destitute of that unholy glamour
imparted by so many superficial, flippant, and thoughtless
writers.

It will be perceived from the foregoing that the ordinary
work of the reporter is varied, arduous, and responsible ; but
it is an admirable training-school for the higher work of
journalism, and it leads to a thousand avenues of literary
influence and usefulness.

In regard to shorthand, I believe that several forms of
stenography may be recommended. Personally, I prefer
phonography, but phonetic spelling, which it was originally

designed to introduce, is an abomination to every really cultured mind, and would inflict frightful loss to philology. It must be observed that Pitman's shorthand is quite or nearly useless for verbatim reporting in its *early* stages. It is only in its *developed* and advanced forms, as perfected by such masters of the art as Mr. T. A. Reed, that it can be safely used to take a rapid speaker verbatim. The forms of the sixpenny instruction book do not, I think, suffice for any great speed. The beginner should not lose heart when he finds, as he must in practice, that a reportorial style cannot be acquired in a few months. There is no royal road to excellence here, and nothing but patience, perseverance and great practice will enable the novice to attain to a *fluent* phonographic style which can alone yield perfectly trustworthy results in the shape of " notes " which are really legible.

V.—LEADERS AND LEADER WRITERS.

The leader is said to derive its name from the fact that it is a *leaded* article—*i e.*, between the lines a *lead* is placed, so that the bottom of the type of one line shall not touch the head of the next line. Any way, originally, newspapers, as shown in another section, did not contain aught beyond *news*, but when comments began to appear, it was thought well to make them prominent by spacing out the lines, hence the term *leaders*. Now it is undoubtedly the leading or guiding part of the journal, and for the supply of these a vast quantity of original writing has to be done; for this work, in the case of the best papers, the remuneration is good.

There are here, as in most other departments of press work, many grades. Some leader writers, indeed, rank high in literature, while others, as those who " do " the weekly article for some local news-sheet, are but the lowest journeymen workers of the press.

There is, however, in 'l quarters a marked disposition on

the part of newspaper proprietors to raise the quality of leading articles wherever this can be done, and it is noticeable
that many trade journals now employ writers of a far higher
class than of old, so that altogether the out-look generally for
the leader writer is decidedly encouraging

There are, first of all, the general leader writers, men who
claim to be able to write effectively on *any* topic under the
sun.   These writers are highly useful to and much valued by
the minor journals, where funds are limited, but they rarely
obtain any of the higher class of work, except in some
special department they may have made their own.

On the best journals sub-division of labour is the guiding
principle, and, while one writer is retained for politics,
another is confined to social subjects, and so on ; while
politics may be divided into home, colonial, and foreign

On the London morning papers the staff of leader writers
has to call each morning except, perhaps, Saturday, when
they receive their subjects, this being the great function of
the editor to settle, and without much trouble the topics are
all fixed on, and the writers separate, each to perform his
task in the best way he can.   Most of the "copy" is ready
by the early evening, and then comes into the hands of the
editor or sub-editor, but during Parliament the political
leader writer may have to attend the House, or, any way,
the office, and a political leader is often composed at the
last moment, and deals with some subject before the House
on the morning of the issue in which it appears.   The readiness and cleverness of the practised leader writer are at
their best remarkable.   It is said in illustration of this, that
on one occasion when an editor replied to a certain leader
writer's query as to what he had to give him for subject
with the one word, "nothing," the gentleman thus curtly
dismissed soon returned with an article which was in prose,
a good deal better than Rochester's famous verses on this
seemingly hopeless theme.   Besides "leaders" there are

shorter original articles of the editorial type to be written, and finally, "notes," all of which belong to the same category Examples of all three types may be found in the London *Globe*, which, in what is quaintly termed its "turnover," exhibits a type, too, of the best kind of newspaper essay: one of these, under some interesting title, appears in the *Globe* daily, always occupying the last column on the first page and turning over into the next page. Leaders always come in specially wide margined proofs to the editor or sub-editor, and frequently are greatly chopped about. Here, indeed, comes in the great art of editing, and in this the late Delane of the *Times* was said to excel. A typical leader should consist of just *three* paragraphs, the *first* setting forth the subject in as attractive and incisive a way as possible, the *second* advancing the various arguments for or against, and the *third* clinching the whole, or, as is often found best, leaving the question still open for further development. It is well to remark here that a great fault of young leader writers at first is too great a disposition to be final, and not to leave an opening for occasions that may arise for modifying the views advanced. Many of the best leaders are quite of a composite type. It is said that *three* writers have been separately instructed each to do his *best* with a certain subject, and when all three articles came up in proof, a *new* article was made out of the best passages from each! This, however, is a costly and elaborate form of editing special to the "Thunderer" alone

The leaders constitute to a great extent, if not altogether, the *power* of the Press. As in the case of the preacher from the pulpit there is virtually no reply to the leader writer, who now occupies very much the same influential position once exclusively held by the pulpit itself.

Among some of the results of this is the propagation of much mischievous fallacy in the name of party or class

interests, and then some reckless writers, urged on to make
their journal as saleable as possible, frequently indite matter
whereto few writers would like to affix their name, as, for
example, when a writer in a great morning daily made
hideous fun about one of the most appalling subjects that
can engage human thought—the end of the world—and
joked about this "planet bumping up against a comet and
vanishing, squib-like, in a flash of fire". This is the very
degradation of writing, and should be avoided by all who
seek to attain to real excellence. As things now are,
however, to the majority of people the daily paper is a sort
of Scripture, and the leader writer a Pope who not only
claims to be but is infallible.

I know that some will immediately object that it is no
part of the duty of the Press to preach morality or to en-
force the fundamental principles of religion, but then I
reply that the Press has no right to do all it can to systematically *debase* the one and to bring contempt on the other.
Here, indeed, comes in the great question of liberty *versus*
license, and decidedly many sections of the popular press
have done very much evil through systematically sneering
at Christian theories and opinions. This need not be
noticed here, but for the fact that every day over a thousand leaders appear, which go far to form the opinions of
the nation, and exercise a far more determining influence,
being repeated six times a week, than the weekly sermon,
especially as church attendance—and no wonder—is so
rapidly declining.

But to return to our subject. Leader writers are rather
a class by themselves. To a great extent the art of the
leader writer is to say but little that is positive (I refer to
political and partizan leaders), and to envelop what is said
in a nebulous mass of smoothly written sentences, running
but a little over the head of the average intelligent reader,
thus delicately flattering him, and leaving an opportunity to

revert again to the topic.   It does not do to be too
definite.

Too many young writers fancy that a leader is but a
brief essay, and occasionally, especially now, there will be
seen in the leader page of the newspaper articles of this
type, but these are not *leaders* proper, and are really literary
exercises put in to gratify the general reader, and because
there chances to be space to fill.   Frequently the tyro will
produce a paper using up enough matter to last a professional leader writer for a dozen turns, and I remember
that one writer of this type having a topic given him
said naively, "Oh! yes, I know that subject and have
threshed it out to a final issue.   I'll polish it off finely."
"But, you mustn't shut it up like that, we shall have to
revert to it again and again   Don't close it whatever you
do."   "Why, isn't that what you want?"   And when gently
reminded that this particular subject was of the hardy
annual sort, the gentleman loudly complained that a journal
which existed by keeping subjects perpetually open, was
simply propagating ignorance, and he for one would be no
party to such a course!

This is a specimen of the impracticable writer.   Another
I knew used to make such a fuss when he found how his
leaders were trimmed and pruned into newspaper shape,
that he was dismissed, although his matter on certain subjects was exceedingly valuable, and a far inferior writer took
his place   In the newspaper office it is even found that the
practical adaptable writer who keeps his common sense
about him, frequently ousts the man of talent, of brilliant
ability, and very often even poor genius has to retreat
fuming at the absurd density of editors, who will not
place their columns absolutely at its changeful and often
eccentric disposition.

To be a good leader writer, however, a versatile and
fact-stored mind is essential, and the more that mind is

enriched by multifarious reading the better. The leader writer is often *ex necessitate rei* the adroit plagiarist, and any way all is prey that can be caught up in the glittering intellectual web he spins. I would, however, earnestly warn young writers not to borrow from other leaders. Let them " work up " their reading wherever it can be made to tell. Sometimes the essence of a chapter in some book, cognate to the subject, may be tagged on in a crisp summary to a leader, or worked up in its very texture ; but do not in any way or case copy from contemporary printed matter. First of all, it is not honest ; and secondly, it will probably be detected and entail disgrace, and, perhaps, the loss of work.

Printers are discerning men, and as severe on shams as Carlyle. I knew a case of an editor who regularly " worked up " the original part of a cleverly written contemporary which came out just in time for his purpose. A cruel compositor, to test the matter, stole the paper while the editor's attention was engaged, and he being really afraid to openly send a boy for the paper in question, was at his wit's end, and that week his original writing was singularly lifeless and bald.

To write an ordinary leader is not really difficult. Let the tyro recollect that here practice is all in all and at first his employers will not expect him to do anything wonderful. The beginning is trying to the beginner, but it never troubles the old pressman. Until the tyro acquires confidence and has had practice, he may resort to the common expedient of opening his article with a pithy saying, a proverb, a very brief anecdote, an historic allusion or the like. Thus, taking care, of course, that the citation is in harmony with the subject, he may begin by remarking, that " as Carlyle says," or " we believe," " Sydney Smith has a story," or " as that scathing but unhappy satirist, Dean Swift, once declared," or, perhaps, like this,

"Voltaire in one of his most satirical moods asserts "— obviously these and thousands of other cut and dried phrases form quite a ready stock-in-trade for professional writers, and once the article is started, it will be found that, as Lucian says in one of his famous dialogues, "The beginning is indeed half of the whole".

So soon as the tyro has had a little practice let him cultivate the allusive art. It always adds a special charm, and is relished by all classes of readers. If you frequently remind your readers of the pleasant things they have read you make them *pro tanto* pleased with *you* Thus a writer will perhaps say "he was a type of the habitual, but at bottom good-hearted grumbler like Boythorne in *Bleak House*," or "she had that inner intellectual beauty which illuminates a plain face, as in *Jane Eyre*". These are but rough examples, yet they may indicate the way wherein a well read writer may judiciously powder his work with tiny brilliants in the form of apt allusions ; and after a time the writer may find himself adding to these from his own previously unsuspected originality. All work of this kind must be imitative. Note in the lives of all great artists, how at first they had to *copy*, *copy*, and do nothing but *copy* the antique. In his early days the young writer will probably have to adapt the work of others. Much of the matter in many publications is made up by converting into new "copy" various items that have already appeared in print, and very often this is taken over without acknowledgment. Then it must be "worked up" anew, and the general sense preserved, but made to run, so to speak, through a new verbal mould Facts, once published, are obviously open to all, and often a paper needs the facts that appear in a contemporary, but does not choose to adopt the words. When, however, facts and words are both taken over, even though partially altered, due acknowledgment of the service should always be made.

VI.—EDITORIAL.

Successful editing is obviously the higher function of journalism. The editor often rises from a "sub," and sometimes he is the only man on the paper who never writes! Tact, sound judgment, a most rapid and clear way of surveying things in general, and of solving complex problems almost instantaneously, are among the qualities involved. On the morning paper the editor does not usually appear on the scene until the day is advanced, but thence until past midnight, he is kept on the stretch, and among his special functions he must focus in his mind all the views of the hour at home and abroad, and be alert to treat all salient topics in accordance with the tone of his journal. He it is who instructs the leader writers and gives them the useful hints, and he it is who has to deal with the correspondence—always a trying part of the duty—and in one word his time is so occupied in overlooking what others are doing, and in generally grasping the whole of the coming issue, that he has not much time to write himself, and, in point of fact, his literary work is generally restricted to pruning and modifying the articles that come before him in proof. In many cases the editor acts in part as sub-editor, and the "sub" as editor. No beginner in journalism can by the wildest stretch of fancy be supposed to be even near an editorial chair, but the sub-editorial seat very frequently falls early to the lot of a clever and industrious aspirant, and it will be much more practical if we deal here with this branch of editing. The editorial grows naturally out of the sub-editorial, and the former does not call for special treatment in a book of this kind.

The sub-editor is the practical executive of the editor. He sees that the paper, or publication, is properly arranged for press, and that all the desires of his chief have been properly carried out. He is an all-important functionary and, excepting the choice of leaders, etc., he arranges the whole literary contents of the issue, and in truth in some cases writes the leaders in part or whole. On the great papers there are several engaged on this work, one being the chief who makes the rest assist him. Should the beginner get on a daily paper he will have to assist at first in sub-editing. He will probably have reports given him to reduce, articles to summarise, statistics to bring into popular form, and a great variety of work of this kind. If he be on an evening journal, columns of matter will be assigned to him to reduce. In all these tasks the great points are to be quick, accurate, and honest ; that is not to *shirk* the trouble of finding out the meaning of some long paragraph, and boiling it down into what one of Dickens' plain speaking characters calls "a mouthful of English". Let us take a working example. The following is a piece of telegraphic foreign intelligence. It runs—

CONDITION OF CRETE.

DISARMING THE CHRISTIANS.

(FROM OUR CORRESPONDENT.)

CANEA, Thursday.

Chakir Pasha is disarming the Christians. Yesterday three mules laden with guns were brought to Canea from the provinces of Kydonia and Kissamo. Simultaneously fifteen Christians and yesterday eight more from Apokorona were brought to Canea in chains. A battalion has left for Sphakia.

The soldiers are committing fresh excesses. A Christian, named Maralaky, has been killed at Klima, in the district of Apokorona.

An official paper containing thanks for the Sultan's firman is demanded from the Cretans by the Turkish authorities.

The Cretan chiefs in Athens, I am informed, are organizing a general rising in the island, which will be most welcome to the inhabitants.

(THROUGH REUTER'S AGENCY.)

ATHENS, DEC. 12.

The Cretans resident here express great indignation at the terms of the Sultan's firman.

It may be summarised thus : " We learn from a Canea source that Christians are being brought into that town in chains. The Cretan chiefs in Athens are stated to be organising a rising. The Turks are committing great atrocities in the island, and disarming the Christians." This may serve as a type.

We will, however, suppose that our beginner has to gain experience on a weekly publication, which is very largely made up out of the daily morning and evening journals, and we will further suppose that the weekly aims at giving its readers the essence of all that appears from day to day. I will now take one day's turn on such a journal where the " sub " has no assistant.

The base of the work lies in the morning London papers. These I should lay flat one on the other, and armed with scissors, cut out *all* the important news items. This does not appear anything out of the way, but in half-an-hour five or six daily papers have been skeletonised and all these cuttings gummed or pasted on to sheets of white paper of uniform size, leaving a good margin. Some of the cuttings gummed on are over a column, and the *continuation* must be gummed on to the bottom and pains taken not to attach *two different articles*. Place only *one* item in each slip, no matter if it be only a line long. Clumsy amateurs think to save paper, time, and trouble, by filling in, but this leads to future worry and it may be, mistakes, and by confining each slip to *one* subject any item can be *withdrawn* without affecting the rest. Each cutting has to be "edited," that is, it must be shaped for its new place as though it had been written expressly therefor, one example will be worth much precept. In the *Daily News* of Dec. 13, 1889, appeared the following paragraph—

"DEATH OF MRS. BEESLY.—Many of our readers will observe with great regret the announcement in our obituary column to-day of the death of Mrs. Beesly, wife of Professor E. S. Beesly. She was an ardent supporter of the Irish Nationalists, and was the authoress of the much-sung English version of the "Wearing of the Green". Mrs. Beesly, who was only forty-nine years of age, was the youngest daughter of the late Mr. Justice Crompton. She had taken an active part in political work in London for some years past and was president of the Women's Liberal Association of Paddington."

Now the way this would be manipulated for "copy" when pasted on a slip with a margin, might be as follows :— Draw the pen through the words "many of our readers will observe with great regret the announcement in our obituary column to-day of—" and write in the margin "We regret to record". After the word "Beesly" change the period to a comma, and strike out the words "she was". It will then read —"We regret to record the death of Mrs. Beesly, an ardent supporter of the Irish Nationalists". Strike out "and was" and it will read "the authoress of"; strike out "much-sung" and it will read "the English version of the 'Wearing of the Green ". Then at the outset a further carving and change would be judiciously effected by making the opening read "We regret to record the death of Mrs. Beesly, aged 49," while the closing clause may be made to run—"She took an active part in London political work and was president of the Women's Liberal Paddington Association". The reprints may be regarded as a proof to be corrected. You must run a connecting line from your marginal substitutes to the word or words you mean to be altered, and after a little while the eye will become so trained to this kind of work, that two or three columns of reprint will be run over at a glance and the pen will make the requisite alterations in far less time than it has occupied to give the above example. Take out all verbiage. Improve the writing where it is possible to do so without sacrificing too much time, but when you *quote* a paper you *must not alter* the wording. If too long to give *in extenso*, separate the portions between which you have struck out matter by three dots, thus . . . or, if it be found that the portion struck out for want of room is *essential*, to the sense of that given, write in connecting lines thus : "Our contemporary then proceeds to argue that Lord Salisbury or Mr. Gladstone" as the case may be, "was entirely at fault," etc. Then in, say a police report beginning—"a man who gave the name of ' so and so ' was brought up," etc.; change to "a man named," or perhaps simply "John Smith was charged". All these things once clearly understood, come afterwards to the sub-editor as a sort of second nature, a kind of instinct, and he turns out his "copy" as a mill grinds the stuff poured into its hopper. It is best to pile these cuttings as you go, in some sort of order; thus, political items in one heap, crimes in another, accidents in a third, and so on. Many will be found in duplicate or triplicate, and, of course, the *best* is selected, and then any essential details are added from the others. The sub-editor must *discriminate* between *pending* and *final* news. What is pending must be put by

4

for additions. Many pieces, too, will be useful only as pegs on which to hang remarks. Thus you will obtain hints, texts, and suggestions for such headings as "Chat," "Gossip," "Notes," "Talk of the Day," "Entre nous," "En passant," etc.

In the result the manipulation of the daily papers will have yielded a great heap of "copy," some of which, being definite and final, may go to the printer at once. Much care must be taken not to reproduce *libellous* matter (libel and copyright will be found fully dealt with in separate sections), and also to avoid errors. In the most careful work I have used *two* copies of each paper; then the journals must be laid two by two. You take page one of the *first* and page two of the *second* gives the continuation. This prevents the trouble from having good matter on the *back* of cuttings, for all copy for press must be on *one* side of the paper only. In extraordinary cases as in MS. letters on both sides of the paper, which still have to appear, and for the copying of which time is wholly wanting, printers will set up from both sides; but the real difficulty is that such "copy" cannot be cut up. It must go to *one* man. It is essential to write on such unusual copy "P.T.O." on each side.

The sub-editor has to do more than merely prepare the re-print "copy" and write summaries. He has the exchanges to deal with—that is, journals wherewith he exchanges copies. These sometimes come from all quarters, not only the provinces, but from abroad and the colonies. In the case of *American* journals it is very unsafe to take over literary matter, especially if very good, for it may be, and often is, pirated from English publications; and although our Yankee friends can and do appropriate with impunity the best fruit of English brains, you may find yourself in an awkward position when the article you deemed original to the *Cincinnati Cormorant*, turns out to be a paper plundered from some great London magazine, and copy-right here!

The sub-editor will have to deal with the letters that come, and many of these are exasperating. Subscribers will ask for a stupendous amount of information on the strength of sending a stamp or two, and others will be angry because the last number did not contain some insignificant piece of news which *they* wanted. Tickets will come for theatres, con-certs, public meetings for all kinds of purposes, political, social, philanthropic, and scientific; samples will be sent in to be reported on and described, and generally a vast number of most miscellaneous tasks have to be got through somehow, and that at once. Beware of postponements. Everything in the sub-editorial department must be done strictly *pro re nata*. Disaster and appalling confusion will soon convince the man "who puts off" that the newspaper office is no place for *him*.

There will be books for review, and, as only a limited number of papers give reviewing to specialists, the sub-editor will probably be expected to review most or all of the books sent. Reviewing, however, is fully dealt with in a separate section, and need not detain us here.

We will imagine that our typical sub-editor has managed to get through his preliminary work, and that "making up" and "going-to-press time" is at hand.

"Making-up" is the term used to describe the arrange-ment of the different portions of the paper into pages, and this, although a terrible thing to some young and nervous journalists, need cause no uneasiness, as the printers, assum-ing that the "copy" has been properly prepared, practically do this part of the work.

The various items of news—the articles, correspondence, etc.—composing the paper are laid up in the metal in long, narrow trays, having ledges to keep the outside type from falling down. These trays are termed "galleys," and hold a column or so, according to the length of the page to be filled. The foreman-printer, or his representative, furnishes a statement of the *quantity* he has, and if this is less than what is required to fill the space at command, more "copy" has to be provided ; and if too much has been sent in, and set up, then a portion is omitted. A statement may run something like this—

Notes,	...	...	...	$5\frac{1}{2}$ cols.
Leaders,	...	...	...	$2\frac{3}{4}$,,
Law, ...	...	...	...	4 ,,
Crime,	...	...	...	8 ,,
Accidents,	...	...	...	6 ,,
Music and the drama,		...	2 ,,
Reviews,	...	...	...	3 ,,
General news,		...	...	4 ,,
Correspondence,		...	...	2 ,,
Fill-up pars, ...	...	...	2 ,,
Advertisements,		...	...	10 ,,

$$49\frac{1}{4} \text{ cols.}$$

Required, 48 cols. ; excess, $1\frac{1}{4}$ cols.

Of course, measurements vary. They may run to one-eighth of a column, and the excess may be considerable ; or the reverse may be the case, and matter may be wanted, but the principle is the same. The sub-editor will indicate to the printer what is to be left out, if too much has been composed, or he will give in fresh "copy" to "fit". Then the order of the "notes" or leaders will be indicated on the proof by numbering them, and it will be found in practice that all the details come, as it were, of themselves. Occasionally, when an article falls awkwardly, the printer may require a few words or a few lines to be cut out, or even an addition to be written in. One example may suffice. Commenting on the death of Robert Browning, the poet, in December, 1889, a writer in the London *Echo* wrote—

"Browning was essentially a Christian poet. The optimism of a clear and exalted Christian faith filled him through and through, and sometimes, as in ' A Death in the Desert,' he argued it out with the sceptics, in a somewhat laboured and painful manner; but he was at his best when simply expounding his faith in such poems as ' Rabbi Ben Ezra,' ' Abt Vogler,' ' Saul,' and ' Instans Tyrannus '. These are poems which the world will not willingly let die, and which will endure long after the dismal caterwaulings of the ' life-not-worth-living ' school are buried in oblivion."

Now, suppose this were found in making-up to fall awkwardly, and needed reducing, you might contract the latter sentence by striking out the words "which the world will not willingly let die," and making the sentence read "These are poems which will endure long after the dismal caterwaulings of the ' life-not-worth-living ' school are buried in oblivion ". If it be desired to *add*, you might make the close read, "long after the dismal and *exasperating* caterwaulings of the *palpably insincere and childish* ' life-not-worth-living ' school of *contemporary pessimists* are buried in *well-merited* oblivion ". This is not given as a specially good example. It is simply to *indicate* the kind of thing that may come up, and the way in which such difficulties should be met. Of course, much good taste and sound judgment must be exercised, and some articles must *on no account* be altered, but adjacent matter may be shifted or altered instead. These are things to be acquired in practice, but it is well to warn the embryo journalist of some of the tasks that may be his.

Always remember that printers—a long suffering and much enduring race of patient and generally very hardworking worthy men—will *always* give the young journalist every possible aid, if only he does not give himself undue "airs," and will bear himself considerately towards those

who have it in their power to make matters very smooth or
very rough for him according to his seeming deserts.

Sometimes the sub-editor may, especially when on a weekly
journal, be required during the intervals of the weekly issue
to visit and describe places, report on processes and inventions, attend and report meetings, and be generally useful
in the interests of the publication. All this should be regarded
as a means for gaining fresh and valuable experience.
Let it be borne in mind that the great aim of the really
able and practical journalist should be to emulate with his
professional mind the trunk of the elephant which picks up
sixpence or lifts a balk of timber with equal dexterity
and serenity of temper. The true journalistic art is to
appear to know *everything*, and when ignorant of how
something is to be done, which *must* be done, to know
where to find the requisite information   Let the aspiring
journalist who means to rise, take care that he is at all
seasons quite ready to direct a jet of exact and yet popular
information on any topic that may suddenly be sprung on
him, and this whether he has only to pen a few lines, or to
supply many columns   The working journalist must, as
occasion arises, be a lawyer, a clergyman, a soldier, a sailor,
a policeman, a man of sentiment, a practical philosopher
with no nonsense about him, an artist, an architect, a
man of science, a statistician running over with dry figures
to be popularised into readable periods, a merchant, a
stockbroker, an engineer, a critic of painting, music and
old china, and not to catalogue too far, he must be the
Protean genius of contemporary life in its many activities
and in all its multifarious phases. He must be full of
general information, or know at once where to get it when
his own fails, and he should have at immediate command
ready to flow off his flying pen, crisp, well worded and
luminous expositions of all the principal political, social,
industrial, artistic and economic theories of the day. He

must be ready at an instant's notice to write a special article, which shall imply that the writer is perfectly familiar with Comte, and knows that his original was Confucius, or to suggest that he, the writer, is quite up in Plato, Aristotle, St. Augustine, or Henry George and Professor Harrison of our own day. He must have a working acquaintance with the Talmud and the Koran, and be able to discriminate, when required by the exigencies of his subject, between the nominalistic and the realistic schools of the middle ages. He should know something of the "venerable Bede" and be able to refer to Duns Scotus or to Martin Luther, as though he were a theological student. History, science, and geography he must know, and when he has a brief telegram from some out-of-the-way quarter, he must know under what country to put it, and it is well if he can add a crisp line or two informing the ignorant reader that such and such is the place in question, and that it is famous for so and so. I may here mention that writers are some-times specially engaged on journals to elucidate and illustrate foreign telegrams. But this, though much, is not by any means all. A practical journalist should have a rudimentary knowledge of physics; he should understand agriculture, have some acquaintance with our staple manu-factures, comprehend the principles of commerce, possess an insight into foreign and colonial affairs, have a smatter-ing of commercial law, and be versed in finance, know something of bi-metallism and a thousand and one other things For are there not games of all kinds and sorts? and then there is *society* with all its unwritten codes. All these various subjects have their *special* organs and these organs have their special journalists, but in *general* newspaper work a little of each is often required, and that little the journalist who means to succeed must be prepared to supply Never say to an editor, or to a newspaper manager "I don't know," or "I can't do it". Go and find out, is the golden rule. In nearly every case you will succeed, and doing this you will be readily pardoned for an evidently exceptional failure The great and master faculty to cultivate is to bring all your power to bear at once on any subject that may be set you, and this faculty once acquired, you may confidently feel that you can go on any paper and hold your own. In a word, the model journalist is a kind of intellectual organ, having as many tunes as there are subjects in newspaper literature, and capable of grinding out at once what is wanted, whether it be a fiery leader on some threatened encroachment on public liberty, or a four-lined paragraph to recommend a new fashion in parasols.

But I think I hear some object it is impossible to acquire all this! Is it? Impossible has no place in the journalistic vocabulary. It will be found on careful reference thereto, that the various sections of this volume combined supply the requisite information whereby any one of average mental ability, united with the necessary painstaking and industrious spirit, *can* actually attain to what seems the ideal state described above The fact is the journalist has to avail himself of every aid that the best books of reference can furnish, and among works which he *must* have in order to work at all times to advantage, are certainly the following —the latest *Encyclopædia*, *Haydn's Dictionary of Dates*, *Cruden's Concordance to the Bible*, *Brewer's Dictionary of Phrase and Fable*, *Walford's Men of the Time*, and others to be duly noted under other sections, not forgetting Henry Southgate's *Many Thoughts of Many Minds*. Thus, to take a pointed example ; suppose you have to write an article on some phase of Industrial Life, in Southgate's work you can turn to " Labour," and find a collection of what some of the ablest thinkers and most eloquent writers have said thereon, some of these extracts may be quotable, and some may suggest to you new trains of thought on the subject, and greatly help in the composition of the article. I say always dispense with such helps when you can, but there they are when wanted

VII.—REVIEWING.

It has been said with much truth that no department of journalism is so badly done as reviewing. Of course this is true only in regard to the great mass of ordinary papers, but even here a marked change for the better is everywhere apparent, and the young writer must prepare himself, as in all other cases, to do well what others have been doing ill ; that is the order of these competitive days for all who mean to rise and to succeed.

According to Mr. Gosse, literary criticism began, so far as the modern idea of the critical faculty goes, with the Restoration, and may be traced distinctly in the prefaces of Dryden. Criticism came, it is said, in 1675 from France, where two Jesuits, Le Bossu and Rapin, had begun to formularise, and apply to modern poetry the rules of Aristotle.

Reviewing, as a method of making books known, is not very modern. One of the earliest periodicals foreshadowing the *Athenæum* and the *Academy* of to-day, appears to have been *The Weekly Memorials for the Ingenious,* and herein appeared criticisms of books. Curiously in those remote times (1681), this periodical complains that the number of books has "now grown almost infinite," and goes on to assert that these cause confusion and distraction of thought.

Of late years the enormous multiplying of books and the universal spread of reading have naturally caused a great demand for reviewing, which in too many cases amounts to "noticing" only the hundreds of volumes continually issuing from the press. The old fashioned idea of criticism is that of a real examination of the subject criticised, but unfortunately the work of reviewing is very often given

to ignorant men, that is men ignorant from an ideal
viewpoint, for the reviewer ought decidedly to know the
subject on which he writes, and especially should he be
well, widely, and deeply read. Where journals are properly
conducted, the able editor deals out the books that come
in for review to men who may be presumed to know
something about the particular thing they are called on to
criticise, but in numerous cases this is not done and the
result is often lamentable. Not a few, too, of our smart
young journalists make woful exhibitions of ignorance here
through their ignorance of the classics, and especially of the
more archaic forms of literature. I have known one of this
type sorely puzzled over the application of the word " silly "
in an old poem, not remembering that it meant " innocent,"
while another could make nothing of the last verse in the
following stanza from old Herrick, wherein he tells us that—

> Some asked how pearls did grow and where,
>   I pointed to my girl,
> To part her lips and show them there,
>   The *quarrelets* of pearl.

Of course this refers to the *quarrel*, the bolt of the mediæval
cross-bow, and is aptly enough used by Herrick in connection
with the teeth.

Then there is the fact that in too many cases, the
reviewer has no grasp at all of the book he is dealing with,
and it must be confessed that the old fashioned eighteenth
century reviews were altogether better than very many of
the miserable and entirely misleading notices found in so
many of the journals of the day.

To me it has always seemed that the whole art of right
reviewing lies in this little formula—find out *what* the book
to be reviewed says, and *how* it says it. And here, obviously,
unless the reviewer is acquainted with parallel literature on
the subject, he cannot *fairly* criticise, for all criticism must
be *comparative*, as all knowledge is *relative*. There have

been cases known when nothing was read of a book but the title and table of contents! Worse still, perhaps, some have been known to simply wait until other reviews appeared, whence they have drawn ideas for their own criticism—a proceeding specially reprehensible. Much misconception exists on the nature and function of reviewing among many people, and Lord Beaconsfield's ill-natured remark that critics are men who have failed in art, has led to great fallacy in the popular mind on the subject. Certainly it is not essential that a critic should be capable of writing the book wherewith he has to deal; and were this really so, then it is to be presumed that the works of Victor Hugo, Tennyson, and some others, could not be reviewed at all—which is manifestly absurd. This idea as to the office of criticism was Poe's, who asserted that, while the critic might be occasionally allowed to play the part of commentator, and, by way of interesting readers, to put in the fairest light the merits of his author, his legitimate task was still to point out and analyse defects and to show how the work might be improved, and thus to aid the general cause of letters, regardless of the individual writer. This is, I think, sound, but extreme. Goethe, on the other hand, maintained that what it concerned us to know about any work or writer were the merits not the defects, and obviously the more perfected form of criticism will honestly combine these two methods. To do this well, the critic should know how to write, and such men as Hazlitt—and many more like him could be cited—show abundantly the manifest, indeed the overpowering, advantage that the critic who can write, as well as read, has over him who can only do the latter.

At first the young reviewer should really read what he undertakes to criticise. This will take time, but save much in the end. Of course, by reading I don't mean that every sentence is to be studied like a text book, but practice here will soon enable any one, who is apt, to take in the general meaning of pages on pages, and in numerous cases the reading of one book is an aid to the understanding of another. The experienced proof-reader can detect a turned letter in the middle of a page at a glance, and so the experienced reviewer soon acquires the faculty of rapidly estimating the true merits of a particular book, and especially will he be able to discriminate a poorly written work, and to deal with it accordingly.

Too many reviewers however, and some of the clever sort, too, unfortunately think far more of airing their own smartness than of doing justice to the work under consideration, and this accounts for the fact that in many cases everything that is just and right is sacrificed to make a point or to give an epigrammatic turn to a paragraph.

In the earlier stages of reviewing the young writer will find it well to keep closely to giving the best account he can of the work, and neither to praise nor censure *unless* he is quite sure of his ground. Most readers of reviews, especially in newspapers, want to know what the book in question *is* rather than what the reviewer imagines it to be from a very superficial knowledge thereof, and the young writer can, at anyrate, determine to give a fairly exact account of the book before him. One or two examples must be worth many precepts. I have before me as I write this, a History of Warwickshire, by Samuel Timmins, F.S.A.

Turning over the first page I find that this is the fifth of a series of county histories, and then chapter I., headed—General History, naturally starts my review if I so please, by quoting Drayton's line in his Polyolbion referring to Warwick as that shire—

Which we the heart of England well may call.

I go a little way on and am reminded of the fact that Warwickshire is one of the most interesting of all English counties, for is there not Coventry and Lady Godiva, and are there not the Barons' Wars, those of the Roses, the closing conflict with the gunpowder plot conspirators, the Battle of Edgehill, and the rise of Birmingham? Then we have Shakespeare, Drayton himself, and a host of worthies; and chapters are given on the legends and folk-lore and the Roman and Saxon antiquities of this region, while a special section is devoted to its castles—Warwick Castle of king-maker fame and Kenilworth with its Elizabethan splendour, as set forth in the magic pages of Walter Scott, to say nothing of much interesting matter of reminiscences of George Eliot. Lo! here we have a review in outline. Of course this is not the higher criticism which would *compare all* the principal statements made with the original and best authorities, and perhaps find some errors, but *that* form of reviewing is not here under notice. It is specialist work, and has no place in the great mass of current criticism on contemporary literature in the journals of the day

Fiction must be read, and this remark applies to all works of pure imagination, but, after a while, it will not be necessary to read *all*. As to what may be called the filling-up writing, a glance, after experience has been gained, will often fully serve to show what is the real value of the writer's style. Take these two extracts from current books—not necessary to name specifically—as two very distinct styles in preliminary description, and both occurring in the opening page of two purely-fictitious narratives. The one runs: "A July sun, high in the cloudless sky, poured its heat down upon the country. . . . The farm labourers were all resting in drowsy day dreams after their mid-day meal. The old grey horse in the paddock, past work, lay outstretched under a spreading elm . . . The horse was old; and the farmhouse which overlooked the paddock was old; so was the little, quaint Norman church; so was the picturesque rectory, with its gabled roof and trellised porch. Everything was old at Linwood, and these far-spreading, stately woods were the growth of centuries." In the second instance, we have the following : " It was a wild, stormy night, and the wind howled over the housetop and rushed impetuously down the chimney. . . The sea thundered on the beach . . . the casement rattled ; and the scudding clouds obscured the moon. . . . On a low, velvet-covered stool in front of the fire sat a tall, graceful woman." After further telling us that her eyes were blue, and her throat white, it is added " her little feet, clad in heelless satin slippers, were such as a sculptor would have gloried in ". Now, in both these citations we have examples of conventional descriptive writing, the former piece being the least pretentious and the better. It will be noted in each—but especially in the latter—that the writing does not give us a *single new idea.* The "wild, stormy" night has been used to open thousands of romances ; and the sea has "thundered on the beach" in many a melodramatic tale. As to the lady—there is not a really distinctive trait about her. She is tall and graceful : so are many women. She has blue eyes and a white throat and small feet : so, indeed, have many millions of women. But, if we turn to the portraiture in, say, such a book as *Shirley*, we shall find a very different sort of writing, as in Charlotte Bronte's Mr. Helstone, with his "hawk's head, beak and eye"—a clear portrait drawn in five words ' I say, then, by comparing books, and exercising judgment and *thinking* about what you read, it will soon be practicable to obtain a general idea of the style of a writer, which is the great object of a reviewer, who is not expected to spend the same time in examining a melodramatic, sensational novel, only meant to be read once—a spasm of a more or less morbid idea—that should be given to such a book as Mr. Froude's *Two Chiefs of Dunboy*, for example, to cite a recent work.

All kinds of knowledge are of immense value to the reviewer. In fact, to do his work well, he cannot be too well informed. How many superficial so-called reviewers on the ordinary journals of the day are likely to perceive—and, perceiving, be able to correct—such an error as that in Milton's *L'Allegro*—

> Then let Hymen oft appear
> In saffron robe ?

Now it was a yellow *veil* which Greek and Roman brides wore, the *robes* being *white*. This is but a type, of course, yet it will soon be clear to the thoughtful student that a vast substratum of sound information ought to be in the possession of him who presumes to stretch a book on the Procrustean bed of his individual criticism. Of unprincipled, indolent reviewers who will not take trouble, but go wholly by the name of the author and praise or blame as they deem it safe, I only say do not imitate them, and do not drop into the equally bad way of having certain cut and dried forms for criticising favourably or otherwise. Remember that the best reviews, other things being equal, are those which have in them the greatest amount of *original writing* The old-fashioned reviews in a less hurried and more thoughtful age, were really essays, and in Macaulay's these are found perhaps at their brightest and best, although it must be remarked that Macaulay was not at all impartial. As matters now stand, in numerous cases all that is wanted for a newspaper review is the title of the work, author's and publisher's name, and a brief statement of what the book is about, with any remarks that may naturally suggest themselves. This, however, is reviewing made easy with a vengeance, and the young writer who is making his way, cannot expect to obtain any credit off such perfunctory work If reviewing is really well done, it is of value to the journal in which it appears, as parts may be quoted in announcements of the work, and the review may secure an advertisement. Editors and publishers are ever alive to

literary merits, let people say what they may to the contrary,
and the young writer who can get so far as to have a book
given him to review, may feel that he has one foot on the
literary ladder, and he should thoroughly exert himself to
ascertain both the merits and the demerits—if there be any
—of his author.   Let him be as impartial as a judge and
then he can be fearless.   Do what is right so far as lies
within your power and then go ahead, that is the way to
succeed in literature, as in any other department of the work
of life.   When novels or any kind of fiction have to be
dealt with, it is best to give, unless, of course, particularly
instructed not to do so, a synopsis of the plot up to a certain
point, but not so far as to spoil the reader's enjoyment in
the book afterwards.   There is art in turning off neat little
vignettes, so to speak, of a story with two or three crisp,
apt extracts thrown in to clothe part of the skeleton you
have drawn.   This art will come with practice.   Above all,
in every kind of writing do not be afraid of the beginning.
Determine to get over that first sentence difficulty, and if
needs must be employ such forms as these . "Opening
pleasantly in a romantic part of Cornwall," or elsewhere, as
the case may be, using a suitable adjective to fit the occasion,
"we are early introduced in this story to so and so," or,
"The writer of this novel does not lose any time in setting
his plot in motion," or, "Very charming is the idyllic description, at the outset, of the village where the heroine has
her home".   These are but hints, and are meant as
suggestions, not to be actually adopted. but they will set the
mind of the young writer in many cases in the right course,
and show "how it is to be done'.   In the early stages, it is
as well to look up the name of the writer, if one of note or
fame, in *Men of the Time*, or some good biographical dictionary.   This will gradually increase the writer's store of
information and will in many cases help him in writing the
review by suggesting some fact or allusion about, or in,

connection with, the author, which may be "worked in" with the notice and generally improve it. And here I would add a word on the necessity for doing your best always and writing all you know on every subject that comes before you.

Think not that this is the way to rapidly "use up" all you have in you. If it *should*, then you will the earlier have an unmistakable warning that literature is *not* your vocation. The more you pour in from the page, and the more you pour out from the pen, the more will you assimilate and secrete for reproduction, and the writing-faculty will be strengthened, like a muscle is by use. I have known young writers talk about their original ideas and their fresh powers being worked up in profitless and anonymous work, but we may depend on it, that such sickly sentimentalists could not hold their own in any part of the great field of competitive literature, and only he who gives generously full and overflowing measure of his best, is likely to climb up the steeps into the fair table-lands of recognised success.

Finally, one word on prefaces. These are useful enough to the hurried reviewer, and especially to the journalist who is "filling-up" time at this task. Prefaces, as a rule, are seldom wise, however, except where they are confined to *facts*. In numerous instances the preface is only a thinly-veiled review of his own work by the author. It is meant to influence the reader favourably, and to check the reviewer, although too often that functionary is only provoked thereby to criticise more sharply than he might otherwise have done. The blunders made in prefaces are often glaring. In one to what is really a good romance, the preface commences, "The launching forth of a book on the sea of literature is always an important event for the writer, and not without anxiety," and so forth. This is enough to make a testy reviewer cast an ill-natured eye on the whole performance.

5

Mock modesty is a mistake, too, and so is the absurd defiance
of, and absolute indifference towards, all criticism expressed
by some writers who had far better say nothing. If the
book is good it needs no preface, and if it is bad, no preface
will help it in the smallest degree.   How hollow and false
prefaces sometimes are is instanced by the following anecdote,
which may be accepted as authentic. Mr. Richard Edgcumbe
communicated to the *Athenæum* of March 6, 1886, an
account of an uncut copy of a book entitled *Greece in 1823
and 1824*, containing the letters of Colonel Leicester Stanhope, and a preface by the editor, Mr. Richard Ryan
While cutting the leaves of this old book Mr. Edgcumbe
found in it a manuscript, undated and unsigned, in the
caligraphy of the earlier part of the century, and most
obviously containing the heads of instruction to Mr. Ryan
for writing his preface   These are as follows—

" Eulogise the Greek cause and the assertions of Stanhope,
and show the apparent certainty of the Greek cause being
victorious   State the probable progress the people have
made in literature and civilisation by means of the presses
established by Col. S during the conflict. *Blaze away* about
the Greek cause appealing to the breast of every Englishman,
and wind it up by showing the Greek cause to be of permanent importance to everybody who has any right idea of
decency and propriety.

"State the usual lie of the publication being undertaken
more with a view of serving the Greek cause than of profit,
and *splash* away about 5,000 other fine things which just
now I cannot think of.

" Mem.—If Lord Byron is spoken of, let him be praised,
and *gammon* us well about his loss to the Greek cause."

No doubt all this was well and faithfully done. It certainly served as a hint, and indicates how little dependence
can be placed on prefaces. These are best when confined
to necessary matter-of-fact statements, and are most objec-

tionable when they are, as it were, officious, anticipatory reviews, expressly meant to win over the professional critic, which, however, they always signally fail to do.

VIII.—DRAMATIC, MUSICAL, AND ART CRITICISM.

Each of the departments mentioned above is a speciality. The two first are frequently combined in the same writer; the last usually stands alone, or may be combined with general reviewing. To criticise *music* properly it is essential that the critic understand music; although, unhappily, all these several functions of criticism—dramatic, musical and artistic—are sometimes exercised by the same writer, who is at bottom equally ignorant of all three. Here, as in all other departments of journalistic work, the more previous knowledge that the writer brings to bear on his work the better. Let us take the drama first. Dramatic criticism is not, as some falsely suppose, the work of cliques, who agree on a certain attitude to be observed towards each new play. Each critic, as a rule, stands very much alone; and, in working for a daily paper, it will often be found a hard task, as the criticism must be written the same evening that the play is seen, in order that it may be published the next day! Most decidedly the dramatic critic ought to be well versed in the history of the drama, and he must know the principal plays of the past and the present. All criticism must be comparative; and for a man to write critiques on contemporary plays who had never read, say, the *Rivals*, the *School for Scandal*, the *Lady of Lyons*, *Money*, the *Ticket-of-Leave Man*, and a score of others, is simply absurd. It is needless to observe that a thorough knowledge of Shakespeare, the principal Elizabethan dramatists, and those of the Restoration, is simply essential. Some acquaintance, which may be obtained through the medium of good translations, with the French, Spanish, Italian and German stage is equally requisite. The splendid plays of Victor Hugo, Schiller, Calderon and others must all be studied ; and the older continental dramatists, such as Molière, Racine, Corneille, etc., must also be familiar as the works of Dumas Fils, Sardou and other contemporary writers for the foreign stage. When it is remembered that we go abroad for the substance of most of our plays, the need for this reading will be the more apparent ; and then, too, besides what is the purely literary side of the work, there is need for the critic to possess a knowledge of the technics of the stage, and of much that lies outside the province of mere books, which will, however, be gradually acquired ; for the dramatic critic, though partly born, is partly made. Let it be remembered that the upholstery-play, as it has been termed, is gaining ground ; and a writer in that periodical *East and West* has lately drawn attention to the fact that, while interest in matters dramatic has much revived of late, there is general apathy on the part of the play-going public towards the purely literary side of the drama. This is, I think, only what might be expected. The novel long ago, in a manner killed the narrative poem, and, in like manner, what once gave literary beauty and power to the play is now expended on fiction. Thence dress, " property," and other material attractions are all important on the contemporary stage. Still, there are many examples of successful plays possessing great literary merits, and the critic must be alive at all times to both phases of the drama as it comes before him. Let it not be forgotten that, in criticising any piece, two things have to be considered : the play and the playing thereof. Do not confuse these ; and be always tolerant ; and, when censure has to be meted out, let it be done in a refined and thoughtful—not a coarse and obviously slap-dash—way. The one will raise your reputation, and the other just as surely lower it. Bear in mind what Pope says as to the impartial spirit of true criticism, when he reminds us that

A perfect judge will read each work of wit
With the same spirit that its author writ;
Survey the whole, nor seek slight fault to find
Where nature moves and rapture warms the mind.

And, then, as to the value of being oneself a capable writer, it is well to bear in mind the fact that a writing critic should understand how to write; and, though every writer may not be exactly called on to prove himself a good critic, every *writing* critic is bound to prove that he can write effectively.

Of course, much depends on the character of the publication for which the criticism is required. In some cases the great thing wanted is an intelligible account of the play or piece, and of the general "mounting," as it is called—that is the way in which it is put on the stage. In other cases stress must be laid more especially on the acting; and, if you are engaged on a *theatrical* journal, naturally the task is one of far greater difficulty than if you are simply writing for an ordinary newspaper, which only requires a general account to lay before its readers.

I need hardly remark that the position of a dramatic critic is one peculiarly open to "undue influence," and if this be yielded to, let it be well understood that persistence in biassed criticism will end at last in ruin and disgrace. Be incorruptible from the first and resist all attempts, however subtle, to warp your judgment, and if wise, avoid convivial meetings as a *preparation* for scribbling your criticism. The stage has advanced very much of late years, and it is well that its critics should advance too.

In musical criticism, properly the critic should be himself a musician. In any case he positively must have an ear for harmony and a knowledge of the principles thereof. A love of music in England is greatly on the increase and beyond all question the sphere for the competent writer on music is widening. Long ago we were told that music is the only sensuous gratification which may always be indulged in

without any hurt to the moral or the religious feelings, and
rightly has it been said that the meaning of song goes deep
and that it is a kind of unfathomable speech which leads us
to the very edge of the infinite, and even gives us a glimpse
of that itself!   Conjoined with mere technical knowledge
of harmony—and the more there is of this the better !—there
should be a competent acquaintance with the history of
music, ancient and modern, and the would-be critic ought
to know, roughly at least, the main principles whereon the
principal musical instruments are constructed.

I now pass on to art criticism, and this opens out a very
wide vista indeed, for the drama and music are confined
within certain bounds, but the picture practically includes
all things imaginable, and sculpture is much the same.
Painting in truth speaks the universal language, and as was
long since remarked, while

> The poets are confined to narrow space
> To speak the language of their native place ;
> The painter widely stretches his command,
> His pencil speaks the tongue of every land.

Before venturing to criticise any work of art, the young
writer should have studied the subject generally through its
literature, and supplemented that study by examining as
many pictures of all kinds and statues as may be within his
reach.   It is essential to read the lives of the principal
painters and sculptors, and those of the classic and mediæval
times must be familiar to the critic as well as those of the
day, with whom he may have more particularly to deal
There are many phases of art.—classic, mediæval and
modern, and these have to be sub-divided, and its history
during the successive epochs of its evolution must be
thoroughly mastered.   Art in its symbolic aspects is, Ruskin
rightly tells us, an incarnation of fancy and is a sort of
petrified poetry.   Then it is well to remember for bases, so

to speak, in dealing with different works to be reviewed, that Egyptian ornament is thoughtful and ever allegorical, Greek is full of invention, Byzantine is composite, and Gothic is imitative.   Then there are the rich oriental types to be studied, such as the Moorish, which has been beautifully called by Ruskin the poetry of geometry; the Indian, the Persian, the Arabian, and the modern Turkish.   If the young writer be in London or any large city, having art galleries, he can easily study first hand.   The great thing is to read up art, and then to verify the result of that reading by the intelligent study of actual paintings and statuary, etc. Access can often be had to studios.   Endeavour to visit as many of these as possible.   In London and elsewhere there are ever artists who, if courteously asked to allow their studios to be inspected, will readily grant permission. More is learned thus than would be readily imagined by many.   I know that I gained enormously myself by personally visiting studios and occasionally getting really instructive lessons in art from painters and sculptors.   Many excellent painters and sculptors have neither the time, inclination, nor the requisite literary training to enable them to write on their art, but some of these will discourse in their studio in a way that teaches more than most of the professionally written papers published in the best art journals of the day.   I need not give names here.   Let it suffice to say that the young writer who desires to properly qualify himself for the functions of an art critic, had better write to some of the painters and sculptors whose names are before the world, and though some may refuse him, he will receive invitations to call from others, and then when he has a commission to go and describe some painting or collection of pictures, he will be fortified with a certain amount of technical knowledge and will not feel so much at a loss as some do the first time they enter an art gallery for the purpose of reporting thereon.

IX —SPECIAL CORRESPONDENTS.

It is striking to find, if we will only probe deeply enough, what a unity of common purpose runs through vocations so frequently very unlike each other.   In truth from one point of view the reviewer and the art critic are but reporters of their mental impressions of certain things placed before them, and the special correspondent is but a writer sent to give his entire attention to some one thing, and to concentrate all his powers thereon in order to present in words as nearly a perfect representation thereof as it is humanly possible to give.

One of the higher walks in reportorial journalism is that of the war correspondent, who is with each new war coming into active request among us, and ever receiving more honour and general consideration.   He is the historian of the hour and must possess qualities physical, mental, and moral, which are but rarely combined in one man.   In a word, he need be a soldier who writes in place of fighting, and he must, to succeed, have much sympathy with all phases of military affairs.   To go anywhere, like Lord Clyde, at a moment's notice, to be ready to encounter all the many hardships of campaigning, he should have, like Dr William Russell, of Crimean fame, or like Mr. Archibald Forbes, those *personal* qualities which secure to the possessor friends wherever he goes, and yet with all this there must be the will and the determination to make duty a paramount consideration when occasion arises.   We all know how Dr. Russell's fearless letters in the *Times* served the cause of our soldiers in the Crimea, and since then we have had several cases of a similar kind.   A war correspondent should know how to ride well ; he must be a linguist, and should possess good social qualifications. With the constant development of the telegraph, and the growth of enterprise among newspapers, he must expect to find his work harder. As I write this, comes the announce-ment of the *Daily Graphic*, a new experiment in journalism. and in the prospectus appears a fanciful, but perhaps prophetic illustration of a war correspondent riding on a well equipped carriage, unwinding in its track a thin telegraph wire, enabling the war correspondent (for shot and shell are flying about), to transmit to his paper an immediate picture of what he is actually witnessing.

The reward for work of this kind is great. There is both money and honour in it, and in the near future I anticipate a large increase in the number of writers thus employed owing to the competition among papers. Remember, a war correspondent runs the risk of being killed or taken prisoner, and for those who have in their blood, as many, the thirst for adventure, few occupations can be imagined that are really more fascinating. How to obtain work of this kind is no doubt the question with some of our hot youth, who feel that they could wield a note-book and pencil in the field as enthusiastically as a sword. Well, there is Mr. Forbes himself. He had to work his way up from being a hanger-on of the daily press, to becoming eligible for sending abroad I knew one of the war correspondents of the *Pall Mall Gazette* during the Franco-German War He was but a contributor, but when war breaks out inquiry is made all round, and every man at all suited to the work has a chance of putting in his claim.

But we are not always at war, and after all the war correspondent is rather the exceptional form of journalist Special correspondents, however, are always in request, and a great and an increasing number of these are employed. If Mr. Forbes is the ideal of the best type of war correspondent, then Mr George Augustus Sala is most certainly the prince of "special" correspondents. He has been round the world; Australia, India, America, and many other regions have been the scenes of his triumphant labours, and perhaps

in the whole circle of nineteenth century journalism, there
has not been anything yet at all equal to his wonderful
graphic charm and facile style.

The "special" must be a thorough all-round capable
man, and one who can stand any amount of physical
fatigue. He ought to have good nerves, too, for he may
be sent to the scene of a frightful railway accident, and he
must not hold back, if he would do his duty properly and
honourably earn his salary, on account of something that
may make him feel sick with horror. Nor should he
venture to rely on second-hand or hear-say statements,
unless compelled by necessity. He should investigate
everything with his own eyes, and act exactly as though he
were a vigilant coroner holding a most important inquisition.
Let him remember that he represents the public quite as
much in his newspaper capacity as a member of Parliament
represents his constituency, and his motto must be *thorough*
"Specials" are sent literally everywhere. To define the
work of the "special" would simply mean sketching an
encyclopædia, for his range of subjects is universal, as all is
fish that comes in these days within the net of the newspaper Now and then the "special" will be put on some
work for which he has special fitness, and then he ought to
shine, for he has a far better opportunity than most
journalists to make a mark and individualise himself.
A good number of writers are retained generally in this
capacity, but are not called on to write until something
arises within the sphere of their special knowledge, while,
on the other hand, some "specials" are kept on the "move"
and required to furnish constant "copy". Those regularly
retained may be, and are often called on, to make very
distant journeys, and while it may be only to Yorkshire,
it may be to China, for once it is said Mr. Sala himself
had but an hour in which to make his arrangements for a
trip to the celestial empire itself!

The "special" must be full of "go" and vivacity. He should be very enterprising, and must not on any account "hang back". Industry is a prime qualification, conjoined with integrity System too is half the battle. Few men in these days have such splendid opportunities as a "special" for seeing men and women, places and things in all their newest and most striking aspects. A prudent writer, when sent to do a particular thing in a particular place, will not miss noting other points of interest too, and these, held in reserve, will often prove very valuable on future occasions, and may form the basis of acceptable articles to be written in dull seasons.

Obviously the work of the "special," like that of the war correspondent, leads us to consider the question of descriptive writing Descriptive writing is the one thing imperatively demanded of this type of journalist, and by that is meant more than a mere skeleton, dry-as-dust account of what was done or said, or how some place happened to look at a particular season. Life and colour must be imparted, and the mere reportorial style will never do. It may serve a turn, but it will win no credit for the writer, and unless he can invest his account of what he sees with a true descriptive and narrative charm, he is certain to fail and give place before long to one more eloquently gifted by nature. Just think what this means and it will be perceived that it is quite true that no other section of journalism affords such opportunity for good literary work as descriptive reporting. More, too, is it essential that the writer who is resolved to succeed, should be generally well informed and extensively read and that not only in new but in *old* literature also. Here we have the new journalism or the realistic manner of newspaper writing in full force, and other things equal, this will always be accomplished better by the writer who possesses a really intimate acquaintance with *books* as well as with places, things, men and women, and children

of the time, for this is the day of children, as we all know,
and we are fast arriving at the point indicated by Dr. Lyman
Denton, in his novel, *Under the Magnolias*, wherein he
speaks of " our young men of *fifteen*—intelligent, educated
and patriotic ".   But to return.   The *Amateur Casual's* experiences of Mr. James Greenwood, of the *Pall Mall Gazette*,
were decidedly a turning point in descriptive journalism,
and in truth initiated quite a fresh school of writing.
Originally the news sheet was put forth exclusively for the
information without any great regard, if any, for the amusement of the reader ; but all is changed, and contemporary
writers on the press strain might and main to render their
journals as interesting, and if possible more, than the
literature of imagination, and truly there *is* a vast deal of
very imaginative work now in our leading papers.   In this
department zeal often outruns discretion, and no man can
divine what may be the next move of the aspiring new
journalist, who is ready to get himself all but killed, if only
he can thereby give his particular paper something exclusive,
startling, and altogether novel.   There has been much said
as to the origin of the phrase " new journalism," but I
believe it is pretty certain that it was first used by Matthew
Arnold in the May number of the *Nineteenth Century*, 1887.

In point of fact, the " new journalism " is greatly due to
American newspaper enterprise, which is often in a direction
not exactly in harmony with right ideas of what is honest,
much less what is honourable and refined.   It is from
America that we borrow our " screaming " headlines and
the practice of helping the reader to devour a particularly
sensational report by the aid of cross-line sub-titles.   In the
leading American journals a man is kept entirely to write
these headlines, and sometimes an article is half titles, the
pith of the text being summarised into startling headlines
plentifully provided with exclamatory notes   By the way,
it may be interesting to note that the first American news-

paper was published by Benjamin Harris, at Boston, on September 25, 1690. It was the intention of Harris to issue his sheet, which was entitled *Publick Occurrences, Both Foreign and Domestick*, monthly; but the sheet was suppressed by "authority". It was not until a full century later that the first American newspaper of importance—the *Boston News-Letter*—began to appear.

A very special department in journalism is that filled by the "sporting prophets" and others connected with newspapers devoted to sports. Many men, no doubt, manage to do their work in some sporting—*i.e.*, racing—journals with honesty; but this is certainly a groove in periodical literature that I do not advise the young aspirant to seek to "qualify for". The less said about the horse-racing Press the better, and in any case, however determined a man may be to keep honest, he must make up his mind, if he takes work on a racing journal, to come into contact with some of the vilest characters in Christendom. The so-called "tips" are rarely aught but guesses if they be honest, and they are not always *that;* but, undoubtedly, some men of great resolution and ingrained probity do manage to write for the racing Press and yet preserve an honourable reputation. This is rather the exception than the rule, and the young man whose literary longings direct him towards the sporting press should beware.

Very different, of course, from this special section of the Press is that devoted to general sport, such as cricket, boating, cycling, and the like. The number of these journals is much on the increase, as athleticism is spreading far and wide, and being taken up by young England with an enthusiasm worthy of ancient Greece. Indeed, the extremes whereto athletics are now pushed is the fact that in some public schools football is as compulsory a sport for the boys as are any of their regular lessons, and that notwithstanding the fact that even under the Rugby rules death sometimes results from the determined scrimmages that take place at critical points of the so-called game Meteorology is a subject, too, receiving increasing attention in most newspapers, and probably other features connected with the practical application of science to the everyday affairs of life will follow. The outlook is very wide, and there is all possible encouragement for the young aspirant who has steadfastness of purpose and ability.

I have here and in some of the previous chapters insisted on the absolute need there is for the journalist who would succeed being well read. This is really essential, unless he is content to remain a mere "liner" and a writer at everybody's beck and call, to do just those things that bring no literary credit when done, and serve nothing to advance the writer in his vocation. The question of reading will be found fully treated under a separate section, as are also the various rates of remuneration and other practical matters.

X.—FINANCIAL AND TRADE JOURNALISM.

The city editor is the functionary who presides over the "money market" columns of the morning paper; and his special duty is to survey the whole world of finance and trade. and to note each event of interest or importance occurring therein In the case of the great daily papers, he has his own office in the city near the Stock Exchange; and there, in touch, as it were, with the vast concerns that engage his pen, he is the great autocrat of the journal. All other writers on a paper are liable to have their articles more or less trimmed , but even the editor himself would not venture to meddle with the "city" article; and thus it follows that the writer who furnishes this matter occupies a peculiarly favoured position. He is also exceptionally well paid, so that there may be no temptation to dishonest practices; and his work, though arduous and very responsible, is not of a very brain-exhausting character.   It is cool, clear labour and is not done in a hurry; neither has the writer to go hither and thither, like the "special," to obtain food for his pen.

In a daily journal, of course, the responsibility and dignity of this post are of great magnitude, and only men tried and true and specially gifted can hope to fill this particular and coveted chair of daily journalism.   The city editor must not only understand finance generally, but he must be a thorough master of currencies, of the nature of money, of the higher laws of mathematics and their application to banking and other cognate operations; and he must understand public companies in all their phases, and be versed in the law thereof, as well as in all practical departments of commercial law.   He must have a good knowledge of commerce and trade—and that, too, in their international aspect—and he must have a current knowledge of the courses of all the great markets of the day.   It is needless to add that such subjects as wheat, wool, metals, textiles and the like, must be familiar to him as his ABC.   He is a journalist who works, as it were, isolated from all others; and he may—and does sometimes—write for more than one paper.   He has his assistant, and it is in this capacity that a young man possessing ability, a sound knowledge of theoretical finance and commerce—such as can be acquired in a good school, or, better still, college course—may obtain his initial experience. Among the duties of the city editor is the dealing with the prospectuses of new forms of joint-stock enterprise which are ever appearing, and on these he must look with a most vigilant and critical eye.   He must not take any statement on trust, but must apply to all the assertions put forth the touchstone of his own knowledge.   He must be competent, too, when requisite, to make intricate calculations to test statements put forth to induce people to take up shares; and he must, above all, be incorruptible, and avoid, especially, the frequent temptation offered him of making money by buying some stock or shares to sell again at a premium. As a rule, the city editors are men of integrity; and their salaries are so large as to elevate them high in the social scale.

Lately there has been a very marked increase in the disposition to expand these money market articles into a whole newspaper devoted to finance alone, and hence such journals have arisen as the *Financial News* and the *Financial Times*. Besides these, there are a host of weekly and monthly journals devoted to railways, banks, insurance and other cognate subjects. Many of these papers admit articles of a broader range than could be conveniently inserted in the more absolutely financial organs. The *Economist* and the *Statist*, for example, unravel some of the most tangled problems in political economy, and admit into their columns essays on topics similar to those discussed in works like Adam Smith's *Wealth of Nations* Altogether, in this department there is much increasing activity, and a widening sphere for the writer who draws his inspiration from facts and figures, and has views of his own to propound.

Thence we pass on to a very multifarious and exceedingly important department of periodical literature — trade journalism pure and simple. Here we find almost all industries, arts and manufactures, professions and vocations duly represented by an organ especially devoted thereto, and ignoring every other interest but the one actually represented. In many cases there are several, and sometimes many organs on the same subject, and thus the opportunities for the young writer are increased, and a post on some of these many publications can generally be obtained after a time by a young writer of ability willing to adapt himself to such conditions as may be required of him. The range is very catholic, indeed, and includes something fit for every taste.

The accountants, to take these in alphabetical order, have two organs, then follow the auctioneers, bakers, boot and shoemakers, booksellers, brewers, builders, butchers, and so on through more than sixty trades and industries. A good many of these publications are small, of very limited circulation, and of but little moment to the trade they represent ; others are really great papers, like the *Engineer*, the *Miller*, the *Caterer*, the *Chemist and Druggist*, the *Ironmonger*, the *Builder*, and the *Brewers' Journal*, or the *Wine Trade Review*, and employ men of proved ability and of literary reputation to edit, sub-edit, and write them. Some, however, are what may be called one-man papers, the editor doing all the work, and being himself the staff. In other cases, however, there is an editor, sub-editor, and there are contributors, and all is conducted very much as in the case of an ordinary newspaper. An introduction to this department of journalism may be often obtained to assist in the sub-editorial department, and there one of the duties will be to open and examine the exchanges— *i.e.*, the various papers sent to the office in *exchange* for the one in question. By sending his paper to a number of other journals, the editor thereof receives perhaps a hundred or more journals, which he lays under more or less contribution. It is usual to confine a trade journal very strictly to its own particular subject, and thus, suppose you had to work up matter out of a number of exchanges for a paper which dealt only with metals, you would cut out of the exchanges only such paragraphs and articles as related to the subject, or something subsidiary thereto. In cutting out it is best to have plain paper of uniform size—about that of an octavo page—and gum or paste each cutting on one of these. Write the name of the paper and date at the top, and do not put more than *one* cutting on each slip. Paper is cheap enough, and you will soon find out the practical reasons for this when you are making up "copy" for the printers.

Trade journalism offers many inducements to the young

writer, but let him remember that once embarked therein, he is likely to find himself practically shut out from *general* newspaper work, unless he be greatly gifted and possess friends or influence on the daily Press. Still, in trade journalism there are some prizes of their kind, and some of the editorial chairs—as in the case of the *Builder*—are invested with ample dignity and importance. Then, too, the great tendency of the times is to elevate the general plane of trade journalism, and a far higher tone and much more intellectual power are being infused into its original literary department. It is only right and logical that this should be so, for, examined rightly, trade journals deal with the *productive* and *distributive* forces of the nation; and politics and general news, although interesting enough to the reader, are in nine cases out of ten of infinitely less real importance than is the "visible supply" of wheat or the crop of beetroot. The great political sheets deal chiefly with what Tennyson calls "the windy ways of men," which are but—

> Dust that lightly rises up,
> And is lightly laid again;

but the trade journalist is the true practical political economist, and, in the case of the more powerful and really influential organs of some industries and trades his utterances have a wide-reaching influence, while his paper enables the individual to understand the character of his own calling far better than he ever could without it, and in numberless cases the pages of the trade journals are fraught with matter of sterling business value to those for whose use they are specially intended. Another noteworthy point, too, in the literature of the trade journal is its rising tone of refinement and the much greater finish that is now found in most of the original articles that appear in class papers. All these are very hopeful and encouraging signs of the times, and they render a career in trade or class journals more attractive by far to the young journalist ; but let it be carefully borne in mind that if more is offered in the way of a higher possible literary reputation, very much is required. The times have long passed when any sort of writing would do for the trade sheet, and those who look to make their way upward in trade journalism must equip themselves thoroughly for the work before them, and especially must they combine business habits with a good literary style and unlimited stores of exact information on all points of the subject wherewith they have to deal.

This it is essential to bear in mind. The successful trade journalist must be a good man of business. He must be painstaking to a degree and possess a rapid eye-power for taking in detail. He will have, as among his most ordinary functions, to report on all kinds of inventions and improvements in existing inventions, and he will have to visit factories and large establishments, and he has to be a good descriptive writer, while at the same time he must be mathematically exact when describing a piece of mechanism, or say a chemical process. Exactitude, clearness, and pithiness are great requisites in doing this kind of thing well, and above all, versatility is essential. The more, too, the writing can be made agreeable the better—agreeable by allusions to relevant matters, and by giving, where it is necessary, preliminary introductions bearing on the subject in question and pleasantly working up the interest of the reader in the matter to be dealt with.

I have known an expert writer at this kind of work turn off excellent descriptions of the most opposite things in rapid succession. Some trade journals like the *British Mail* or the *British Trade Journal*, for example, are co-extensive with commerce and productive industry. They, therefore, include in their reports and articles all kinds of subjects. I knew one writer who, after going over large iron works at Millwall, and describing in exact technical

terms the machine tools in "the shop," would walk into
a place like Jackson & Graham's, and after half-an-hour's
look round, would go home and post off the same evening
a paper describing the principal pieces of furniture and
work, in such apt, allusive matter in art and history as to
make a trade notice on a level with a magazine article.   He
had a most imaginative way of looking at all details when an
article of this kind was needed, and a few chairs and cabinets
in the style of the period would draw from him a series of
interesting paragraphs on say Louis XV. and his court, or
he would work in bits from novels and romances, and all
this was done in a perfectly natural manner so that it seemed
a part of the subject.   I cite this because it is desirable
that the young beginner should have an idea of what *tells*
in this department, and of the kind of work he ought to do
if he is to rise in trade journalism.

XI.—How to Work for Many Papers.

There are not a few journalists who are practically "Free
Lances," as they have been aptly called, and who write for
any paper that will accept their "copy". Usually such
writers are more or less retained on some publication for
certain work, and for the rest they watch each opportunity
that offers to put in suitable matter for each passing occasion.
This department in literature may be so worked as to bring
affluence and much reputation, or it may result only in
present poverty and ultimate failure.   I have known a
journalist engaged at once on as many as *nineteen* publications, doing all his work with but slight exceptions, at home,
and remaining practically his own master.   But success of
this kind is based on ability and built up on system.   The
writer in question, and his business history is instructive,
began young on a trade journal which he eventually edited.
The paper did not pay so well as was expected, and he was

dismissed, as the proprietor found he could not pay the salary, about £200 a-year. The editor thereupon, having thoroughly mastered the details of the paper, offered to do the requisite writing for £5 a-month, if allowed to do it in his own time and way. He then soon obtained contributory work on another trade journal, and, on a new monthly organ appearing, offered to provide all the original matter. This offer was accepted; he organised a series of exchanges all round, and having papers in all departments of class and industrial journalism under his eye in a body, and possessing an exceedingly rapid method of turning out accurate work, he soon found other journals ready to take from him special items. The thing worked out thus: One trade journal, perhaps, had say 30, another 50 exchanges sent to its office. Well, the papers whereto he supplied the matter sent him all these papers, and thus he aggregated to himself sources of information possessed by few individual editors in this department of journalism. His principle was all for one and one for all, and thus those who resorted to him found that his information was copious and exact, and could always be obtained just when and where it was wanted. Year by year he extended his reputation in this direction, and eventually made a very good income. The work, however, was exceedingly arduous. System was the secret throughout of the success attained. Each journal wherewith the writer was connected had its set of pigeon holes, and, in going daily over the various papers, cuttings were deposited in each set bearing on the subjects of the journal in question. Articles that *could* be written in advance were turned off and laid up. Each month all stale stuff was thrown out; and thus, by bringing quite a book-keeper's business routine to bear on the literary work, my friend managed to get, and keep, in advance of his very heavy work, and could always find time to supply any unexpected demand, and occasionally to produce better work for the literary magazines on topics of which he had a special knowledge   To many the mere examination of the newspapers and periodicals forming the base and starting-point of all this work, or the mere proof-reading, would have been too much; but here, as in all other things, practice makes perfect, and piece-work greatly quickens the worker.   Those who have to attend a newspaper office daily and devote their whole time to one journal know well how much of that time is uselessly consumed in "waiting" between periods of pressure, in "gossip" and mere idle talk, in going to and fro, and the like.   In the case cited above the golden and guiding rule was, to do each thing *pro re nata*.   My friend could turn from one thing to another with an automatic indifference.   He would take a cutting as a text, and write a leader for a paper devoted to cereals in three-quarters of an hour; and then produce half-a-dozen crisp notes for a journal devoted to beverages; and afterwards write an "original" article (aided by the encyclopædia) on, say, the food-producing palms; and spin out a dry and technical description, from a trade catalogue, of a wood-working machine; and afterwards write a pretty little bright article on a new process for reproducing oil paintings, wherein he would discourse as one who knew the old masters, was thoroughly familiar with modern art, and had quite a touch of Ruskin in his style; and even this was not exhaustive of a day, as commercial articles and trade reports had to be dished up, and a number of miscellaneous paragraphs trimmed into form.   Indeed, if I gave here a full and particular account of what could be, and *was*, done in a single day by one pair of hands, eyes, scissors, a single pen, and the well-stored pigeon holes, fortified by a large library of books of reference—it would be held as incredible by the ordinary reader.   Still, done it was.   Such was the intellectual thrift observed that facts and figures were laid up weeks and months before they were wanted.   Summaries that were only needed at the close of the year had each its pigeon hole, into which cuttings likely to help in their production went directly they were made, and all this enormous mass of work was conducted without any hurry or confusion, and with the most admirable smoothness and ease. This was working on a system wherein each thing done went straight to and exactly hit the proper mark. The worker, as he said, claimed to have no special ability, but he would quaintly say in his dry way that he always had the small beer of practical journalism on draught to any extent, while those who professed to give wine were frequently found to be quite out of that article, and had not the beer even to fall back upon! I know that, as a matter of fact, this writer succeeded a very gifted and brilliant journalist in supplying original editorial notes to a leading family paper, simply because the brilliant writer, after scattering intellectual diamond dust on his notes for two or three weeks running, would find himself "pumped out," and send in really wretched stuff. My friend was never "pumped out," and could always be depended on for exactly the kind of "copy" he had contracted to supply This was, doubtless, a case of a journalistic free lance of a somewhat uncommon type; but it is quite within the capacity of any young aspirant to follow in these tracks The work of class papers grows wider and more complex every year, and method, tact, hard work and ceaseless application are essential to success upon them.

Let it not be supposed that the journalist described above carried all before him even with *his* "copy," which was ever in proper form. He had many articles returned, but then he put them by and frequently found them come in afterwards. He had neither fits of despondency nor of elation; he worked on, grinding out his enormous daily task, and drawing in the proceeds with the indifference of an automaton. His returns were generally large, but, of course, very fluctuating, and as he confessed, often difficult to collect. The beginner in this branch of journalistic literature must often expect trouble in getting paid what is due to him People will pay for everything sooner than for mere writing. Office rent, wages, paper makers, and ink makers, and— sometimes the printer—are all paid by a certain class of journals before the contributor There are, of course, many papers conducted on really admirable business principles, and a writer who gets his matter printed therein is certain of receiving his fee without any trouble whatever It is not always so, however, and truth must be told, as the object of this book is always to help, not to simply please its readers. It cannot be disguised that one of the early troubles of many writers in the press is that of getting paid. Some of the magazines pay pretty punctually others are irregular, and a few take such long credits that the publication has been known to stop before the date came round of settlement for contributions.

Magazine writing is a good branch if only you can get enough of it, and when that happy period arrives, you can probably—paradox as it seems—do much better in other ways At first a few guineas may be earned, but it is hardly possible to make up an income thus, and it is to the journal proper that the young and struggling writer should look for his support A magazine usually comes out monthly, and few writers could expect to have a paper in each number, so that the amount thus raised cannot well be great, and naturally a magazine article takes more time and trouble to write as a rule than a newspaper contribution which is to serve only for the passing moment, and is the true literary ephemera.

Naturally, assuming that the young writer has found his capability to lie in the direction of general all-round writing, he must make a study of the character and probable requirements of each journal to which he proposes to send his matter. There are many things that the novice would send which the man of experience *knows* to be useless, as they *must* be done by the staff, or not done at all. Very great acumen is needed here. I will cite an instance to show what is meant. A new trade journal was started devoted to bread and confectionery. A certain writer who shrewdly guessed that the staff did not include any very classical scholars, turned to his *Deipnosophists,* or the Banquet of the Learned, of Athenâeus, and wrote thence a series of pithy, pointed articles on the bread and pastry of the ancients, which is all duly set forth in Book III. of that curious work, and shows by the way that our pagan friends had really excellent bread and most artistic pastry. These papers were readily accepted and ran some time. They were dressed up, of course, so as to interest and indirectly flatter bakers by showing in what estimation these were held in those days. Ay, but I hear someone object, suppose a fellow does not know Greek; what then? The writer, however, managed very well with the literal translation of Athenâeus, which is to be found in Bohn's excellent classical library, and has before now worked out excellent matter in a like manner from the Latin, French, German, Spanish, and other languages !

This is a hint and can be practically followed up by those who have wit and industry. Speaking of industry reminds me of the great necessity there is for this in literary work, at all events in connection with journalism, although some heaven-born geniuses—in their own estimation—imagine that they need work only when the spirit moves them. The writer was at one time much pressed, working a combination of class journals, and among the number was one devoted to fire extinction. It was a monthly publication, and gave an epitome of all the fires at home and abroad during the interval. A young aspirant for journalistic work had the task of compiling the fires for one month, which

was quite an easy thing, as he had only to look over the
principal daily papers, cut out the records of each fire and
gum each on a slip of paper, putting them under different
heads: Metropolitan, Provincial, Colonial, American, and
Foreign.   If he did this satisfactorily, he was to be sub-
editor   Yet it will hardly be believed that he had not the
perseverance to carry out this task, and when, towards the
end of the time, he was asked for the work, he had virtually
nothing ready !   He had, I believe, some vague notion that
he could pick up all the items at the last moment, and consequently failed altogether, besides causing much trouble.
Yet he was well educated and possessed of some decided
literary ability, but he could not learn the old lesson that a
man must prove himself faithful in little before people will
care to trust him with big things.

No; to succeed here, attention must be paid to small
details, and the young writer must not presume to measure
the relative importance of different departments of labour
by *his* ideas, which he will find eventually very greatly modified by the magic hand of practical experience.

It will be noted that I have not said a word on the subject
of fiction in connection with the periodical press.   This subject properly belongs to the production of the book, and not
the journalistic form of literature, and will be found duly
dealt with in the second part of this work.

XII.—THE ANONYMITY OF THE PRESS

There has been very much controversy of late on the
subject of the anonymity of journalism.   Truly, much may
be said both for and against the existing practice; and it is
well known that on the continent the custom prevails for
each writer to sign his work—and he must, indeed, do so
by the press law existing, although he is not compelled to
sign his own name.   On the side of anonymity, it has been

contended that the English press stands first in the world, and has all along been perfectly anonymous; and this anonymity is further asserted to be the secret of its power; but obviously this is an argument quite open to the attack that the English press may be the most powerful in the world not *because* but *in spite of its perfectly anonymous character.* In leader writing, no doubt, where the writer has to express the opinions of the paper as a whole in which the article appears rather than his own, the argument against signing each article may be more cogent; but it cannot be consistently denied that on many grounds the existing plan of silence and secrecy as to the writers of articles, and reviews especially, is open to certain objections. Practically, too, it should be remembered that signed articles are generally much better written than those which appear anonymously. Special articles and leaders are, no doubt, well written; but then they are well remunerated. It cannot be truthfully denied that much ordinary writing is, after a time, done by the staff journalist not as well, but rather as badly as possible, consistently with the retaining of the work. But then comes the question of the morality of the anonymous plan. As things are, the writer in each great paper carries with him in each original article the entire weight and influence of the journal; and, although he may not be a powerful or even a very good writer, his work will *tell.* It has appeared, let us say, in some great daily sheet, and thence it must be very good. Now, anyone would allow that by making original writers, as a rule, sign their work, those who are clever would advance to better things, and the dull and inapt scribe would very soon be squeezed out altogether. The barrister and the physician are both personally associated with their respective work; and now, when the press generally has risen to such a height of power and of ever-increasing influence, it is well, perhaps, that the general reader should know a little more of his leaders in thought and his guides in ethics. Take an extreme case · some leader lauds Darwin or Huxley as the only true intellectual lights of the age—and this, emanating from a great daily paper, is swallowed as gospel by the majority of readers; but, if the article were signed, readers would know much better whether the writer was exactly one who could justly be held as superior to Paley in the past or to Sir William Dawson in the present! Then, the plan of signing articles would, in a measure, put a stop to the un-principled practice of men writing on both sides of the same question. I know it has been argued that this is justifiable on the principle of the advocate, who must do his best for his client. But the cases are quite different. The barrister takes each case separately and without relation to anything else, whereas in politics and in all forms of public ethics, there is *continuity* of subject; and the writer who aims at doing both sides is in the proverbial false position of him who attempts to serve two masters. Of late years, indeed, there has been a growing tendency to break through the anonymous rule, and decidedly the able writer benefits wherever he can place his name. In ephemeral newspapers, which some one has not inaptly called the grave of much unrecognised genius, a writer may go on for years pouring forth really good, instructive and popular matter, and, at the end of all, he is not one whit the better for it. He has had to live on the fees earned, and when he stops writing, another steps in and fills the place, and the former scribe sinks beneath the waters of oblivion. This is, indeed, the cold shadow of newspaper anonymity. Take a case. I know a journalist who conducted a class organ of real importance for nine years. During that period he wrote every original contri-bution that appeared in it, and produced over a thousand articles all directed more or less towards certain ends which were ultimately in part attained. Had the writer's name appeared during this time, he would have been known to, and liked by, thousands of readers, and his pen would have become a power, for it was ever consistently employed in a good and great cause. The net result is that *he* would have become a power, whereas the *journal* became the power and could cast him off, and resign the direction of the momentum he had given to other hands. Here I conceive we hit the core of the whole dispute. The man makes the newspaper after all, but the capitalist who runs it naturally desires to absorb the individual into the editorial "we," because this principle, to a great extent, limits the reward which the writer might obtain for his work. In France, it is well known that many writers of fame and fortune owe both simply to the fact that, being industrious writers, they have kept their names constantly before the reading world, and should editor or proprietor act unjustly or ungenerously towards such men, they have but to take their pens to another paper, knowing that numbers of their readers will follow them. It is very different in England The truth and justice of these remarks is after all accentuated by the fact that journals are very glad, as in a prospectus now lying before me of a new coming paper, to dwell on the ability of known writers who are to contribute to their columns. When a writer becomes great, he is allowed to sign; how is he to become great? By signing all his original work and so having the greatest of possible incentives to do good work. But then you will not let him sign! It is like the old story of the author in manuscript who sought to place some little thing in print and was told by all to whom he applied, that he must have some published work to offer as evidence of his qualifications! "Where shall I go?" he asked in despair. "Ah! that is *your* affair, succeed and we will listen to you with pleasure!"

Another point of very great moment in the interest of public morality, is the question of a common line of action among the great journals on certain topics in which the public is specially interested. At present it frequently happens that, from a family point of view, the great daily papers become for a time unspeakably objectionable, owing to the fierce competitive race between them as to who shall give the fullest details of something utterly abominable, or some virulent and foul attack on morality and religion generally The excuse offered in detail by the editorial offenders is the everlasting one in England, viz.—business. An editor says frankly he is grieved, but if *he* limits his reports, and especially if he expurgates them, his rivals will at once transfer thousands of his readers to themselves ; in one word, he has before him the alternatives of doing what is right and ruining himself, or simply falling in line with his contemporaries and sharing with them the moral responsibility of corrupting the people and disgusting all thoughtful and right-minded persons.

Surely in so associative an age when such rare facilities for organisation exist, it would be easy enough to establish a National Council of Editors of the United Kingdom, whereto every editor would *ex officio* belong. Chosen delegates thence could meet from time to time to discuss all large questions of editing ; and as emergencies arose, special means could be devised for enabling editors to agree to a common course of action By this means, when matters arose which are clearly unfit for general reading, all the leading papers would agree to do as the *Times*, to its honour, has done on not a few occasions, viz, decide on giving only a bare statement of the facts and no more. Probably there would be some vile prints that would seek to serve up such matters in detail, but these might be left to their own shame. Many persons will gloat over an abomination in a daily London paper, who would be ashamed to be caught reading such a paper as *Town Talk*. This is no piece of idle moralising. As I write these lines the prospectus of the *Daily Graphic*, that remarkable feature in nineteenth century journalism, lies before me, and I read therein the following significant sentence relative to the editing: "It shall contain nothing from pen or pencil which a parent would wish to conceal from his family". This can, as the prospectus goes on to observe, be undoubtedly effected without making the paper either "prudish" or "namby-pamby".

Certainly if all respectable editors were associated together in one great connected body, on national lines only, not political, for *that* could never be in this country of party strife, they would find no real difficulty in deciding *pro re nata* on a common course of action in treating matters clearly against public morals. The good to the nation in general, and to the young in particular, that would result thence would be enormous, and how much, too, the press would be augmented in dignity and increased in power; for after all, power derived from action that is right and good always far transcends aught drawn from base appeals to the worst propensities and the lowest tastes of mankind.

That I am in no way singular or eccentric in my views on this head may be seen from the subjoined extract from an article that appeared in the *London Echo* for December 27, 1889, written by Mr. John Page Hopps, which run thus—

"It is a delicate question, but the time has fully come for asking whether newspapers are justified in so entirely ministering to the morbid curiosity of the worst side of poor human nature. It is, of course, necessary that the brutalities of the world should be chronicled. How else could they be fought? But it is one thing to chronicle, and another thing to revel in details, and details of late years have been far too common. Under a thin veneer of deprecation, there has been a discreditable eagerness to supply and dish up the ghastly details of Whitechapel murders and the beastly details of the divorce courts It is easy to distinguish between what ought to be known and what need not be known by everyone —what, as a painful necessity, must come into the house; and what has no more business there than a pailful of slush or a bucket of blood. We are passing through a fiery ordeal of publicity. It is a perilous experiment; but we need not make the furnace hotter than is necessary by catering for the cads."

This, in substance, is exactly what many have been urging for years past; and with each passing year the need for press reform becomes greater. But to take one more case in point. On December 28, 1889, there appeared in the *Athenæum* an elaborate review of Lord Tennyson's *Demeter and other Poems*, wherein the reviewer, after dwelling on the fact that Tennyson was the greatest poet of the age, alluded to the piece in the volume entitled "By an Evolutionist," and thereupon remarked—

"Many of the readers of this poem will recall the terrible shock the doctrine that man was descended from the brutes gave to all of us. It had the fascination of a horrible repulsion. It seemed to mock at poetry, mock at art, mock at the charm of womanhood, mock at religion, mock at everything that the idealist's soul had previously cherished. There seemed to be no possibility of reconciling idealism with such a hideous reality as this. Thousands of thinkers passed through this ordeal. The refusal to accept the inevitable destroyed Carlyle as a thinker, and destroyed Browning, and many another. And yet it has to be accepted, and idealism has to be reconciled to it."

Now, this *dictum*, appearing as it does in the first review of the greatest nation in the world, naturally carries tremendous force with it. It is the *Athenæum* that speaks, but we should certainly prefer to know *who* is the all-knowing sage who thinks that, because Carlyle refused to subscribe to evolution, he was "destroyed" as "a thinker". It were better in all ways that the writer of such a statement should reveal himself. Otherwise, he gathers to himself all the weight of the talent, ability and genius that has lifted this famous review to a plenitude of power and authority. By the way, turning to Canon Bell's work, *A Winter on the Nile*, published about the same time, it is worthy of note that the result of *his* personal investigations of the remaining relics of ancient Egypt goes to show that in the early grandeur and high mental attainments of the ancient Egyptians we have an actual witness *against* the theory— for it is *only* a theory—of the evolution of man, as suggested by Haeckel and others of his school. The truth is that evolution is wholly *speculative*. Authentic history abundantly shows that nations have *descended* from civilisation to barbarism, and, as Sir William Dawson says, "the speculations as to the derivation of man from lower animals obtruded by some popular writers on a too-credulous public . . . have no basis in archæology or geology, since no transitional form between man and beast has been discovered". But it is needless to say more; only, when such tremendous assertions are in question as those quoted above, it were certainly well for the *name* of the writer to appear, that, as already said, we might know *who* thus presumes to impose a *new dogma of his own* on the world at large Science is confessedly a progressive, as theology is a fixed branch of intellectual knowledge; and it is not, to say the least, for even an unbeliever in the Holy Bible to write that evolution *must* be accepted. Far better for such a writer to sign his name, and say, "*I* think so". Then he would be above criticism, for opinion is free.

XIII.—CORRESPONDENCE.

There is, besides the various other departments already noticed, one, that of special or occasional correspondent, which is very decidedly worth cultivating, a department of

newspaper work for which there is certainly an increasing
demand.   As the editor of the *Times* is to the editor of the
smallest local sheet, so, of course, is the foreign correspondent of the great dailies to the rank-and-file of " our own
correspondents ".   To be a newspaper correspondent in a
foreign capital involves a host of qualifications rarely found
in one individual, and then, too, a man must be in the
" track " of this choice department of journalism to even
hope for such an exceptional position.   Usually the gentle-
men who fill these posts hold them for life " during good
behaviour," and they are singularly favoured positions of great
honour and profit to the man who is fond of society and is
capable of maintaining his place in the highest circles.   The
pay given for this kind of work is very liberal, but the positions are limited.   Mr William Beatty-Kingston, writing on
this very subject, remarks : " Of all the European realms,
England is the one in which, through the agency of a free,
wealthy, and enterprising Press, popular interest in matters
political (foreign as well as domestic) has been the most
generally stimulated and developed.   Englishmen of all
classes bestow more attention upon the politics of countries
not their own than do Frenchmen, Germans, Russians,
Italians, or Spaniards, not to mention the less important
European nationalities."   The same writer dilates on the
way in which the English newspaper-reading public is
dependent on its foreign correspondents, and cites some
notable examples of men who have raised this branch of
newspaper work to a very high level indeed   Among those
named are General Eber, Count Arrivabene, and Dr. Abel.
The latter is, I believe, the master of some score of languages,
living and dead, and is even capable of writing, as well as
reading, Egyptian hieroglyphics !
    It must be evident from this that very uncommon mental
attainments are indispensable for the man who has the
ambition to write a foreign letter.   The *Daily Telegraph*

Paris article giving the news and gossip of that city from day to day, however, is a sign of the increasing popularity of this form of journalism, and in time to come, doubtless, more journals will compete to produce good foreign letters from resident writers. It is practicable, too, for a young man having some linguistic skill and literary ability to obtain employment as an assistant to a foreign correspondent, and thus experience may be acquired

But without flying thus high, there is abundance of work of the kind to be done, and London news-letters and the like now regularly appear in many of the best provincial papers, while many of the Colonial journals are following suit. Much of such work is paid for very badly, but then an expert can often make his facts serve for several quarters, varying the style and verbal clothing, and thus render this branch fairly remunerative, while some newspapers pay very well. The writing is in the first person usually, and this is in itself a great facility. London letters or other forms of special correspondence are not difficult to compose, while practice should soon lead to proficiency. In some cases the writer has to obtain his matter direct. He must interview the people likely to afford him information, go round to the picture galleries, and run over the newest books, have a sharp eye to the shop windows for novelties, perhaps for paragraphs on dress and fashion, and so forth. Some papers require their letters to commence with politics, and then to descend through social items to art, literature, and perhaps at the end there is a little domestic information that the ladies like to read. Many letters are supplied by men who are engaged as Parliamentary reporters, and really *are* in the House; but others are "concocted" and cleverly evolved out of information derived from the daily papers or retailed second-hand from those who are really behind the political scenes. Audacity marks many of these productions, and pleases editor

and readers too, especially in obscure corners of the
country where it seems grand to read that "our correspondent" thought "Gladstone looked younger than ever and
was inclining to a smaller collar," or that Lord Salisbury
"had an anxious and very care-worn expression," when all
the while the writer has, perhaps, never looked on either of
these illustrious men.   One thing the correspondent must
be, and that is smart and vigilant above all   Wherever he
is out and about he may find food for his pen, and he
should ever be ready to assimilate all that comes in his way,
and to store up in the right memory-cell just what will run
off nicely at the pen's point when he is writing his letter.
Thus, to illustrate this point, when once supplying special
correspondence for Australian readers, I saw, while hurrying
along, in a tobacconist's window, the legend "Australian
Bird's Eye".   I bought half-an-ounce, ascertained that it
was of Queensland growth, that it was being experimentally
sold, and had been approved by several customers.   Need
I add that in my next letter, there appeared a fine flourish
about Queensland Bird's Eye in London, and this was, of
course, written in a way to afford information and pleasure
to the Australian reader, and to prove that Queensland will
one day be a great tobacco producing region   Again, in
passing through Leadenhall Market I saw some Tasmanian
apples on sale and thence secreted as it were, by an instinct,
a paragraph on the progress now making of Australian
fruits in London.   I noted one day some swans, cats, and
small cage-birds in a corner of the same market, in remarkably close quarters, and thence easily evolved a paragraph.
Indeed after a time, the writer who properly cultivates his
faculty of observation, in harmonious conjunction with the
writing art, will find that to see anything at all out of the
common is practically to write it down in his memory
whence it has only to be transcribed when required.

As remarked above, there is much scope for the work of

the general newspaper correspondent. He will, when once he gets on a journal, often find that this form of contribution may lead to his obtaining other work, and if only he proves himself trustworthy, he is likely to be permanently employed. I say—if *trustworthy* This is vital. Never be tempted on any account into exaggeration, or writing aught that you know is not true. It is possible you may escape detection, but the habit once contracted (apart from its being *morally* wrong) will cling to, and eventually get such a hold of you, that in the end you are pietty sure to come to complete disgrace, and perhaps, cut short your whole career on the Press.

If you are living in the provinces, you may by perseverance get put on by the local paper to report the district, and this may lead to a sub-editorship; or you may, if you are in an industrial centre, be retained by some trade journal. Do not despise a humble and ill-paid opening. Honest work is always worth doing well. It may appear to the village genius who writes blank veise on the fields and woods nearly up to the ordinary level of James Thomson, or who can rhyme on the lambs better than the author of the *Farmer's Boy*, a terrible falling off to indite a weekly report to an agricultural journal as to how the crops are looking, or to send to a trade journal an account of the new machinery in the neighbouring flour mill, but this work is that which *pays*, work it is which may lead to independence, and it may some day even lift the writer into a sphere where there will be an actual demand for his verse, which he will write a great deal better when he has mastered as a writer on the press all the details of literary technics If it be objected that by that time all his poetic faculty has been killed, then he may be sure that leisure and idleness would have ultimately proved that it was either a *weed*, or such a weakly plant that it was not worth cultivating! These may seem harsh facts, but facts they are, and those who doubt them now, will in due time come to see their force and application.

In many cases it will be found that small, humble beginnings of journalistic work are the best in the end. Many a young writer is forced too early into a position really beyond his capacity. He finds that journalism has much hurry about it, and to him, in his inexperience, much confusion. He consequently blunders, and is blamed, and perhaps has to "give it up," whereas, had he graduated from small things, he would have been in a very different position. The truth is, there are many "incapables" in the journalistic world whose comparative uselessness is due to the fact that they have never been grounded in rudimentary matters, and have been placed on the top of things of whose bottoms they are profoundly ignorant. In my own case, when very young, I saw at a certain printer's a journalist periodically preparing produce market reports for a large and important commercial publication It was careful, good work, quite out of *my* line then, and yet it struck me that it would be well to be able to do it. I therefore watched, and occasionally asked for a little information, and soon found out something of the way in which the market reports were "dressed up" and made intelligible; and, although it was many years before an opportunity arose to *apply* this information, the time came which brought some specially well paid work, at which a guinea can be earned in two hours But without a thorough *grounding* in the essential principles of such work, instead of two hours it would more likely have taken two days to do it, and then it would have been "botched". In reality, as a rule, I have always found in practical journalism that *rapid* work is the best. The reason is clear : the experienced and able writer *knows* his work, and why should *he* delay it? The inept, half-trained scribe *does not know* it properly, and he hesitates, tries back, crosses out and writes new matter, and generally hashes up the whole thing; while the other, who has early acquired the technics, so to speak, of the matter in question, simply runs off the "copy" with a flying pen, and it comes up in proof in correct form. In this case, however, finish and speed are the natural result of years of experience, of careful practice, and of a determination only to attempt in journalism what one can really do.

XIV.—ILLUSTRATED AND COMIC PAPERS.

The true Volupük is found in the picture. Painting, indeed, is the real passigraphy, the universal language, and as Campbell wrote—

> Possessing more than vocal power,
>   Persuasive more than poet's tongue;
> Whose lineage in a raptured hour,
>   From Love, the sire of Nature, sprung.

The progress of late years of the illustrated press, culminating in the *Daily Graphic*, has been simply extraordinary. Not to mention the higher artistic types such as the *Illustrated London News* and the *Graphic*, and excluding comic and humorous or satirical sheets, to be considered presently, there are now some hundreds of illustrated papers, and every year the tendency is for more to appear, and for journals that have hitherto disdained the graphic art to adopt the plan of giving illustrations For one cause of this there has been a vast diffusion of art among the masses, and the picture is such a rapid and easy form of reading. It is exactly suited to an age of hurry and sensationalism, and in due time the reportorial pencil will quite rival the reportorial pen. There may be much evil in this, as when the daily papers shall begin to give us sketch outlines of atrocious crimes; but much good must also result, and those journals which foster true art and aim at evoking the

higher and nobler sentiments, undoubtedly, will deserve well
of the nation. The great success of papers like *Scraps*,
however, is due probably to their comic character, and with
the coming improvement in the mechanical agencies for reproducing sketches, we may look confidently for better
things than smudgy pictures of more or less stupid practical
jokes. Here lies an opening, and one likely to widen, for
those who can combine artistic with literary skill; and just
as shorthand is now looked for as a matter-of-course accom-
plishment in the young journalist, so the day may come
when to *sketch* may be a qualification frequently required,
and one of which the possession will be of great importance
to the career of many. It must be remembered, too, that
the Australasian press has a strong leaning towards pictorial
art, and here too, openings will occur, and altogether the
prospect offered to artistic talent by illustrated journals is
very encouraging.

There is nothing new under the sun. The comic and
humorous press are ancient as Aristophanes who employed the stage in place of a printing press; and then
again, the "fools" and jesters of the mediæval period were
in a great measure to their generation what the comic press
is to us now. In truth, what with wandering mummers and
strolling minstrels the Middle Ages were well supplied with
plenty of verbal fun and much quaint fancy. If we turn
but to some of the records of old English poetical facetiæ
we shall find abundant traces of this; and this is, by the
way, a field which would be well worth a thorough literary
exploration. In such a piece as "The Schoolhouse of
Women," printed by Wyer in 1542, we find a severe satire
on the sex, and then came "The Praise of all Women,"
printed by John Kyng, and intended by Gosenhyll the
author as a corrective to the former work. Here the writer
feigns a vision of woman as he lay asleep, and the fair
dames depute him to undertake their defence. Venus her-

self is one of the characters. Even here a sly satire peeps out as in the following passage, which is, I think, unique of its kind—

> Some say that woman had no tongue
> After that God had her create,
> Until the man took leaves long
> And put them under her palate.

The closing passage is particularly noteworthy for its satiric ingenuity—

> An aspen leaf of the Devil he gate
> And for it moveth with every wind
> They say women's tongues be of like kind!

But to return. The comic and humorous press of our own day is largely based on and derived from caricature, which carries us back to Hogarthian days. The very word coming from the Italian *caricare*, to overload or overcharge, indicates the inherent exaggeration of the thing, and, in truth, caricature is the antithesis of idealisation, and depends for its success on the disproportionate development of some special characteristic of the subject treated. It is, therefore, quite destructive of the idea of harmony, which is the prime essential of the ideal, and when employed on persons bears about the same relation to true pictorial art that the farce does to the true drama. It will be remembered that once when in his declining days a lady expressed to Hogarth a desire to learn the art of caricature, the great master thereof said, " Alas! it is a faculty not to be envied. Never draw caricatures. By the long practice of it I have lost the enjoyment of beauty. I never have the satisfaction to behold the human face divine." There is much truth in this, but as we know, the comic illustrated press of to-day has an infinitely wider scope than in the days of James Gillray, who first reduced Hogarth's satirical method to the level of periodical publication, and much ingenious fancy, much true poetic taste, may be found in the best productions of papers like *Punch, Judy*, and *Fun*.

The famous *Charivari*, established in Paris in 1832, preceded our *Punch* by nine years. The derivation of the word *Charivari* is usually given as a French term signifying a great tumult, or the inarticulate cries of a noisy multitude. The German corresponding word is *Katzenmusik*, which evidently refers to the midnight yelling of cats !

Punch has been and is a great power in this country, and truth to say, that power has been uniformly exercised in the right way, and has on occasion been productive of distinct national good.

Australia has of recent years developed a corresponding comic press Both Melbourne and Sydney, and Brisbane, too, the capital of Queensland, have each a *Punch*, our antipodean contemporaries being equipped in a manner corresponding to the Colonies, and " Toby " giving place to the kangaroo. In these days the tendency is very strong towards the further extension of the comic and satiric press, and especially to introduce columns devoted more or less to what is purely amusing, funny, and witty in the make-up of ordinary journals. It is, therefore, well for the young aspirant to inform himself somewhat on this head, to read up at least a little in wit and humour, and fit himself properly for the task of selecting items of this kind for the paper he is engaged on, a task that may befall him at any time in the course of varied sub-editorial work. Many journals here draw largely on American sources for this kind of " copy," and others simply make selections from the current comic press. When we note that even the *Grocers' Journal* now dishes up weekly a selection of jokes to lighten its serious trade articles and commercial intelligence, it will be perceived that this sort of " spicing " for the newspaper must be very general indeed. This is the case, and it will be incre singly s .

In regard to the production of comic, humorous, or even satiric "copy," no amount of book instruction, or, indeed, of teaching of any kind, could possibly help the young writer, beyond putting him earlier into the best way to employ his gift, so far as it goes, for this kind of light literature. You could no more teach anybody to be comic than you could teach him to be a poet. Yet, as in the latter case, the mechanical part of versifying can be taught to *anyone* willing to learn and to take the requisite pains, so even in relation to comic "copy" a good deal can be suggested and defined by judicious study of the works of professed humourists, and he who has learned to discriminate aright between wit, humour and satire is *pro tanto* the more likely to find his own observations run in channels which *may* evolve something of the kind, and surprise himself quite as much as others. The faculty for perceiving the anomalies, the discrepancies, and the disproportions of life all around us, and for noticing hidden points of resemblance in things superficially quite dissimilar and the reverse can be cultivated. Men like Tom Hood, Mark Lemon, or even Theodore Hook, are born, not made, and still even these owed much to *culture* and to early training. An old and neglected English poet declares that—

> All things are big with jest, nothing that's plain
> But may be witty if thou hast the vein.

The word "humour" comes remotely from the Sanscrit *ama* (moist); and, as the ancients thought—not without some reason—that the temper of mind in the individual turned on the state of the fluids of the body, so the word *humour* came to indicate the tone and direction of mind itself, as indicated in such expressions as he had a fit of ill or good humour. The main difference between wit and humour, which often interpenetrate, appears to be that the former is less provocative of laughter than the other. In

An Analysis of Wit and Humour, by F. R. Fleet, the
writer says "Three phases constitute risible matter—of
imperfections in beings possessing, in reality or in our
imagination, the capacities for pleasure or pain—these
phases being, (1st) really or apparently involuntary retro-
gression in respect of welfare by loss or pain, (2ndly)
experience of obstruction of legitimate progress, and (3rdly)
inferiority to certain standards of perfection". A little
reflection, and a brief reference to any "comic" publication, will illustrate these views; and, for one thing, we may
note how largely the comic fancy revels in putting serious
and eminently "respectable" persons in positions of pain,
peril and ridicule. This is humour, no doubt, although it
be of a kind that does not always commend itself to the
moralist.

Wit, coming from the Saxon *wit* or *ge-wit*, undoubtedly
signifies, in a primary sense, the understanding, and includes,
therefore, the great faculty of apprehension. It is difficult to
correctly define wit in its special sense. Originally the word
meant simply wisdom, and anciently the man of *witte* was
a *wise* man Pope tells us that wit is a quick conception;
Locke says it consists in quickness of fancy and judgment.
The nearest approach to a satisfactory definition seems to
lie in stating that it is a peculiar faculty, connected closely
with imagination, and especially shown in the setting forth
of remote resemblances between dissimilar objects, or an
unexpected likeness where nothing of the kind is looked for
in opposite things In humour, properly considered, the
result is more risible, whereas, in wit, the effect is usually
more intellectual; and we are pleased by the ingenuity of
the saying as in the well-worn couplet—

> Immodest words admit of this defence—
> That want of decency is want of sense.

Those who are interested in this subject should consult

Hazlitt, Sydney Smith, Coleridge (who has very fully discussed the principal points of the subject), and Leigh Hunt.

By reading up, much will be gained, as in all other departments of journalism, and much may be suggested to the student's mind which may open to himself unexpected sources on which to draw.

Wit has been called the pupil of the soul's clear eye, and, certainly, it is, among other things, inherent to the clear vision, and thus comes close to, if it be not partly identical with, the poetic faculty itself

XV.—THE NEWSPAPER PRESS AND THE PRINTING OFFICE.

Some obscurity rests on the actual origin of the newspaper. It has been said, with obvious absurdity, that a French physician invented the journal, having found his gossip more welcome to his patients than his medicine! This worthy applied to Cardinal Richelieu for a patent to publish the *Paris Gazette* in 1622. But we must travel farther for the germ of the newspaper, which certainly existed in the famous *Acta Diurna* or *Acta Publica* of ancient Rome. These were government gazettes which appeared daily and gave an enumeration of the births and deaths, some account of money paid into the treasury, and information as to the supply of corn, thus anticipating our *Mark Lane Express* and *Miller* and *Agricultural Gazette* of to-day. In addition to all this there were extracts from the *Acta Forensica*, being edicts of the magistracy, and a variety of other information highly important for the good citizen to know.

It is generally said that the modern newspaper began in Germany, soon after the invention of printing. There seems good ground for believing that when Charles V. conducted an expedition against Tunis, a number of *Zeitungs*, *i.e*, newspapers, appeared from the period 1536. and it is

universally admitted that small sheets were published at
Augsburg, Vienna, and Nürnberg during the sixteenth
century.   The contents of these sheets clearly confirm their
claims to be the original newspapers of Europe, for they
relate to the discovery of America, conflicts with the Turks,
executions, inundations, and other like events.   In the
next century the Venetian Government issued what was
known as *Notizie Scritte.*   These contained accounts of the
wars of the republic, and being sold for a coin called a
Gazeta, gave rise to the word "Gazette".

As to the earliest English journals, much doubt has existed
as to what is really the initial issue.   It was supposed that
a *Mercury* was published in the reign of Elizabeth with an
account of the Armada, but this print has been demonstrated
a forgery.   It is said that the earliest English newspapers
belong to the time of James I.   A writer in the *Gentleman's
Magazine* states that with the Long Parliament originated
appeals to the people, a series of *Mercuries;* one of these
appeared in 1644, entitled *Mercurius Fumigosus.*   Evidently
even our slow-going ancestors, as many deem them, had
some notion of sensationalism and thought that a paper
"smoking hot" would be popular.

I am much inclined, however, to think that some newspapers existed at a very much earlier date, for it is on record
that in the 36th year of the reign of Henry VIII., a royal
proclamation was made to call in and prohibit "certain
bookes printed of newes of the king's armies' successes in
Scotland".   All these for some occult reason were called in
and burned.   The newspaper even now is a very perishable
form of literature, and it was quite practicable in those
tyrannical times to wholly suppress and utterly destroy any
sheet obnoxious to the governing powers.   A small paper
was issued for Mr. Newbery in 1619, called *News out of
Holland,* and three years later there appeared a print
entitled *The Certaine News of the Present Week,* edited by

Nathaniel Butler.   But for a long while it was hard to distinguish between newspapers and pamphlets, and no doubt
the first regular English journal was founded in 1663 by Sir
Roger L'Estrange, and entitled *The Public Intelligencer.*
This ceased on the issue of the *London Gazette*, which
appeared 1665, and then succeeded other sheets.   Difficulty,
however, was felt in those days by those who had to fill
them, and passages from the Scriptures were put in, and
frequently a blank left, so that the reader might write thereon
a letter when passing the precious journal on to a friend !
Until the reign of Queen Anne few journals appeared more
often than once a-week ; but war changed all this, and the
campaigns of Marlborough stimulated the press so much
that seventeen journals appeared thrice a week.   In 1709,
the *Daily Courant* commenced and the *London Daily Post*
established in 1726, became in 1752 the *Public Advertiser*,
and acquired historic fame as being the medium in which
the celebrated letters of Junius first appeared.   The earliest
English provincial journal is said to be the *Norwich Postman*,
which came out in 1706 at a penny, but quaintly and naïvely
informed its readers that " a half-penny would not be
refused ".

It is, however, the present century that has developed the
newspaper into the fourth estate of the realm.   Looking
back some fifty years, we find the newspapers of the United
Kingdom were some 400 ; now they number, roundly calculated, 2500 !   Then the journals were high-priced and very
restricted as to sources for news, and in the provinces were
usually circulating when the news they contained was quite
stale.   Now, if we glance at any good newspaper directory,
we shall find nearly every calling and interest—almost every
thing concerning men and women—duly represented by
some special press organ.   The trade journals reckon up
to about 100, and are increasing.   Then, if we turn to the
magazine—a form of literature allied to the newspaper in

many ways—we find that, whereas in 1861 there were 481 magazines, there are now 1600 magazines and reviews. These are enormous numbers, when we consider the amount of intellectual activity that they represent, and when we reflect on the great army of writers that must necessarily be employed to supply the immense quantity of matter required to fill what are veritably millions of pages. As to what has justly been designated as "Greater Britain," it appears that in 1889, in round numbers, there were in the United States and Canada no fewer than 15,000 newspapers and periodicals, of which 2000 were daily. Then Australia and New Zealand have already many hundreds of papers, while India and South Africa have many more. In a word, the number of publications of the periodical class produced in English is stupendous, and constitutes a power that, great as it is now, is yet only in its infancy. The circulation of all these sheets is past conception, as the figures are much too great for any ordinary mind to even faintly realise. As long ago as 1880 the circulation of the world's press was put at the unthinkable figures of 10,600,000,000! Most decidedly we live in a newspaper era; and, now that the literary workers in this department of literature are to be reckoned by thousands in even our own country, it is evident that a field is offered for the young as fair and as promising as in any other of the recognised vocations of life.

There can be no manner of doubt but that the British and American press stand first, and occupy, indeed, an eminence high above that of all the rest of Europe. The British press is in the very van of progress, and must be reckoned as first among the great intellectual powers of the age. And, now, let us turn to the printing office, without which the periodic sheet practically would cease to exist.

It is curious and true that, while literature could very well dispense with the printing office, the newspaper is the creature of the invention of printing, which has done wonders for the diffusion of literature, but has had very little to do with its highest phases. Obviously *all* works of transcendent genius would still be written if printing did not exist, just as was the case before the art was even thought of. The newspaper, however, could not appear, and is distinctly the creature of the printing press. One word may be in place on the method for reproduction of copies of any literary work that existed anterior to Fust's movable types.

The word *book* comes from the Anglo-Saxon *boc*, and is believed to be identical with *beech*. At all events, it is curious that some of the early northern nations wrote on slips of wood, engraving the letters with an iron or some kind of metal instrument. *Biblos*, the Greek for book, is derived from the Egyptian name of the *papyrus*, which, being rolled round a wooden stick, formed literally the *volume*. I believe that the honour of breaking up the very inconvenient "roll" into pages is due to Julius Cæsar, and his brief notes, laid one on the other something like the modern book, were termed *paginæ*, and thence we obtain the word "page".

Under the Roman Empire in its palmy days there were certain persons who organised bodies of copyists, who sat and wrote around a reader, who gave out what the author had written syllabically. By this simple means each "reading" yielded as many copies as there were copyists. As the batches of manuscripts were turned out they went to men called *librarioli*. These were persons of taste who put in ornamental scrolls and "got up" the manuscripts in as attractive a manner, no doubt, as the price agreed on permitted, and thence the copies went to *bibliopegi*, who bound up the sheets. Finally, the books were sent to the *bibliopola*—viz., the actual bookseller. Thus it will be seen that, after all, there was some kind of parallelism between the ancient and modern methods of putting forth a book. The copyists, of whom some of the great Roman publishers re-

tained fifty or even a hundred, answered to our modern
compositors, and it is probable that an edition, say of 500
copies of the *Odes of Horace* or the *Æneid of Virgil* could
be turned out by the Roman publisher promptly if not as
quickly as now by a house in Paternoster Row In the
middle ages the monks in the seclusion of the cloister were
much occupied in copying various works and generally
multiplying manuscripts, and with them the art of illumina-
tion was brought to perfection.

Modern printing offices vary greatly. Some, indeed, are
fitted up in quite a grand style, and those engaged
in any form of work involving attendance at the printers'
find well-furnished and very comfortable rooms at their
disposition. This is not, however, always the case, and
in some it is difficult to discover a place to sit down in.
Work, such as proof correction or making-up of "copy," or
writing some late original matter must be done standing at
one of the iron tables on which the compositors "impose"
the "formes," and comfort and quiet must be dispensed
with completely. The principal parts of a printing office are,
after all, the composing-rooms, where the compositor stands
(some sit on a stool) before what is called his *frame*. This is
a wooden structure having wooden trays at the top called cases
(hence the term "at case"), which are divided into as many
little shallow compartments as there are types in the fount.
The trays rest one above the other slanting, but each within
easy reach of the compositor's arm. These are known as
upper and lower cases. The former contain capitals and
small capitals and figures. The latter hold the small letters
and punctuation marks. The compartments are so arranged
that the type most in use are the nearest to the compositor's
hand. Standing before these cases the compositor places the
" copy," as it is called—that is, the MS. or the reprint piece
he has to " compose "—in a convenient spot, and takes in
his left hand a tool called a composing-stick. This has a

slide to regulate the length of the lines, and is otherwise like a metal box of oblong form, having one of the sides omitted. Into this receptacle the compositor places one by one the types as he picks them out of their respective compartments, and when a word is completed, a piece of metal called a space is inserted to make the white, or blank, space that we find between the words in a printed page. When a line has been composed, if it be not quite long enough, and it is not desirable to begin another word at the end, spaces are put in to "justify," and to separate the lines well from each other thin slips of metal called leads are put between. When the composing-stick is full—a matter of half-a-dozen lines or more, according to the size of the type and the amount of leading—the whole is lifted out with great dexterity and placed on what is called a "galley," a tray having a raised ledge to support the type and prevent it from falling down. When the galley is filled the type is tightened up with a piece of wood, and the surface being inked by a roller, it is placed under a press with a piece of paper on the top, and an impression taken. This is known as the proof, and is further proof in slip. Sometimes this is omitted, and the matter made up into pages before proofs are pulled.

To make up matter into pages the compositor adds to each page the "running head"—that is, whatever title has to appear on the top of each page, and also the number indicating the number of the page, known as its folio, and under the last line of the first page of every sheet is the letter or figure called the signature. The reason is this. When the book has been printed, as many sheets as make one copy have to be laid up (a process called gathering), and it is of course important to see that there are not two copies of one sheet. This might be done by examining the folio. If the last page of one sheet bore the figure 16, the next should be 17 and so on, but in practice it has been found more convenient to print on the first page a letter of the alphabet.

This is the alphabet "of signatures," consisting of all the
letters except A J V and W. There are some other points
that might be noted, but these are simply technical and do
not concern any young writer for the press. As a page is
"made up," a piece of strong twine is tied round to secure
it, and after proofs have been pulled the pages are taken to
the stone or iron table on which they are arranged or
"imposed" so as to print off in the right sequence. The
pages are wedged into their places by pieces of wood or metal,
for if they fall apart they come into what printers call "pye,"
and this may necessitate resetting. The wedges, etc , are
called "furniture," and the whole is fastened into an iron
frame called a "chase," and then the whole is a "forme".
The mass of metal, which may contain many thousand
separate pieces, is tightened and finally "locked up" by
driving wedges called "quoins" between slanting pieces of
"furniture" known as "side sticks," and all is ready for
printing. There is a good deal more to be described to
render the technics of the printing office complete from a
printer's view-point, but the above is quite enough for our
present purpose. The young journalist will now understand
how spaces are left by filling in a piece of furniture in a
column to be filled by later news which, when set, can be
dropped into the blank made by withdrawing the furniture.
In "making up" newspapers at the printers it is often
needful at the last to provide for some exigency, owing,
perhaps, to some item being withdrawn at the last moment ;
in which case something must be composed to fit into the
vacancy. The rough description I have given of the compositors' frames at which the "copy" is put into type, will
show the desirability of not writing, when it can be avoided,
on paper of too large a size. If the separate sheets are very
large they necessarily cover some of the type-boxes, unless the
compositor fix up a holder, and then this often puts the MS.
too far from his eyes, so that altogether a moderate size is best.

It is highly desirable to keep the sheet or slips uniform for convenience in "casting-off" quantity. Very often in press work time runs short, and it is important to know how much a particular MS. will make. This is quickly done by counting the words in a slip and then multiplying by the number of slips. Lined paper is good to use as it imparts a greater uniformity and makes indifferent writing more legible. Only *one* side of the paper must be written on, and white paper is to be preferred. A new paragraph is marked thus "["; and if insertions must be made that cannot be clearly written between the lines marked in the MS. at the place where the new matter is to come in, write "See slip A," and in the next "See slip B," and so on. If more than one slip have to go in at "A," number them thus, "A1," "A2," "A3," and on the slips to be inserted write on the top, "to be inserted where marked in slip 7," or whatever the folio may be of the MS.

Such words as are required to be italicised have *one* line scored under ; small capitals are indicated by *two* lines, and large capitals have *three* lines scored underneath.

After a little practice with printers, even the novice will soon pick up all he requires in the printing office, and if he treat them with courtesy and consideration he will find the normal printer the most obliging of men. Besides the composing-room, most printing offices have little rooms for the "readers" who, aided by a lad who reads the "copy," checks on the "proof" the accuracy of the compositor in setting up. Small printers keep but a reader or two, and I have known local sheets "read" by a compositor told off for the purpose, but in the better offices there are several readers, often men of considerable mental attainment ; and in the case of the great daily papers where much matter has to be "rushed through," the allowance of "readers" is very large. At the *Daily Telegraph* printing office I was much surprised to find the great number of reading closets all round the noble composing-room, where, during the small hours of the morning, may be seen a very extraordinary sight and a degree of intense activity without the least confusion or apparent hurry, which results only from an admirable organisation and a thoughtful study of every detail.

Formerly printing offices were very ill conducted, and they long deserved to be called what Benjamin Franklin declared they were · "sinks of iniquity". Now, however, things are quite different, and printers will be found a most steady, industrious, patient and hard-working set of men, possessed of uncommon intelligence, and often having men of real merit in their ranks I know personally of two men taken out of Spottiswoode's composing-rooms to fill editorial posts, and first-rate and most worthy men both were; and, thus, in journalism it is quite possible for even the working printer to rise from "case" work to fill eventually the editorial chair.

In point of fact, the great world of journalism is most essentially a true republic, where every boy employed may become a president if he possess the requisite ability; and any young man who can write, if he once get into the printing office side of a paper, may feel sure of getting on if only he perseveres, waits, and seizes each opportunity for self-advancement as it arises

Some journals—especially the minor prints devoted to trades, or to class or local interests—have to be worked most economically, and only those willing to "rough it" can expect to maintain their position. Thus editing even has often to be done under personal difficulties, and in the midst of the noise of the machinery, the clatter of "locking up," and other disturbances peculiar to the printing office. Then, too, the young sub-editor may have to send out, the last thing, for the evening papers, to cull thence and put into his paper any late item that affected it. Thus, suppose you were "making up" a journal devoted to flour milling, and at closing saw in an "evening" paper that a cotton mill had been burned down that morning, and that enormous damage had been done, you would take no notice thereof; but if you read that a one pair of stones' flour mill had been burned down, you would insert that item as giving the finishing touch to your number. If you read, however, a telegram announcing such an appalling catastrophe as that of the fearful explosion at Minneapolis (the great American centre of flour milling), you would, if possible, write a few lines stating that "we have just been telegraphically informed of a terrible disaster," etc., and winding up by promising full details in "our next". In like manner, if you were closing up a journal devoted to sugar confectionery, and saw in the "evening" a report of the coming beet crop, you would put that in; but you would take no notice of any subject that was foreign to the scope of your journal. In sub-editing there is much scope for cleverness, and also ample opportunity for ineptitude and stupidity. It is a duty of the sub-editor to see that his paper does not contain two or more versions of the same thing. Some journals are badly managed, and have too many "editors" about. Properly, all "copy" should pass finally through one man's hands, and he should keep an account of all. Some write down the items. Others carry all in their heads, and this is best for those who can do it safely. A retentive memory and a clear judgment are two essentials to good sub-editing. I have known every item in a large journal carried in the memory so completely that a piece of "copy" coming in late would be thrown out directly as "a double" and superfluous, being already in type. Editing is an art, and at the printers and in "making up" for press the rudiments are learned. Endeavour to have all possible corrections made in the "copy," and as few in proof as possible. Do not allow, as far as your authority and influence extend, *after-thoughts*. Some persons connected with the press are very fond of "correcting in the metal," as it is called. Indeed, I have known a case where rough "copy" was sent in and composed, and then in proof extensive additions were made, and again, and again, until the thing was made right, which should have been done in the "copy". One result of this slovenly and wasteful way of working is expense, and another is much increased risk of printing errors. On the journal in question, at the last, when judgment might be required for some point of policy, everybody's time was taken up in looking after corrections and additions, all of which might have been easily avoided by the requisite care in preparing the "copy" properly for press.

Editing is a consummate art, and cannot be taught through the medium of any book, or by any other teacher than experience, but much may be gained by hint and suggestion ; and the direction in which one should incline in editing can be clearly indicated on paper. First of all, a paper must be made harmonious to and consistent with its avowed policy, and the judicious editor will not permit anything to appear that can possibly *compromise* the character of the journal for *consistency*. If he have, for example, an article thrust on him (as sometimes happens) that ought to go in, and which is yet likely to pledge the paper to some undesirable course, he can convert the article into a " letter to the editor," or he can make it a *signed* paper, and even add at the bottom " we do not necessarily agree with the writer of the above," or something of an equivalent nature. These are but stray hints, but they may sufficiently indicate what is meant by editing, which is obviously the most difficult of all journalistic work.

A word as to type may fitly close this section and may be useful For books usually there is a choice of about twelve kinds of type, although in practice only two or three are in use ordinarily. These types are Great Primer, English, Pica, Small Pica Long Primer, Bourgeois, Brevier, Minion,

Nonpareil, Ruby, Pearl, and Diamond. The last three are
so exceedingly small as to be rarely employed except for
notes, etc., or in the smallest prayer books. Most of the
above have two kinds each, old style and modern The
sizes are arbitrary—six lines of pica and twelve of nonpareil
equal one inch. The width of pages or columns in printers'
language is reckoned according to the number of "ems".
An "em" is a pica *m*, that is the square of the depth of
pica, and a page 24 " ems " wide equals 4 inches.

XVI —LIBEL.

It is a well-known though not sufficiently regarded fact,
that ignorance of the law does not excuse the wrong-doer,
and this should certainly induce journalists more than it
appears to do to study somewhat the legal aspects of their
vocation To the journalist, and, indeed, to the literary
worker generally, some knowledge of the elements, at least,
of the existing law of libel is essential. Foolish is the man
who seeks to be his own lawyer, and once involved in anything libellous, legal aid becomes a necessity ; but I propose
here as succinctly as possible, to show what constitutes a
libel, and to indicate how at all events the young journalist
may keep himself clear of what may be very serious indeed
to his prospects, viz., an action against his paper for libel,
consequent on his own indiscretion.

The Law of Libel is still very perplexing and it remains
difficult to define in many instances exactly what constitutes
a libel, but undoubtedly that which tends to degradation of
character in anyone is a libel.

Technically, a libel may be construed as a false and
unprivileged publication by writing, printing, etc , which
exposes any person to hatred, contempt, obloquy, or
ridicule, or which causes him to be shunned, or has a tendency to hurt him in his occupation

Any person libelled, has two legal remedies. First, he may bring an action of damages against the libeller, and if the obvious tendency is manifestly libellous, as in a case when someone has published that A or B is a man of straw, proof of special damage is not required.

In the second place, the person libelled may prosecute the libeller criminally by indictment, and the punishment, if the case is proved, may be very severe.

The defences to an action for libel are numerous enough. The statute of limitations may be one, but is probably never urged, as no one would wait over six years before taking action. An agreement may be arrived at and apologies accepted, or, it may be urged that the matter complained of was true in substance and in fact. This obviously is a good defence, but it has been called a dangerous one, as if it be not sustained, it is likely to aggravate the offence. Then again, under the Law of Libel Amendment Act, 1888, fair and accurate newspaper reports of proceedings in courts of justice, or at public meetings *bonâ fide* and lawfully held for a lawful purpose, are privileged. Then too, by the same statute, the order of a judge in chambers is required to authorise the prosecution of a person for libel.

In olden days the law was very harsh, and the terrible punishment inflicted on William Prynne merely for writing *Histriomastrix* is matter of history. The work in question was a condemnation of stage plays but it was ingeniously construed into a libel on the Queen (1633), and entailed on the writer dreadful sufferings.

As a rule, newspaper reports of public matters are privileged, but towards the close of 1889 a very important case occurred, which puts quite a new aspect on this privilege. This was Kelly *v* the "Star" newspaper, and the facts appear to have been the following :—A certain Mr. Thomas Martin Kelly attended a meeting on the 10th of April, 1889, and read a memorial in favour of the Sugar Bounties Con-

vention Bill. The meeting, according to the evidence of
the plaintiff himself, was attended by three hundred people,
and was, in the language of the Act, "bonâ fide," and "lawfully held for a lawful purpose" While the plaintiff was
reading the petition in support of the Bill for which he in-
vited signatures, he was assailed with a running chorus of
hostile interruptions The chief point of these interpolated
remarks was that Mr. Kelly was not really a working man,
and had no right to speak for the class. It seems some of
the observations made were exceedingly rough on Mr.
Kelly. The *Star* newspaper proprietary set up for defence
the contention that the remarks had been actually made,
and were correctly reported. This plea was not seriously
contested by the plaintiff's counsel. Mr. Lockwood called
witness after witness from among those who had been present
on the occasion, and had themselves interrupted the plaintiff
in the manner described. In point of fact it was virtually
admitted that the report *was* accurate, and, therefore, one
would suppose, fully privileged. Quoting from the Act of
1888, we find that it provided that "a fair and accurate
report published in any newspaper of the proceedings of
a public meeting . . . . shall be privileged, unless it shall
be proved that such report or publication was published
or made maliciously . . . provided . . . that nothing
in this section contained shall be deemed or construed
. . . . to protect the publication of any matter not of public
concern, and the publication of which is not for the public
benefit".

Now this should, one would have supposed, protect a
newspaper simply publishing a *report*, but Baron Huddleston rules otherwise, and his summing up amounted to this
in effect, that, as the law now stood, a newspaper was
privileged in publishing a report of any public meeting, provided it was fair and accurate, and provided that the matter
was one of public concern, and that the publication was for

the public benefit—not, as Mr. Lockwood (counsel for the defendants) said, for the public interest.

Here we have the whole distinction in a nutshell A report is most certainly "privileged," if it be for the public good, but not necessarily if only for public interest, and as the matter complained of was undoubtedly libellous, the *Star* lost the day, and had to pay damages, although only to the moderate amount of £5. Naturally this ruling gave occasion for much criticism, but even a newspaper cannot fight the law of the land, and thence, in cases where reporters put down libellous matter, its publication can be justified only on the grounds that it is calculated to *benefit* as well as to *interest* the public. As such a plea as this could hardly ever be sustained, it follows that much of the privilege that formerly covered an honest verbatim report is practically cancelled.

This typical case naturally evoked much discussion, and as the *Daily News* in particular objected to the judge's ruling, and raised the question : What is a libel? a correspondent sent that journal a letter on the subject whence I extract the following, as throwing much light on whereon much obscurity, popularly speaking, still exists. The writer referred to says :—" The question whether the truth of a libel is or is not an adequate defence for its publication depends upon whether the proceedings are civil or criminal In a civil action truth is, and always has been, a complete defence. For the action is brought to recover damages for loss of character, and a man has no right to damages for the loss of a character which he did not deserve. In a criminal prosecution, truth could not be pleaded as a defence at all before 1842. For the prosecution was supposed to have for its object the maintenance of the peace, and it was held that the publication of a defamatory truth might be more likely to cause a breach of the peace than the publication of a defamatory falsehood Hence the maxim 'The greater the truth the greater the libel,' which has been practically obsolete since the passing of Lord Campbell's Act. For under that statute, now forty-seven years old, the truth of a libel, if proved, justifies the libeller, provided that in the opinion of the jury the circulation of the libel was for the public benefit."

This seems very much to the purpose. But it will be more satisfactory for the fuller elucidation of these knotty points to turn to the *Law Times* in which the *Star* case was very fully and ably threshed out, and here we read that in the opinion of that journal, the direction of the judge was this : "That, in order to enable a newspaper to claim the protection of privilege in the reports of public proceedings, which without the privilege would be libellous on an individual, it must prove, not only that the report was accurate and of public interest, but also that its publication was for the public benefit. The provision of the Newspaper Libel Act of 1881, s. 4, is that, 'a fair and accurate report published in any newspaper of the proceedings of a public meeting, or (except where neither the public nor any newspaper reporter is admitted) of any meeting of a vestry, town council, school board, board of guardians, board or local authority framed or constituted under the provisions of any Act of Parliament, or of any committee appointed by any of the above-mentioned bodies, or of any meeting of any commissioners authorised to act by letters patent, Act of Parliament, warrant under the Royal Sign Manual, or other lawful warrant or authority, select committees of either House of Parliament, justices of the peace in quarter sessions assembled for administrative and deliberative purposes, and the publication at the request of any Government office or department, officer of State, commissioner of police, or chief constable, of any notice or report issued by them for the information of the public, shall be privileged,

unless it shall be proved that such report or publication was
published or made maliciously'; and for the purposes of
that section public meetings are interpreted to mean any
meeting *bonâ fide* and lawfully held for a lawful purpose,
and for the furtherance or discussion of any matter of public
concern, whether the admission thereto be general or
restricted   In a recently published work by Mr. Hugh
Fraser, he makes these comments upon the above section,
which we think correctly state the law and justify the
summing-up of Mr. Baron Huddleston :—' It is not enough
that the report is fair and accurate, and that it is for the public
benefit that the reports of all meetings of the same kind as
this particular meeting should be published, *e g*, that it is
an accurate report of a political meeting—to obtain protection
it must be proved that the publication of the very words
complained of is for the public benefit.   This imposes on
every editor the duty of editing the whole of the paper ; he
must not trust to the proved accuracy of his reporters ; he
must himself read through the report and be careful to
eliminate all blasphemous, seditious, and obscene matter,
every unfair attack upon a public man, everything defamatory of a private individual.   No doubt this is almost a
practical impossibility in the case of a daily where the type
has to be set up with the greatest possible speed ; but,
nevertheless, it seems to be clear law, according to the
decision in Parkhurst *v.* Sowler, that unless this is done the
proprietors will be liable to an action for libel '"   This is,
I think, conclusive.

Various typical cases might be cited bearing on other
points of the law of libel, but they are technical and would
only confuse the reader.   The main point to bear in mind
is this, that anything calculated to injure a person in reputation or in pocket, or to bring that person into contempt
and ridicule, *is* a libel.   It is best, therefore, for the young
journalist to make up his mind that he will not libel any one

himself, and that when in matter coming under his *final* notice he detects a libel, or aught that is suspiciously near one, he will point it out to his superiors and repudiate all responsibility *himself*. I can speak from many years' experience, during which I put thousands of issues to press, and on some occasions when libellous matter came in and appeal could not be made to the editor or proprietor, I then acting as sub-editor, simply "held the matter over," and was greatly thanked afterwards for my caution. Here, indeed, the young journalist is safe if he acts on the golden rule in press-work of a responsible character that the way to err, if err you *must*, is by OMISSION and never by COMMISSION. "When in doubt, blot it out," is good reason as well as rhyme. Many journals give lists of bankrupts, etc., and here is a pitfall since a mistake of a name may entail serious consequences. The publication of a bankruptcy gazette *is* privileged, but it *must be accurate*, and it is exceedingly dangerous to permit any carelessness in preparing the "copy" for the printer, and each item ought always to be carefully checked. The mistake of putting "J" for "I" before the name of a bankrupt to my personal knowledge once cost a paper a large sum. A certain *Isaac had* failed —never mind the surname—but *Jacob* had not. Jacob brought an action for having been damaged in his business consequent on his name being given in the list of bankrupts and he received a large sum. It is noteworthy in these cases which occasionally occur how the plaintiff will magnify the importance and circulation of the offending paper, although, perhaps, he had previously refused to advertise therein, not deeming it a print of the least consequence. Here, as usual, circumstances greatly alter cases!

Then again, and this is a point that all journalists might well bear in mind, a libel is always a mistake, seeing that it puts the writer in the power of the person libelled, and that the writer of the libel might very well have produced just the same effect by employing legal language. There are many ways of using the legitimate weapons of effective irony, mock deference, incisive sarcasm, and scathing satire, without resorting to vulgar forms of abuse, or raking up scandalous things which in the issue generally recoil on the writer.

It may be well to add here that a libel may lie as much in the pages of a novel as in those of a pamphlet or a newspaper. Fiction has no privilege, and individuals must not be pilloried in a story in such a way that an ordinary reader, being acquainted with the persons, would at once know *who* was meant. Even a transparent change of name will not shelter a dastardly writer who attempts to injure or distress those against whom he has conceived an enmity; thus and in like manner, he must not attack one who in his opinion is a public enemy or an offender against some fancied ideal of his own.

XVII.—Copyright.

Some general notion of the law and nature of copyright in literary work is decidedly necessary for the young writer, as otherwise he may suffer much loss through his own ignorance, and may possibly be led into doing something illegal through not understanding the general principle on which periodicals deal with paid contributors. Strictly defined, copyright is, of course, the sole and exclusive privilege of indefinitely multiplying copies of a literary work. It is, perhaps, needless to add that no copyright can exist in any libellous, immoral, or irreligious work, although the latter might be extremely difficult to define in these very lax days, seeing that those old-fashioned people who absolutely believe in the plenary inspiration of all scripture, would unanimously pronounce *Robert Elsmere* to be irreligious. As to the period during which copyright lasts, the term is always for the whole of the author's life and for seven years beyond. If, however, it happen that the author die before the period of forty-two years has elapsed from the first publication of the work, the copyright runs for the balance of the forty-two years. Thus, if an author died ten years after the first issue of a book of which he retained the copyright, the right would remain with his representative for thirty-two years.

Generally speaking, the whole subject of copyright is enveloped in much intricacy.

The Act regulating copyright is 5 and 6 Vict. 45, 3. When a book is pirated the remedy lies in an action. In the case of articles, essays, poems, and matter generally contributed to and published in periodicals, the right of reproduction lies with those papers for twenty-eight years, and then lapses to the author if he is so fortunate as to be alive!

The general rule is, that matter specifically *paid* for, is, unless otherwise expressed in writing, the property of the publication in which it appears. If the writer desire to reproduce any matter thus paid for, he must ask permission; but if the matter was contributed gratis, and no assignment made of the copyright, the writer retains complete right over the matter in question.

To secure copyright, due registration must be made at Stationers' Hall; the fee is only five shillings, and here the inquirer can obtain all the information necessary. Of each *new* book issued, copies (one each) must be sent to the libraries of the British Museum; the Bodleian, Oxford; the Public Library, Cambridge; that of the Faculty of Advocates, Edinburgh, and to Trinity College, Dublin. Copyright can now be secured with France and some other continental countries; but, as is well known, not with the United States, and thus, unfortunately, great hardship is sustained by popular English writers, whose books are reprinted in America without asking leave of the writers. This is a wrong that will, doubtless, be remedied in time by an international congress. As things stand now, much matter is pirated by American periodicals; and, coming over here, many young journalists run a risk in copying out of such publications, as what *seems* an original American article *may* turn out to be an English magazine paper which is protected by copyright law in this country.

As matters now stand, the law is far from being satisfactory, but in Great Britain the author is fairly protected. When disposing of any of his literary work, he should always have a clear understanding as to what he is selling, and on what terms. Many rash sales are made on occasions which come after to be the subject of bitter repentance. Victor Hugo in his early days made a foolish bargain over *Notre Dame*, one of his finest and most original efforts; and I have known a despairing, unrecognised author sell three copyrights of as many original fictions for £5. Soon after he succeeded, obtained good commissions for his work, and naturally repented his precipitancy

It is best, if possible, to sell for periodicals the right simply to print, leaving all other rights with the author. I have found myself that this is much the best way with serial fiction, and it enables matter to be thoroughly well tested as to its value before it is finally disposed of.

XVIII.—REMUNERATION.

The question of remuneration in the various departments of journalistic work is naturally a vital consideration to those who join the profession with a view to living thereby. First of all, it is noteworthy that the range, from the minimum to the maximum earnings, is very great indeed, ranging from a few shillings a-week to fifty pounds and more. In a word, salaries run from, say fifty pounds to several thousands a-

year, so that here, as in medicine or law, there is ample
encouragement for those who possess ability and industry.
The two are really necessary, the one to the other. Then,
the journalist who earns a good salary on a good paper may,
and often does, write for other publications; and he may
possibly run imaginative matter through various papers,
receiving a royalty from each; and thus his total gains may
mount up to a considerable sum in the year. As to imaginative work, however, and the gains that may be derived
thence, that belongs properly to the book and its production, which will be found very fully dealt with in the
second part of this work.

It is said that an eminent journalist received for his first
fee on a well-known London paper the sum of ninepence,
the price of a small paragraph, the same paper afterwards
paying him at the rate of more than a thousand a-year!
How to get on a paper, indeed, may be summed up as the
art of combining ability with industry and tact. Write what
is marketable, and put it into good form, and adapt it to the
character of the journal whereto it is sent. I once became
connected with a good evening journal by writing notes of
the day on current foreign and colonial news thus-wise: If
I saw a telegram from some little known part of the world,
I looked up the place in a cyclopædia, and tacked on to the
news a few lines giving, in the fewest and most picturesque
words, some interesting historic, physical or generally interesting facts about the place, and making it harmonious with
the intelligence conveyed.

To make this plain. One day I saw a statement that
the Dutch were about to negotiate a loan. I seized on
this as a text, and having looked up Holland under "Foreign
Countries" in *Whitaker's Almanack*, and referred to the
encyclopædia, I turned off the following note, which duly
appeared in the *North Times* (Manchester) for Friday,
November 3, 1882 .—

" The Dutch are busy negotiating a big loan, to be issued at $3\frac{1}{2}$ per cent, and amounting to nearly 85,000,000fl. The redemption of this loan is to be obligatory, and in all probability the money required will be forthcoming It should be remembered, however, that the Dutch National Debt is large even for so thrifty and generally well-to-do a people. The total amount of the public debt of Holland is, we believe, £79,548,000, and this lays a charge of £20 11s. 8d. per head per annum on the total population. Holland proper has an area of 12,718 square miles, and a population of 3,865.4456, or 304 persons to the square mile. The colonies, however, are very important, and are reckoned to include an area of 666,700 square miles, with a gross population of nearly 24,000,000. This is especially an era of colonies, and the vast and increasing development of the world's mercantile marine renders colonies ten-fold more valuable to the countries to which they belong than they were of old In Holland, too, further and important progress is, we believe, making in the reclamation of fresh land from the sea, and the draining of the great Haarlem lake, now inhabited by 12,000 persons, has of late years done much to stimulate fresh efforts in this direction. It appears further that of late years the commerce of Holland has very materially developed. During the year 1880 the imports amounted to no less than 9,851,573 tons, and the exports to 9,477,120 tons, being an increase of 880,032 tons, and of 544,000 tons on the two items respectively for the previous year."

I am not putting this forward as in the least a model of literary work. It is very ordinary, indeed; but then it happened to be work that was accepted at once, inserted, and *paid for*. Take another case. I read that ivory was likely to "go up". I at once sat down and wrote a few lines stating that at the late sales prices had advanced, and then drifted into the following, which was duly published.—

" Ivory was once the name given to the main substance of
the teeth of all animals, but now it is properly restricted to
that modification of *dentine* which, in transverse sections, exhibits lines of different colours running in circular arcs and
forming lozenge-shaped spaces. By this true ivory is distinguished from all other tooth substances and from bone
counterfeits. It is curious that the teeth of the elephant
alone possess the proper signs of pure ivory, although such
animals as the walrus and hippopotamus have teeth and
horns of such density as to approximate to true ivory. The
best comes from the tusks of the African elephant, and Herr
Holtzapffel states that in Northern Siberia he found fossil
elephant tusks of 186 lbs weight From remote antiquity
elephant tusks have constituted an important article of commerce, and mention of these is often made in the Old
Testament. With the ancient Greeks ivory was an important
material, and Phidias, the great sculptor, made his famous
Olympian Jupiter entirely from this costly material. The
art of working ivory is of oriental origin. The value of true
ivory is in proportion to the soundness and size of the tusks,
and when under the weight of 5lbs. each they are known
commercially as *scrivelloes*, and except in these dear days
should not exceed five shillings a pound, but the price of
good ivory used to be about ten shillings a pound. The
price of good tusks has risen lately enormously—from £2
to £4."

An examination of these samples of published work which
was duly paid for will at once show that the writing is within
the capacity of anyone able to write at all. In fact, the style
is not as good as it should be, and I advise all young
journalists to aim high in writing, but not to attempt ornament or rhetoric Plain, nervous, vivid, familiar, and yet
refined English is what is wanted by the respectable journals,
and this style can be acquired by taking pain and reading
good authors.

Take another example The subjoined appeared in the *Financial Times*—

"It seems as if the next great company boom will have oil for its object. Petroleum perhaps more than anything else has made the United States rich, and around the Caspian it has also raised a stupendous industry But within the borders of our great Empire we possess oil fields of at least equal magnitude and richness. Those in Athabasca and the Mackenzie Valley in the North-West are probably the most important yet discovered, the Burme e deposits are almost similarly extensive, whilst New Zealand is not unlikely to regain prosperity through this latent wealth."

This was "worked up" by a writer of an article in the first person thus—

"Oil is the fuel of the future. There can be no doubt as to that Everywhere I hear rumours of syndicates to 'exploit' more petroleum deposits, and I would remind those whom this may concern that if New Zealand came early into the market it would be well. There are great deposits of oil in the Britain of the South, and this latent wealth may set New Zealand booming once more "

In another instance I chanced to see that the number of pilgrims to Mecca in that year (1882) had fallen to 20,000, as against 100,000 in the preceding year. That was enough for me and I turned off the following, which was at once accepted—

"MECCA.

"It is rather singular considering the present perturbed state of the Mahometan world that the number of pilgrims to Mecca this year has fallen to about 20,000 against 100 000 last year. As a rule, when Islam is greatly excited the pilgrimage gains popularity, but now it appears the otherwise. Mecca, literally called by Mahometans *Om-al-Kara*, Mother of Cities, the birth-place of Mahomet, is the capital of the Arabian province of Hedjaz, and formerly the number of pilgrims was rarely less than 300,000. The principal building is the Beit Ullah, containing the Kaaba, or house of the Prophet. This mosque is entered by 19 gates, and is constructed of marble, granite, and beautiful porphyry. Quite an ecclesiastical army is attached thereto, consisting of Katibs, Muftis, Mueddins, etc. The inhabitants are among the most courteous and lively of Arabs, and, mixing as they do with strangers from all quarters of the world, are true cosmopolites. It was at Mecca, so it is fabled, that the greater part of the Koran was brought to Mahomet by the angel Gabriel The Kaaba is the special shrine of the famous blackstone, a relic of Paradise, and has to be devoutly kissed by every pilgrim Burckhardt, the great Eastern traveller, who penetrated into this sacred fane, says that the effect of the scene with mysterious drapery—no doubt suggested to Mahomet by the veil of the Jewish temple—the gorgeous profusion of gold, and the intense awe of the adoring pilgrims, surpasses anything he could have imagined."

These specimens may serve to indicate the kind of thing that is likely to be acceptable Such work is profitable too, and £2 or £3 a-week can be earned off a *daily paper* without very much outlay of time. Quickness and vigilance, and ready faculty for seizing on the salient and popular side of a subject are the main requisites, and especially knowing *where to stop*. Not one of the " notes " quoted here would have gone in had they been, say, twice as long. The sub-editor who had to deal with them would have seen they contained what he would probably call "some stuff," but they would be laid aside and returned " reluctantly declined," if an unusually amiable spirit prevailed in the editorial department.

The amounts paid for regular staff appointments on journals varies very considerably. On provincial and minor
London papers a general reporter may have to commence
at 25s. a-week, or perhaps, 30s. A sub-editor may range
from 30s to 60s. a-week, and sometimes an editor of a small
weekly may have only a stipend of £70 or £80 a-year
I knew a sub-editor of an Anglo-Indian bi-weekly journal
who received £70 a-year. In these cases, however, the
whole time of the journalist is not nearly filled (of course
some people can make the minimum of work fill the maximum of time), and an able and industrious writer will look
round and seek for contributory work. When this is taken
into consideration it will be perceived that journalism contrasts well with the other liberal professions, seeing that its
mere recruits for places in the rank and file get as much as
most curates at first, and have before them avenues of
advancement that are not nearly so numerous or so unbarred
to the young as law or medicine, or the paid departments of
science; and then, beyond all, there is the entire freedom of
all those examinations, which in these days no doubt
exclude not a few good men from posts they could fill
admirably if excused the ordeal of the public examination.
On better papers a sub-editor will receive, perhaps, £200 a-
year and on a *daily* paper he may range from £250 to £500.

Many monthly trade journals pay their editors £100
a-year, a good rate when it is borne in mind that the editor
has naturally splendid opportunities for utilizing his knowledge in other quarters.

Let us take a few genuine advertisements addressed to
journalists as examples—

"WANTED, for London work, young, smart, descriptive, and verbatim REPORTER. Total ab-
stainer preferred. State qualifications and terms.—237 X."

"REPORTER WANTED, on a Suburban Weekly. Duties will include canvassing for advertisements and book-keeping. Only those who can produce first-class testimonials and show previous success in canvassing need apply. Salary and commission.—State terms, etc., to S. W. R."

The former of these would be the less remunerative perhaps, but it has the better promise for those who are determined to rise. In the second instance the literary work is conjoined with canvassing, which means subordinated thereto. If once the young journalist is much mixed up with advertisements, he must resolve to live by them, and make profit his sole end and aim. Advertisement work and the higher forms of writing are as oil and water, and the man who becomes a canvasser, cannot reasonably expect to be recognised as a member of the Republic of Letters.

Here is another——

"WRITER WANTED, for Short Trade Leaderettes. Address, with terms, W. T. P."

This is an opening of some promise, and the remarks in the earlier part of this chapter on "Notes" apply here, and may suggest that even commercial, financial and industrial articles should be well stuffed with interesting fact, and, if possible, spiced with a happy turn of epigram or allusion.

Take this as a "miscellaneous" announcement—

"TO PUBLISHERS, EDITORS, and PROPRIE-TORS of NEWSPAPERS and MAGAZINES (London or Provincial).— An Author, who has published several volumes of Poems, and who can Write Prose with ease, wishes an ENGAGEMENT. Is a good Accountant, and would be agreeable to assist at or take charge of Books in addition to Literary services rendered. Low remuneration.—Address, J. R."

The above is about as ill-advised and foolish an announcement as can well be conceived   First of all, the statement that the advertiser has published several volumes of poems is calculated only to damage him in the estimation of practical men—and it is to such that he appeals   It is as plain, as if he had so put it, to the experienced, that his "poems" have been published by subscription or at his own expense, and in neither case do they add the least weight to his application   He says he can write prose with ease. Truly, one would suppose he might condescend so far ; and then he is anxious to be generally useful as a clerk, suggesting that he does not feel any confidence in his own literary attainments ; and then he finally bids for *low* remuneration ' The advertisement should have run "the author of several published works," etc , but as it stands, such a confession is enough to spoil any chance the applicant might have of finding a *good* opening.

In another case we find among what may be called miscellaneous literary advertisements, one headed " naval journalism"; while literary ladies are appealed to by the subjoined—

" JOURNALISM.—LADY ASSISTANT SUB-EDITOR required for Catholic Educational Journal, with literary experience, able to write on dress and fashions, and take charge of technical department.—Apply by letter only, with specimens of work, references, etc., to Editor.'

I remarked in my account of the city editor that, as no one gets into *that* position *per saltum*, it is a fine opportunity for a young writer—exact, methodical and industrious—to get into the office of one of these journalistic magnates. Here we read that a

"CITY EDITOR WANTS smart and competent AS-SISTANT who is a good shorthand writer, and can write notes on financial, commercial and general topics. State age, experience, and salary required.—P. K."

Another opening occurs in the subjoined—

"ASSISTANT SUB-EDITOR.—Smart young fellow, who can summarise attractively.—Address, stating salary required, 234 W."

The smart young "fellow" certainly does not sound agreeably to the refined ear, but often these advertisements are penned out of the editorial department; and, if a beginner should find himself in an office where the "fast," jaunty, slap-dash style is in vogue, it does not follow that *he* should adopt it. *Worth*, when combined with *work*, always wins respect; and it will be found that the sole reason why some affect the "new journalism" is simply because they are not sufficiently well read, educated, or solid as writers to attempt the old, and find fluent slang and flippant frivolity, combined with stupid jests, more in their line.

The scale of remuneration for newspaper contributions varies very greatly. For paragraphs the dailies all pay $1\frac{1}{2}$d. or 2d. a line. The per-column rate is very diverse. Dailies may range from 10s. 6d. (very low this) to 15s. and 30s. a column. Some pay for leaders contributed from outsiders

£2 2s. The *Times* gives £5 5s. for an article, and the *St. James's Gazette* £3 3s. Then, when a writer becomes known, he may make special terms Taking one thing with another, a working journalist of fair ability and industry should, after the first few years, be in a position to earn from £300 to £400 or even £500 a-year. Beyond this, for *great* ability—for special qualifications, acquired, perhaps, through the previous ministry of experience—there is the possibility of rising to an income of £1000 or more ; and, when everything is taken into full account, I think it will be admitted that practical journalism is well remunerated, and that it compares well with any other profession, seeing how much encouragement it gives to the self-made man, and remembering the freedom from examinations, tests and the like.

Work, however, is essential to any sort of success No matter how great a writer's genius may be—no matter how fascinating his style—if he will not *work*, he will never do for a journalist. He may be tolerated as a hanger-on, but he will never rise ; and he will probably have the mortification of seeing men possessing not a tithe of his ability steadily rising far over his head, and securing both profit and reputation. Here, above all things, does the well-worn maxim apply, that there is no art too difficult to attain to by dint of industry. The successful journalist is essentially a man of movement. He must be tireless, mentally sleepless, and his acumen must be all-comprehending He must be ready for, and equal to, any emergency, and know the right thing to say at a moment's notice to the most unlooked-for event. Industry makes all things easy , and, if the journalist takes his ease when he ought to be attending to his duties, he will very soon be finally parted from them. I cannot but think that the little-known lines of an old dramatic poet have a good application to the typical journalist —

The chiefest action for a man of spirit
Is never to be out of action; we should think
The soul was never put into the body,
Which has so many rare and curious pieces
Of mathematical motion, to stand still.

Certainly the journalist who stands still is a lost man

I fear that many smart young men of the day possess rather hazy notions of what is meant by hard literary work. They have heard of men of talent "dashing off leaders," like poor Captain Shandon in *Pendennis*, and they imagine something of the kind of men described in the late Lord Lytton's *My Novel*, where Leonard Fairfield, the village genius, is introduced to a gathering of Fleet Street intellectual giants But, be it noted, these men do not get on unless they reform; and the main object of this volume is to teach the young aspirant for literary honours how he can really attain to them In the *Book-Worm* there is an account of how Heyne worked. He was one of those wise men who perceive that *work* is the only way whereby genius can be rendered really effective, so he worked, and this was his method. He lived and worked in one large room. "On the principal wall were two bookcases and a cabinet, containing all the books he used in his daily work. On the opposite wall stood two presses, which held respectively his own and public business papers Near the garden window stood his bed . . . On the remaining wall were two book-cases, holding from thirty to forty pasteboard boxes, two inches deep, and large enough to hold a folio sheet easily. Each box had its inscription

"Through the room were found ten to twelve tables Each was assigned a special duty. One held books to be reviewed, at another Heyne worked at his Homer. A small desk at which he often worked standing, was used specially for reviews, of which he wrote from 7000 to 8000 in his life. All papers relative to works on which he was engaged were placed in these hollow boxes, according to their in-scriptions. also letters, according to their contents; reviews and papers. etc.

"Heyne rose at five in the morning. Having wrapped himself in an overcoat and drank a cup of coffee, he sat down at his writing-table. Author's work and writing of reviews occupied the first hours of the morning. In winter he took breakfast in his own room about nine o'clock—some broth, a glass of wine, or the like, often varying—then he dressed." Then follows an account of his official work, he being then secretary to the Gottingen Royal Academy of Sciences and inspector of the Itfeld School. To resume. "Soon after twelve he dined, and then for the first time usually saw his family. After dinner he slept half-an-hour, but no longer, for he must prepare himself for his lecture at two. After various classes had been attended he lectured on the Greek poets," and having spent a short time with his family, he worked again till after eleven. It is said that besides all this labour Heyne wrote quite 1000 letters in the year. This illustrious German scholar and man of letters was Christian Gottlob Heyne, born the son of a poor weaver, and besides much other work, he executed what has been described as "almost a cartload of translations".

For myself, I find that change of work is a real rest. This was Southey's plan, and it is as applicable to journalism as to book literature. It is a mistake, unless necessity compels, to work for more than three hours on one subject. Those who have either a combination of papers or several departments in one paper to fill will find it a great benefit to change from one kind of work to another, and this is most conducive to force and freshness—the two special require-ments in all phases of newspaper work.

END OF PART I.

PART II

THE BOOK.

I —INTRODUCTORY.

However unattainable in most things, our aim in all we do, or attempt, should be perfection. In literature this is specially necessary, and the writer who aims at ease for himself, is not likely to succeed. Now and then he may, if unusually endowed by natural ability, have a flash of brightness, but he who begins carelessly is sure to end badly; and in these days, with so much that is superlatively good behind us, nothing *can* succeed that is not good of its kind.

Most truly does Pope say

> True ease in writing comes from *art*, not chance,

and it will be found in practice that the *early* formation of good habits in composition and strict attention to style, will result in an immense abridgment of that future toil that has to be undergone by those who neglected or despised advice in their youth, when naturally there is more leisure and aptitude for acquiring good principles. Balzac, for example, had to take incredible pains in correcting his best work, simply because, as a young writer, he had not taken the trouble to study details, and to form a good style. One day of thought and practice before the age of twenty is worth a month after that period with many, for youth is much more plastic to impressions than maturity, and after all, the technics. if I may so call them, of composition, ought to be as familiar to the writer who means to make literature his profession, as the chemical elements are to the practical chemist.

Style is all important; indeed, it is often the main means to literary distinction   The very definition of poetry itself, viz., proper words in proper places. has been applied to style with more appositeness than in the case of poetry, which is very much beyond that   Style has been called the dress of thought, and one way to attain to a good style is to acquire a copious vocabulary and to take care that each word in use for composition is *rightly understood by the writer*.   From Pliny to Macaulay, style has been the great study with all great writers, and in the case of some it can be easily shown that style was really the key to popularity, and the cause of enduring fame   It is necessary to take pains. We all remember the well-worn saying—

> To write with ease may show your breeding,
> But easy writing's curst hard reading

Sydney Smith observes "the multitude cry out a miracle of genius! Yes, a man proves a miracle of genius because he has been a miracle of labour." *Quality*, not *quantity*, should be the early aim of the young writer.   When he has attained the art of producing that which has *quality* in it, he may then think of quantity, if he become a professional writer and his work is in demand.

Style, derived directly from the Latin *stylus*, the iron pen, wherewith the Romans wrote on waxen tablets, comes from the Teutonic *stellen*, to set in place, and may be best described as the special manner in which any writer presents verbal pictures of the ideas arising in his mind.   We talk of a *crude* style, a *dry*, a *loose*, or a *verbal* style, and in a word, the writer's style is made up of the selection, the arrangement and the synthetic junction of words and phrases..

hen there is to be considered the *rhythm* which is far too
uch neglected in contemporary prose, and then we have
ie way in which the writer employs figures of speech, illus-
ations, and many other things which will be found duly set
rth here. Briefly, the main points of an effective style are
arity, perspicuity, vigour, dignity, harmony between the
ords and the ideas expressed, and general beauty of the
hole.

In regard to the matter of style, Pope is the most finished
)et of the English language, and this is due alone to
e exquisite purity of his verbal arrangement, wherein we
? find the best words in the best places. Buckle, the
:mous author of the *History of Civilisation*, devoted years
f his laborious life to style, and took at one time for
iodels Hallam and Burke. The late popular and eloquent
'homas Binney, the well-known preacher, in describing how
e acquired his charming and powerful style of preaching,
bserved that he read the best authors, and that he wrote
iuch poetry as well as prose. Then he goes on to say, " I
:ad the whole of Johnson's *Rasselas*, put down all the new
ords I met with—and they were a good many—with their
roper meanings, and then I wrote essays in imitation of
ohnson, and used them up. . . . I wrote essays on the
nmortality of the soul, sermons, a tragedy in three acts,
nd other things very wonderful in their way. I think I can
iy I never fancied myself a poet or a philosopher ; but I
rote on and on to acquire the power to write with readiness,
nd I repeat with a full conviction of the truth of what I
iy, that having lived to gain some little reputation as a
riter, I attribute all my success to what I did for myself,
nd to the habits I formed during those years to which I
ave just referred." The study of models is important, and
veryone is familiar with Dr. Johnson's dictum, that whoever
esires to attain an English style, familiar but not coarse,
nd elegant but not ostentatious, must give his days and

nights to the study of Addison This, by the way, Dr. Johnson
certainly did *not* do himself, but the advice given indicates
the Doctor's belief that much could be gained by studying
great writers. The great canon, however, of all effective
writing is this, the language used should be that which most
exactly and forcibly conveys the writer's *meaning*, and
as a check to those who affect a stilted style, there is
Aristotle's advice, "to speak "—*i.e.*, write—"as the common
people, but to think like the wise". The meaning being,
of course, that a writer should be, above all things, *intelligible*. Bunyan, in his immortal *Pilgrim's Progress*, gives
us perfectly *clear* composition, and he is remarkable for using
short words and demonstrating how rich our Saxon English
is in its simplicity and directness. As an antithesis we have
Ruskin, with his poetic prose, his magnificent vocabulary,
and his instinct for true rhythm At the same time, I must
warn the young writer against becoming a slave to style
alone. The *manner* is much, but the matter should be
more, and if the *matter* be good, then, *plus* a good manner,
we have perfection, or as near thereto as can be attained.

Below style lies the material thereof—viz , words—and it
is here, after all, that the preliminary toil of the writer who
is determined to succeed chiefly lies. Shall our words be
mainly Latin or Saxon? is a question of moment. Certainly
for individual things, and for *natural* things especially, Saxon
words are best ; but for science and philosophy Latin must
be used, although even here there is room for plain English.
Mr. Herbert Spencer, for example, great philosopher as he
is, must be reckoned as rather obscure in places, as when he
calls evolution "a change from an indefinite incoherent
homogeneity to a definite coherent heterogeneity through
continuous differentations and integrations ".

There is great art, however, in employing a long and
somewhat unusual word in the midst of plain, simple ex-

ssions.   Thus observe in *Macbeth* how the two long words
he third line are used in the following passage—

> Will all great Neptune's ocean wash this blood
> Clean from my hand ?   No ! this, my hand, will rather
> The multitudinous sea incarnardine,
> Making the green one red.

the study of words, as necessarily precedent to that of
, there is much to urge, and young writers should not
dge the time and thought involved in obtaining a really
urate understanding of the meaning and *power* of every
d that is taken into the writer's working vocabulary.   The
st has to mix and prepare his colours, and to pay proper
ntion to many details, before he can give form to his
ceptions ; but, unfortunately, some young writers seem
hink that " the words will come," and that there is no
l to labour over questions of language.   This is why we
 in print so much that is wretched, slipshod, inaccurate,
thoroughly contemptible as literary work.   There may be
culty of observation, a gift of invention, and even much
nality, but all this is often completely marred by a
rty of language which is made more glaringly offensive
ttempts to conceal it through overlaying the style with
ass of slang and conventional expressions.
ne thing is certain, and that is that no literary work will
 unless the wording is really good, and no writer can
loy words to the best effect unless he has studied them
eir separate states.   In a word, here, as in material build-
the builder must possess a competent knowledge of the
rial that he employs.
. the outset of my own literary career, I paid much
ition to words, reading the *Imperial Dictionary* quite
igh, and in order to fix them and their significance
anently in memory, writing out as I went *every* difficult
 and setting down its meaning briefly.   This little by

little formed a useful MS book containing all the more
unusual philosophical or scientific words of the language.
The value of this as an exercise must be obvious   Some of
these jottings are curious—thus, *avernian*, pertaining to Lake
Avernus (an Italian lake famous for its poisonous vapours),
teleology, science of the final cause of things ; *cade*, tame, as
a "cade lamb"; *Ridotti*, public amusements in Italy—
dancing and singing ; *deipnosophist*, one famous for learned
talk at meals ; *nacreous*, reflecting irridescent light ;
penology, the science of public punishment ; *yug*, in Hindoo
mythology, an age ; *Pelagianism*, denial of original sin ;
riant, rire, to laugh ; and thousands of others.   The uses
of these jottings are manifold and often save time in reading,
as although few writers will employ such terms, most of
them will be found among many writers   Scott, plain and
direct as he usually is, writes in one of his final descriptive
poems "tablets *eburnine*" for *ivory* tablets ; and in my own
case I frequently found that the jotting down of an out-of-
the-way word and the writing in of the meaning thereof
was rich in suggestion, opening up new avenues of thought,
and sometimes leading to a new verbal form more effective
than that previously employed for the same end.   The
above citations are given simply as indicative of the *direction*
in which a young writer's *early* studies should lie if he
means to follow literature seriously as a calling.

A good book to study is Black's excellent etymological
and explanatory dictionary of words, derived from the Latin,
and especially should the literary student consult the works
of Archbishop Trench dealing with words – namely, *Glossary
of English Words used in different senses*, the *Study of Words*,
and some others   Shakespeare, the old dramatists, and the
Bible, are also indispensable for this purpose.

After all, however, there is nothing so good, perhaps, as
a preliminary preparation for composition as study in poetry
and actual exercise in versification.   Southey, who excelled

n prose, declared that to write poetry is the best prepara-
ion for writing prose. For poetry he might much better
nave put *verse*, as decidedly *poetry* is not to be produced as a
literary exercise. He goes on to say, with great justice,
'The verse-maker acquires the habit of weighing the
meanings and qualities of words until he comes to know, as by
ntuition, what particular word will best fit into the sentence.
People talk of my style! I have only endeavoured to write
plain English, and to put my thoughts into language
which everyone can understand." It was Southey, too, who
said to a correspondent, "I am glad that you sometimes
write verses, because if ever you became a prose-writer, you
will find the great advantage of having written verse". I
would that this were the case with all who versify and call
the result "poetry," but unquestionably there is an enormous advantage to be derived from poetry in all its forms
as a study, and a subject for actual exercise in composition.
As an aid to expression, its value is incalculable. Equally
important are reading and observation, or the art of storing
up impressions through eye or ear of all that goes on around
us, and secreting it in the mind in such a manner that these
impressions shall fall into their proper places when the writer
is at work on a given subject, just as though they had been
specially culled for the places they fill.

Reading and observing are two comprehensive and vitally
important subjects, as forming essential part of the writer's
training, and to each of these a separate section is devoted.
The purpose of this second part of the "Manual" is to
furnish really *practical* and *workable* advice and instruc-
tions for the successful self-training of the writer or author,
so that all that *can* be done for him in the way of book-advice
may be found here in a handy and available form. Our course
lies, therefore, through poetry in all its phases to prose,
whence we pass to the question of what and how to read,
and thence to that of observation from the author's view-

point. This last includes consideration of the imaginative
or creative faculty. Then follows fiction as an art, with
practical notes on how to succeed therein, with other matters
of interest and value to the young author.

In regard to novel-writing, by the way, as a profession, a
writer in the *St. James's Gazette* has asked: "How is it that
everyone who writes insists on being printed out of hand?
This, without any previous training, and often, as all know,
without any natural gift. Lawyers, doctors, architects, artists
and the like, do not even dream of getting *paid* work until
they have "qualified," and undergone much preliminary
training and study. This is the puzzle. Obviously those
who fancy they have the writers' faculty should first set to
work to *train* that faculty; and *then*—and not till then—
should they essay to find a publisher for their productions."
This virtually justifies all I have said above.

II —POETRY.

A great writer has said that, in a technical sense, by
poetry we mean the expression, in words—most appro-
priately metrical words—of the truths of imagination and
feeling. In a wider sense, poetry is the expression of
imaginative truth in *any* form Then, again, a shorter
definition assures us that poetry is a work of imagination
wrought into form by art; and another definition is, music
in words, which is obviously too limited. A modern poet
writes—

> Poetry is itself a thing of God,
> He made His prophets poets, and the more
> We feel of poetry do we become
> Like God in love and power.

Definitions, however, are notoriously unsatisfactory when
applied to poetry, and are either too narrow or too wide.
Tennyson, after telling us, truly enough, that

>The poet in a golden clime was born,

Adds—

>He saw thro' life and death, thro' good and ill,
>He saw thro' his own soul,
>The marvel of the everlasting will.

And then, again, we have been beautifully reminded that, in dim outshadowings, earth's first poets from the loveliness of external nature evoked spiritualisation. To them the wild forests teemed with aërial beings, the gushing springs rejoiced in fantastic sprites, the leaping cataracts gleamed with translucent shades, the cavernous hills were the abode of genii, and the earth-girdling ocean was guarded by mysterious forms.

For my own part, I think that all that is great, good and pure—all that is beautiful and true—must be essentially poetry, which forms the principal substratum of our life here—the enduring and real spiritual world whence we came, to which we all belong, and whither we are all hastening on the rapid wing of tireless time.

It is simply historic fact that all literature is, in origin, poetic. The very laws of early peoples are found in metrical forms; and all history is, in its beginning, more or less legendary song.

It is unfortunate in many ways that in these days poetry is not more studied and more read. Nothing evinces more a want of proper culture than this disposition so marked in many quarters to neglect poetry altogether. Let it be remembered that poetry, rightly viewed, is no mere luxury of the mind: it is not by any means to be classed as but an intellectual dissipation, as the reading of novels has been quite as wrongly termed. In the Bible itself, the one divinely-inspired book given to humanity, how poetry abounds! Very much of the Old Testament is chronicle and song, and in the New Testament it is much the same.

The Old has that greatest and grandest of didactic poems, *Job;* and the New Testament ends with the vision of the Apocalypse.

Poetry lies, indeed, at the very root of all literature, and this truth has been happily expressed in the following lines—

> I looked upon a plain of green
>> That some one called the land of prose,
> Where many living things were seen
>> In movement and repose.
> I looked upon a stately hill,
>> That well was named the Mount of Song,
> Where golden shadows dwelt at will
>> The woods and streams among;
> But most this fact my wonder bred,
>> Tho' known by all the nobly wise
> It was the mountain stream that fed
>> The fair green plain's amenities.

If only young writers who aspire to do something in verse, or "poetry" as they would term it, understood better what poetry really is, and how its range is co-extensive with all we see, know, think, feel, or imagine—if only they knew that it corresponds with the profound region of spiritual truth which everywhere lies around us, and that it interprets life in its highest and deepest phases—we should have fewer painful stammerings and stutterings in verses, and fewer echoes from half-remembered strains of other writers—fewer imitations, in fact; and those who could do no more than imitate or trifle would learn to remain discreetly silent and listen.

But I have here to consider the vehicle of poetry, *i.e.,* verse technically; and, although some slovenly writers in these days actually manage to get stuff printed as verse which is an outrage to every canon of good composition, the writer of verse is bound to obey certain known and defined rules, otherwise his composition becomes doggerel, and is beneath serious notice

It is strange, however, how very little even many who

write and publish, appear to know about metrical composition. Continually do we see, especially in newspapers, gross violations of all right rules of rhythm, of rhyme, of taste, and of proper arrangement of lines. I once had submitted to me for an opinion, a so-called "poem" on a scriptural subject, consisting of blank verse and some lyrical interludes. I found a part of the work, so far as the versification went, quite correct, and not by any means devoid of ability or interest. The verse was quite equal to very much of that in Pollok's *Course of Time*, but then after turning off some 20 or 30 correct lines, the writer fell into utter confusion, simply writing out very indifferent prose into lines of twelve, fourteen, and more syllables, and so arranged that by no possibility would they scan as verses or metre of any kind. The lyric verse was much the same, good enough in parts, but every now and then unexpectedly breaking down completely. This kind of thing, utterly fatal to literary success of any kind, is the result of ignorance of the laws of metre, and of the various canons that *must* be obeyed in constructing verse. No doubt, halting, imperfect, defective, and altogether bad verses are to be found here and there amid much that is standard literature; but are blemishes and blots to be copied? and shall we imitate great writers in their very worst moods, when from some cause or other they not only nodded, but fell, intellectually speaking, into actual sleep? In these days form is much and finish more still in any composition pretending to be poetical. Imperfect and halting verse is intolerable, and the more so, as it shows a wilful and culpable neglect on the part of the writer, of ready means before him for attaining at least to technical excellence.

From the view-point of verbal and metrical form, we may conveniently classify the different types of poetry, as epic, lyric, and dramatic. Then there is the narrative and pastoral, or idyllic, which often partakes of each of the foregoing, while separately considered, there are the further divisions into the hymn, the ode, the song, the ballad —of which more particularly in its place—the elegy, the sonnet, and finally, humorous, satiric, and comic poetry, and those light verses of society, which have of late years won for themselves a secure estate on Mount Parnassus, and adapted themselves to be a favourite vehicle for expressing the poetic notes of the ordinary nineteenth century mind, which, while revolting from the classic and the romantic alike, has still a certain *feeling* for the true poetic which finds expression in such writers as Locker, Calverley, Austin Dobson, William S. Gilbert, Leigh, F. Locker, and others. Naturally all these many forms of poetry inter-penetrate each other at certain points, but the broad distinctions remain, and we must now consider each in detail.

The Epic.

First of all comes the epic, a form that is virtually obsolete, although for aught we know, the world may have yet another epic. The word *epic* comes from the Greek *epos*, a song, and is often termed *heroic*. It is essentially a form of poetry narrating some story, real or fictitious, or a blending of both, and it must be written in an elevated and dignified style. It must centre on and circle round some great deed or series of deeds, and it, therefore, is essentially the poetry of *action*. It has usually for theme and principal actor, some hero, and in its matter should include incidents, episodes, characters, and moral ; and all these things must be presented in the most splendid, vivid, and picturesque verbal form attainable. The object of such a poem is always to improve the morals and to implant in the mind of the reader a genuine love for valour, virtue, fortitude, and all that is lofty, pure, and true. The great epics of the world are Homer's *Iliad* and *Odyssey*, the *Æneid* of Virgil, Dante's *Divine Comedy*, Ariosto's *Orlando Furioso*, the *Nibelungenlied*, the great German middle age epic, with its hero Siegfried, Tasso's *Jerusalem Delivered*, Camoens' *Lusiad*, and Milton's *Paradise Lost*, which closes practically the epic poetry of the world. There are minor epics, however, of later date, although these will be found to partake of other specific characteristics. Byron's *Childe Harold* is in part an epic, but practically the *novel* (to be fully considered in its place) has killed this great and grand form of narrative poem and remains to us in its highest phases as in the late Lord Lytton, Thackeray, and some others, the prose epic of modern domestic or civil life

Passing reference must be made to the epic poetry of the Orient One of the great Hindoo epics is the *Mahâbhârata*, and Persia has the famous Firdusi, the writer of that great epic, the *Shah-Nameh*, the book of kings.

Lyric Poetry.

Lyric poetry, as its name suggests, was at first sung literally to the accompaniment of the lyre. It is an essential condition of the lyric that it be *subjective;* and here a word of explanation on the distinction between *object* and *subject* in poetry may be of use to the young writer. In metaphysical language *object* is that of which any thinking being or *subject* can be conscious. The subject may be an object, as when one thinks of himself. Now, when in any kind of writing the personality of the *writer* is obtruded so as to be conspicuous, amid the incidents and characters depicted, we call this a *subjective* work. The poems of Byron in his earlier period, especially the metrical tales, such as *Lara*, the *Giaour*, and the *Corsair*, are very subjective. In those works wherein the writer seems quite lost in the detail and general scope of his work we find the objective principle predominant, as in Shakespeare and Scott. Feeling and intense emotion predominate in lyric or subjective poetry.

To dramatic poetry a separate section is devoted.

Pastoral Poetry.

Our next section is the pastoral or idyllic poetry. Originally this related simply to the scenery, sentiment, and incidents of shepherd life, and as pastoral employment was the very earliest form of human labour for the sake of subsistence, the pastoral is probably the initial form of organised poetry. The story of *Ruth* is a veritable idyll. In profane verse we have the idylls of Theocritus, who was imitated by Bion and Moschus. Virgil, with his *Bucolics*, is familiar, but by his time increasing artificiality had rendered the pastoral as far removed from nature as Dresden china shepherds and shepherdesses are from their living prototypes. The mediæval period reduced pastoral poetry to quite a conventional level. Boccaccio reproduced in Italy a form of pastoral from the Greek, and Angelo Poliziano (born 1454), one of the great Italian poets, wrote the earliest idyllic drama known, entitled *Orfeo*. Various works succeeded. Among those was the *Pastor Fido* of Guarini, published at Venice in 1590. After the reign of Charles V., Spanish imaginative literature was quite idyllic, as may be seen in *Don Quixote*. With the grand Elizabethan era England gave forth Spenser's *Shepherd's Calendar* and Fletcher wrote the *Faithful Shepherdess*. Scotland has a remarkable example of the pastoral in Allan Ramsay's *Gentle Shepherd* (1725), while Pope, Ambrose Philips, Gay, and others produced similar works. These later poems are quite conventional, and have as little nature in them as a landscape on a dinner plate. Later still, Tennyson has given some beautiful specimens of idyllic poetry, which ought to be studied by those inclining to this kind of poetry, for which, however, it must be frankly said, scarcely any demand now exists. Thomson's *Seasons* are more descriptive than simply pastoral poems, and have effectually blocked the way for any future attempt to occupy the ground he made his own. He painted nature with a free hand on an extensive canvas, while Wordsworth, who wrote some true pastorals, painted minutely, as in the well-known passage where he tells us that "the daisy, by the shadow that it casts, protects the lingering dewdrop from the sun".

The Hymn.

Properly speaking, the hymn is a poem addressed to the Deity. Among the Pagans it was always a short song addressed to some god. The word primarily expresses a tune. In fact, the word, strictly interpreted, means a certain metrical form in rhythmical cadence. The hymn proper dates from the first days of Christianity. We read in Matthew xxvi. : "And when they had sung a *hymn* they went out to the Mount of Olives". Very little is known as to the authorship of the early hymns. The sublime *Te Deum* has been attributed to St. Ambrose, St. Hilary, and to others. Modern hymns are multitudinous. A few, like Heber's, are beautiful, but the majority are wretched if estimated as poetry. Keble is one of the best-sustained writers of hymns. The young versifier who could produce hymns informed by a true and pure spirit of devotion, and of finished form, musical in wording and perfect in rhyme and rhythm, and illustrated by *original*, apt and appropriate similes, metaphors, etc., would probably have the greatest number of readers of any poet living. And here a word as to the *simile* and *metaphor*. A *simile* is a comparison of two things which, different in other respects, have *some* points of resemblance, thus to say the eloquence of some orator was like a rapid torrent is to employ a simile. A metaphor (from the Greek to carry over) is really a simile reduced to a single word. To say that man is a *lion* is a metaphor, but to say he is *lion-like* is a simile, simply. In metaphor the similitude lies in the name.

The Ode.

The next division is wide and elastic, for the *ode* is exceedingly comprehensive, and may be a poem of considerable length. Originally it was like the lyric, designed to be accompanied by the music of the human voice, for in days when MSS. could not be readily multiplied every kind of composition was for the most part read *aloud*, a mode of publishing a work which had, no doubt, certain advantages. The ode, properly speaking, is a far more lofty composition than the song. It is full of energy, and should be changeful in metre, the changes corresponding to the various moods of the poet. One of the very grandest odes is the song of *Moses*. The Psalms include the very finest of all. Among others may be cited Dryden's *Alexander's Feast*, Gray's *Bard*, Collins's ode to the *Passions*, Shelley's *Skylark*, and Wordsworth's sublime *Intimations of Immortality from Recollections of Early Childhood*.

Structurally considered, the ode is composed of verses varying in length, and arranged in stanzas and divisions known as strophes. As to the latter, it is only a division, and derived its specific name from the fact that originally the reciter *turned* while declaiming that part of the poem, and afterwards turned round and sang the succeeding section, which had to correspond in length, and was known as the antistrophe.

The Elegy.

The elegy is a mourning, a lamenting—or, at all events, a plaintive, melancholy—poem, and a perfect example is to be found in David's beautiful and affecting lament over Saul and Jonathan, one of the most powerful and pathetic poems in the Old Testament.

Elegiac poetry serves, like all true poetry, as a discipline of feeling, and its pivotal point is sorrow for the dead. Rightly, however, from a true ethical standpoint, this sorrow should be tempered and ultimately eliminated by joy for the life to come. It is curious, by the way, that Gray's *Elegy*, which has achieved such an extraordinary success, has the Pagan-like defect of never *once* proclaiming the immortality of redeemed man. It is this that really mars what might otherwise have been a perfect poem. How different is Schiller in his splendid elegy, which is probably the finest work of the kind extant. It is, like that of Gray, on the death of a youth. We are reminded that

> Love gilds not for thee all the world with its glow;
>> Never bride in the clasp of thine arms shall repose;
> Thou canst see not our tears, though in torrents they flow,
>> Those eyes in the calm of eternity close!

One noble and pathetic stanza runs—

> Does the aged exult in the works he has done—
>> The ladders by which he has climbed to renown?
> Or the hero, in deeds by which valour has won
>> To the heights whence the temple of glory looks down?
> When the canker the bud doth already decay,
>> Who can deem that *his* ripeness is free from the worm?
> Who can hope to endure when the young fade away?
>> Who can count on life's harvest—the blight at the germ?

Then, after dwelling on the melancholy of early death, with all its unfulfilled promises, the elegy proceeds—

> Earth and heaven, which such joy to the living one gave,
>> From his gaze darken'd dimly!—and, sadly and sighing,
> The dying one shrank from the thought of the grave,
>> The world! oh, the world is so sweet to the dying!

This is but an inadequate rendering of the fine original, which alone stamps this elegy as the finest of the kind—

> Earth to earth may return—the material to matter—
>> But high from the cell soars the spirit above,
> His ashes the winds of the tempest may scatter,
>> The life of eternity lives in his love!

The translation here given is by the late Lord Lytton.

Bishop Heber may be studied in this department ; and, of course, the beautiful poems of Tennyson in his profound *In Memoriam*. Shelley, unfortunately, devoted his muse to the Pantheism of Pagan Greece, and in his elegy on Keats could find nothing better to tell us than that his friend still lived as a material portion of the universe !

So far this corresponds with Gray's pessimism; how different is Schiller when bidding the dead farewell only

> Till the trumpet that heralds God's coming in thunder
> From the hill-tops of light shall ring over thy bed ,
> Till the portals of death shall be riven asunder,
> And the storm-wind of God whirl the dust of the dead.

Shelley, in his elegy on Keats, can give us no better comfort than by declaring—

> He is made one with nature. There is heard
> His voice in all her music, from the moan
> Of thunder to the song of night's sweet bird

This is of a piece with Byron's fantastic and infidel musings on " becoming a portion of that around him," and

> Existent happier in the fly or worm.

Let the young writer be very sure that poetry, whenever in any sense wedded to the deadly spirit of unbelief, loses thereby its higher vision and cripples its best powers, for the very source of true poetry is in a clear perception of the glories of the creation *because* they are of God.

Mention must be made here of the Pentameter (Greek for five measure). In ancient poetry this meant a verse of *five* feet, as the Hexameter, one of six feet. The two first feet may be either dactyls or spondees, the third *must* be a spondee and the two last feet are anapæsts. The two forms, Hexameter and Pentameter conjoined, constitute what is known as the *elegiac* metre Schiller has some really fine examples of classic metres. The following describes the peculiarity of the ancient elegiac metre in a singularly beautiful manner, the English version here given being from the pen of the poet Coleridge—

> In the Hexameter rises the fountain's silvery column,
> In the Pentameter aye falling in melody back.

The Sonnet.

The sonnet is a special form of verse, and so special is this form in its most elaborate phases, that a volume might easily be filled on this subject alone. The word comes from the Italian *sonnetta*, and means a poem of 14 lines only. These in the correct forms are composed of two stanzas of four verses each and two of three verses each. The whole must be rhymed, but the rhymes must be interwoven. A sonnet correct as to form, consists of two quatrains, each of four lines and having two rhymes. Then come what are called two terzarimas, each of three lines with a single rhyme. English sonnets are often irregular and generally rhyme the second and sixth lines together, closing often with a clinching couplet. Rhyme is indispensable in a sonnet, and each line must rhyme with some other. The subject must be one leading idea worked out to a result or close, and advancing line by line in force until the end is reached, with all that force focussed in some final thought. Few forms of verse possess such a charm, or are so adaptable to any kind of subject as the sonnet. One thing yet remains to note, and that is that the sonnet must be composed of verses of five feet each, heroic measure, and may have double rhymes, in which case a line will have eleven syllables, but still only *five* accents.

Vers-de-Société.

In regard to what are called writers of *vers-de-société* it is well to study Praed, who was the pioneer of this form of metrical composition half a century since, and after him, Frederick Locker, Henry S. Leigh, Mortimer Collins, Austin Dobson, H Cholmondeley Pennell, and others. There are also special forms of what may be called metrical exotic poems in *Ballades* (not to be confounded with ballads wherewith they have nothing in common), *Rondeaus* and *Villanelles*, called after the French poet *Villon*, and *Triolets*. In its ordinary state the *Ballade* consists of three stanzas of eight lines each. These are succeeded by a stanza of four lines, called the "envoy," or the poem may consist of three stanzas of ten lines each, with an "envoy" of five lines. Each of the stanzas and the "envoy" must close with the same line called the "refrain". Thus, in a poem by Austin Dobson on a fan belonging to the Marquise de Pompadour, each stanza and the "envoy" ends with the line—

> This was the Pompadour's fan—

whereto a different rhyme in each division must be made. The *Triolet* should comprise eight lines or verses worked on but two rhymes. These are all exotic metrical forms. The following is a specimen of the *Rondeau*, and is taken from a recently published volume of very beautiful poems by the Rev. Canon Bell—

> Not for the dead, O Lord, we weep;
> Untroubled is their rest and deep.
>   For them why should we mourn or sigh?
>   'Neath quiet graves in peace they lie;
> "Thou givest Thy beloved sleep".
>   For tempted souls, for wandering sheep,
>   For all whose path is rough and steep,
> For them we lift our voice on high—
>   Not for the dead!
> For all who 'neath sore burdens creep,
> Who sow the wind, the whirlwind reap,
>   Who lonely watch the days go by,
>   For hearts that bleed while eyes are dry;
> For these, O Lord, our tears we keep—
>   Not for the dead!

It may be well, too, for the young writer in metres to try his hand on nursery verses or rhymes for children, or at verses similar to those which have made the "Bab Ballads" of Mr. Gilbert famous. These things when *well* done pay and are marketable, and may lead to better work by-and-by. Those who desire fuller information on this subject should consult the fine and comprehensive series, entitled "Parodies of the works of English and American Authors," collected and annotated by Walter Hamilton.

Metre.

And now let us consider briefly what is meant by metre.

Metre is that regulated sequence of syllables accented in a certain order, of which a certain number form a *verse* or line. Verse is derived from the Latin *verto*, to *turn*. It is a vulgar error to talk of a song of say four verses, when what is meant is a song of four *stanzas* of four lines, or sixteen lines or *verses* Two lines rhyming together form a *couplet*, three lines a *triplet*, four or more lines or verses a stanza.

In English verse metre depends on the recurrence of accented and unaccented syllables. Each English metre, or foot of a verse, *must* include *one* accented syllable and one or two unaccented syllables The metres are arranged in lines or verses; these vary in length, but must have a certain harmonious relation to each other. The stress or accent may occur on the first, second or third syllable. We have, in all, five principal English metres—two dissyllabic, and three trisyllabic. Thus, fólly is a *trochee*, recáll, an *iambus;* terribly, a *dactyl*, confúsion, an *amphibrachys*, and absenteé, an *anapæst*. In general, the usual metres in English verse are trochees, iambics and anapæsts, which are sometimes blended together.

The young versifier should remember that the main technics of verse are *accent, quantity, emphasis* and *pause.*

By *accent* is meant the laying more force on one syllable of a word than on another, as sur*mount*. The *quantity* means the time consumed in pronouncing it, as in the word just used, *cŏnsūmed*—the short time being marked ⌣, and the long time –. *Emphasis* is well understood; and then there is *tone*, which relates to the voice like emphasis, and really belongs to reading. What is known as the *cæsura* is simply a pause in verse designed to render a line more melodious. It divides a verse or line into equal or unequal parts. Pope uses this with great effect. An endless variety of combinations may be formed out of these metres, but the principal types in ordinary use are those known as *octosyllabic* metres, examples of which will be found in Scott's *Marmion*, as in the opening lines—

> Day set | on Nor | ham's cast | led steep,
> And Tweed's | fair riv | er, broad | and deep.

This is an easy form of versifying, and may be varied by introducing alternating lines of three feet each, and in many other ways.

Heroic is the name given to verses each of which consists of *five* metres or *ten* syllables in all. These heroics rhyme in couplets, or, if rhymeless, are called blank verse. A very considerable bulk of English poetry is in heroic verse, rhymed or blank. Nearly all metrical plays are in blank heroic verse, and here a supernumerary syllable at the end of each verse is permitted. This is often found in Shakespeare and Milton. Many of the finest poems in the language are in rhymed heroic metres. Here is an example from Campbell—

> Say, can the world one joyous thought bestow
> To friendship, weeping at the couch of woe?
> No! but a brighter soothes the last adieu—
> Souls of impassioned mould, she speaks to you!
> Weep not, she says, at nature's transient pain,
> Congenial spirits part to meet again!

In elegiac metres the lines are heroic, but the first is made to rhyme with the third and the second with the fourth, and out of this arrangement comes the Spenserian stanza employed in *The Fairy Queen*, and by Byron in *Childe Harold*.

The Ballad.

A familiar arrangement is that of the *ballad*. Here the verses are sometimes each of fourteen syllables, printed in one line. Rhymes in the line occur, as in the following—

Our hero-king—no eagle's wing swept prouder than his arm,
And never Attic eloquence like his could soldier charm!

To the ballad, movement, life and colour—and, above all, dramatic spirit—are absolutely essential. Once the piece opens, there must not be a single pause in its cumulative march to the end. A good ballad to study is that of Oliver Wendell Holmes on "Bunker Hill," wherein the whole episode is panoramic, and moves on from one point of intense interest to another yet more so. The form of stanza is happy, too, and may be studied with much advantage. Describing the second attempt of the British to carry the height, we have the following stanza, which may be taken as a fair example of what I mean when I repeat that, in part and whole, the ballad should always have *cumulative force*—

Now, the walls they're almost under! scarce a rod the foes asunder!
Not a firelock flashed against them! up the earthwork they will
    swarm!
But the words have scarce been spoken, when the ominous calm is
    broken,
And a bellowing crash has emptied all the vengeance of the storm!

The more common form for ballad purposes is what is sometimes termed the eight and six metre, alluding to the syllables—sixteen making a complete line, although the stanza form may be used, as in the battle ballad of *Arbela*, 331 B.C., wherein the rout of the Persian horse by the famous Macedonian phalanx is thus described—

> They came; we broke them on our ranks—
> Those jewelled warriors gay—
> As when the prows of mighty ships
> Spurn billows into spray!

These are but a few of the forms.   Much license exists, and then the skilful versifier will adapt his metres to the varying sentiment and character of the piece.   Instinctively it is felt that a lively metre is quite unsuited to a grave, a dignified, or a pathetic subject, and usually the versifier's mood will determine his metre.

Some mention must be made of the hexameter form of verse, which many English metrical writers have striven to naturalise.   The greatest success has been achieved by Longfellow in his *Evangeline*.   This is the heroic or epic verse of Greek and Rome.   It consists of six feet.   The last of all must be a spondee—that is, *two* long syllables—and the last but one must be a *dactyl*—that is, one long syllable and two short.   The hexameter has been used in German verse, especially by Klopstock and Goethe, but it is very difficult to manage in English.   Longfellow's opening lines, however, in *Evangeline* are good—

This is the | forest primeval. The | murmuring | pines and the |
   hemlocks,
Bearded with | moss and with | garments | green, indis | tinct in the |
   twilight.

This will afford some general notion of the metres used in English verse.   In blank verse it is essential that a high level be maintained, and that the words fall into melodious order, otherwise such compositions have a tendency to degenerate into mere prose printed in measured lengths, forming verse to the eyes, but not at all to the ear.

Rhyme.

Let us now turn to rhime, rhyme, or, more correctly, *rime*, which is, I believe, a Teutonic word, and comes from the German *reihe*—a row. At first rhyme was very loose, as anyone may perceive who turns to the oldest examples thereof, but for our purpose here rhyme means a certain chiming correspondence in the final syllables of words, and is employed to mark the ends of verses or lines. In French verse absolute identity in all the sounds forms what is called rich rhyme, as in *modèle, fidèle,* but in English verse these are not true rhymes at all, and should be carefully avoided. Thus *expire* does not rhyme with *pyre,* or *moor* with *more.* In English syllables that rhyme must at once agree and differ. In each the vowel must be the same, but the consonants before different. For example, *park* rhymes correctly with *bark* or *lark.* In some cases, however, nothing comes after the vowel, as forego, which would rhyme with *O.* Then, in correct rhymes, the keynote syllables must each be accented. Such words as *free* and *merrily* do not rhyme properly. In all cases rhyme depends on sound ; it is strictly a phonetic matter, and has nothing to do with spelling. *Love* rhymes perfectly with *dove,* but imperfectly with *move,* and, of course, *plough* does not rhyme with *rough.*

There are *double* and even *triple* rhymes. In these the *first* syllable must be accented, the rest unaccented and absolutely identical in sound. Thus, turning is a perfect *double* rhyme to burning. In *triple* rhymes it is often necessary, as in double rhymes, to compound the rhymes. Thus, suppose we wanted a rhyme to *fragrance,* it might be managed thus—

Every *day* grants fresher *fragrance,*
Than the early lilies yield—

or, say to *baby*, we might contrive it thus—

> Darling *baby*, may life's *day* be.

In triple rhymes here is an example—

> "Ah," she murmured, "terrible,
>   In a moment such as this,
> 'Tis to hear a merry bell
>   Pealing for a traitor's bliss."

Of course, these are only rough examples, designed to indicate the lines whereon double and triple rhymes should be constructed.

Variety is very essential in these days, as, naturally, readers are tired of the familiar old rhyming forms. I had to write a little piece of verse to the heading "In the Greenwood," and being anxious to avoid hackneyed rhymes, contrived it thus—

> Wandering through leafy cloisters
>   In the days of summer long,
> How the heart with nature's joy stirs
>   Bird-translated into song!
> Under arches green and graceful,
>   Tremulous with sunshine bright,
> Till each scene became a place full
>   Of unspeakable delight.
> O how fresh and O how placid!
>   Pure as Spring's first flowers unfurled,
> Here are sweets to quell each acid
>   Left within us by the world!

This is but a trifle, but it is better than "breeze" and "trees," or similar stock rhymes, which will be found duly satirised in Pope's *Essay on Criticism*, Part II.

For general narrative purposes, I am inclined to favour the use of the quatrain, closing with a couplet, making in all a six-lined stanza. This metrical form is adopted with much effect by the late Lord Lytton in his fine epic poem, *King Arthur*. This six-lined stanza is very convenient for rendering complete ideas hardly adequate for the more ample space

of the sonnet, as in the following relative to the early ages of
England—

> Long was a day in that slow-moving age,
>   A county was a continent in space;
> But nearly all men then read Nature's page;
>   And tho' their wisdom showed the evil trace
> Of superstition—people were devout—
> They lack'd the culture that conditions doubt!

For producing what may be called simple sound effects
I have found a far simpler metrical form, sufficiently expres-
sive, as in this, which relates to the *Spirit of Poetry*—

> I am a fay, and rest on a spray,
>   Or ride on a racking cloud;
> In the sunbeam flit, on the rainbow sit,
>   And sing in the thunder loud.
>
> Sometimes I dwell in the nectar bell,
>   Of the wild flowers of the lea;
> And again I ride on the surging tide,
>   And hark to the booming sea.
>
> And often I lie and softly sigh
>   In a shell by the wave-washed shore,
> And listen at noon to the quiet tune
>   That breaks from the fisherman's oar.
>
> Or swiftly I fleet in the diamond sleet,
>   And flash in the blinding hail,
> And mantle my form in the white snow warm,
>   As I sweep on the winter gale.
>
> At morn I rise, when the sun heaven dyes,
>   I drink his first beams in;
> And often I dream by a silent stream,
>   Then wake in the cataract's din.
>
> By night I stray, in some moonlit way,
>   To bathe in her clear cold light;
> On the lakes I float in a silver boat
>   And am woo'd by the water-sprite.
>
> There is no spot where I am not,
>   All the ways of men I have trod,
> And the false and true alike I woo
>   To the bosom of their God!

There is more, but this is ample to show how good verbal jingle may be produced from simple metres and ordinary rhymes.   It is best, however, to avoid such, and there is ample scope for variety in the interweaving and contriving of double rhymes.   Here is a form that is somewhat unusual—

> Selfishness *narrow*
>   From out of thee spurn ;
> And Sorrow's sad cypress
>   To amaranth turn ;
> Faith blunteth the *arrow*
>   Of Death at the last,
> And no shroud, but bright wings round
>   The Blessed are cast !

I cannot forbear, however, from giving one more example of the way in which a very simple thought may be made exceedingly effective in very simple words.   One of Mrs. Hemans' very beautiful poems is called "The Trumpet".   It opens by declaring that "The trumpet's voice hath roused the land," and then in plain but well-chosen words we are told how " A king to war went past".   The poem then proceeds to give some details of the effects of the summons to war throughout the land in disturbing the ordinary affairs of life. Then the tone changes abruptly, and closes with these arrestive, and, to all who are truly thoughtful and not swallowed up by contemporary materialism, terrible words—

> And all this haste and change and fear
>   By earthly clarion spread—
> How will it be when nations hear
>   The blast that wakes the dead ?

The *Ingoldsby Legends* furnish specially good examples of some of the most ingenious and correct double and triple rhymes extant.

Alliteration is a grace of verse if used wisely.   In old

German, Anglo-Saxon, and Scandinavian poetry it serves in place of rhyme, and combined therewith it is extremely effective. Thus, for example—

> The fair *breeze blew*, the white *foam flew*,
>   The *furrows followed free*;
> *We were* the first that ever burst
>   Into that *silent sea*!

Alliteration is the use of identical consonant sounds, usually at the beginning of words, but sometimes in the middle. What is known as *assonance* is the use of identical vowel sounds within words of which the consonants are dissimilar.

It is said that rhyme was quite unknown to the ancient Greeks, although the ancient Romans were aware of the effect to be produced by what is understood as rhyme, and Latin poems were rhymed by the schoolmen as early as the eighth century. *Alliteration* came from the Scandinavians; and *assonance*, the rhyming only of the final vowels, is peculiar to Spain. Rhyme seems, however, to have been essential to Arabian poetry, and appears to have been borrowed from them by the Troubadours, who made it *the* feature of Provençal poetry. The unit of Arabian verses seems to be the simple couplet, but the Troubadours varied these in a variety of ways, crossing and intertwining their rhymes. In one word, as Sismondi says in his *Historical View of the Literature of the South of Europe*, rhyme was the very groundwork of Provençal poetry, whence it crept into the poetry of all the other nations of Europe. It was the Provençal poets who really first substituted number and accent of syllables for the *quantity*, as it is called, which formed the basis of Greek and Latin verse. In these ancient tongues all syllables were long or short, and the verse was constructed of a certain number of measures termed feet, which marked the rise and fall of the tune; but in the Romance languages *accent* supplies the place of fixed quantity, and the ear alone was the metrical guide. Sismondi tells us that those syllables of fixed quantity mark the cæsura—this pause in the line which, being variously placed near the beginning or the end, prevents the ear from being fatigued by a monotony of verses each exactly resembling its predecessor. Thus, in verses of say ten syllables the cæsura or pause may occur at the fifth or the sixth syllable, or even at other points, as the sense of the passage and the metrical taste and instinct of the versifier may determine. Copiousness of language and a nice sense of the power of words and of their relative value are obviously essential to a good style of versification. Generally, too, the essential characteristics of really good prose writing apply to verse, where perfect and distinct conception is quite as essential as to prose itself.

VERSIFICATION GENERALLY CONSIDERED.

The great art of the versifier is to make all harmonise together and with the subject so that metres, rhymes if any, rhythm, alliteration, assonance if there be any, all go each in its duly subordinated degree to make up an effective whole.

Carelessness in metrical detail is now unpardonable, and the utmost pains should be taken with verse to make it technically perfect. Loose rhymes cannot be tolerated. Words ending in *n* are sometimes made to do duty with those ending in *m*, as gai*n* with na*m*e. Halting metres and slovenly imperfect rhymes irritate the ear of those who know what verse should be. Reviewers are apt to stigmatise a writer's metrical effort as "rubbish" when these defects are seen, and in any case they *must* greatly hinder success even when, which is very rarely indeed, they are found combined with original thought and genuine poetic feeling.

Beware of bad models. Everywhere almost in collections

of standard poetry will be found much that is altogether bad and wrong in form. Remember that the great did not win their laurels through their faults, but on account of their merits. Mrs. Barrett Browning, one of the very greatest female poets of the world, is a great offender in careless rhymes. Her beautiful poem, the *Lost Bower*, is full of faults; thus, she attempts to rhyme *closes* with *losses*, *daily* with *valley*, *hazels* with *dazzles*, *clenching* with *branching*, *said I* with *lady*, *floated* with *suited*, *glory* with *before me*, *waken* with *taking*, *mountains* with *dauntings*, and very many others. All these are absolute blemishes and really ruin the poem from a metrical view-point. Never be satisfied with anything short of verbal perfection in versifying. You may not command great original ideas, or possess a true poetic "vision," but you *can* make your metres melodious and correct and your rhymes perfect. Less than this it is not worth the while of any writer to aim at in these days when the sum of accumulated poetry is so vast and so good. Study carefully, therefore, the true technics of versification and learn to discriminate between the good and the bad in English verse. Be not deceived into fancying *because* a *standard* poet has perpetrated false rhymes, or produced halting metres, that *you* are privileged to do the same. Aim high, and always prefer quality to quantity in verse.

I have before me, as I write, a volume of poems by a writer who has earned a high place in the world of fiction and who presumedly should know all that is set forth technically in this Manual, yet he falls into singular mistakes and fails not only in his metres, but in his figures of speech too. Thus, in a poem composed of trochees, he tells us—

> Not a year of Indian story
>   Matches fifty-seven in fame,
> When the star of England's glory,
>   Almost set in blood and shame.

These are perfectly correct, but the next stanza save one begins—

> When Lucknow's siege-battered splendour—

which is in quite another metre. The same writer declares that for "his lay" he will pluck a *rose* from the storm's dark breast of *thunder*. This is about as unhappy a figure of poetic speech as could well be, and in another poem the writer tells of a *bruised* wave! A wave may be broken, beaten back, cleft, but not *bruised*. You cannot *bruise* water, though you may stain it. It is to points of this kind that the young writer whether in prose or verse should carefully look. Poetry is not insanity or a departure from fact and sense. It is the glorifying and transfiguring of both.

But to revert   Poe, who was as able a critic as he was a poet, wrote an essay to prove that no true poem *could* be very long, and when long, as in the case of *Paradise Lost*, it was really made of several true poems connected together by prose disguised as verse. Be careful, too, not to fall into the frequent mistake of young writers, who compare their *best* verses with the *worst* work of standard poets, and then very naturally do not see much difference between the two ! The very greatest poets are unequal at times. Byron is particularly an example of this. Some of his verse is not poetry at all, and Edmund Young, the author of the famous *Night Thoughts*, printed much that is simply metrical trash. The oft-quoted " poem " of Cowper's on the loss of the *Royal George* is little better than rubbish. He can describe the sinking of the stately warship in no better way than to say—

> She was overset,

and such is his poverty of rhyming power, that he has to finish the stanza with the statement—

> Down went the Royal George,
> With all her crew complete.

Many poet children have beaten this at seven years old. This sort of stuff is rather far away from such a passage of word-music as this one of Byron's—

> She was a form of life and light,
> That seen, became a part of sight,
> And rose where'er I turned mine eye,
> The Morning Star of Memory.

Aim high, I say again. Imitate, the young versifier must necessarily, but he should not imitate obvious rubbish. Byron's *Hours of Idleness* abounds with verse of much the same quality as that found in cracker motto rhymes. Take such a stanza as this—

> The man doomed to sail with the blast of the gale,
>   Thro' billows Atlantic to steer,
> As he bends o'er the wave which may soon be his grave,
>   The green sparkles bright with a tear.

This is sad trash. Now listen to this from the same poet—

> Look on its broken arch, its ruined wall,
> Its chambers desolate, its portals foul,
> Yes, this was once Ambition's airy hall,
> The dome of thought, the palace of the soul !
> Behold thro' each lack-lustre, eyeless hole
> The gay recess of wisdom and of wit,
> And passion's hosts, that never brook'd control.
> Can all saint, sage, or sophist ever writ
> People this lonely tower, this tenement refit ?

Observe the difference. The poetry is pessimistic and cynical, but it is powerful and of very high quality. Even in this fine passage there are blemishes. In rhyming, if possible, the *final* consonantal parts should be *varied*. In the above we have *wall, foul, hall, soul*. The sound effect would be better had the second and fourth lines rhymed on such letters as *d* or *t*. These may seem trivial things, but when studied practically they may make all the difference between success and failure, and every critic is more or less sympathetic with the unmistakable charm and beauty of versification that is flawless in its technical finish.

Poetry, or that which approaches thereto, *must* in these days be exquisite in form and faultless in metrical structure to stand any chance of succeeding. Anything less is not at all acceptable. No one wants it. Mimetic metres—feeble echoes of Longfellow (who is not in any sense a great poet), reminiscences of Tennyson, adumbrations of cynic gloom from Byron—will not pass either the reviewer or the public. Nevertheless, there is such a vast and increasing reading public, that it is certain that the writer who has poetry in him, and will learn how to express that poetry properly, is sure of an audience; for more than ever is poetry a necessity to many amid the mechanism, the materialities, the monotonies of contemporary life. Let it be borne well in mind, too, that although poetry is a gift and the poet is born, he is *made* too, and unless those who seem to have a faculty for verse properly equip themselves for displaying that faculty aright they will inevitably fail to secure any great results, and if ever success comes, it will be far less than it might have been had genius been willing to learn. It has been rightly observed that the objects of a poet's thoughts, and I would add of his feelings, too, are literally everywhere. Poetry should comprehend *all* knowledge, and it is essential that the poet keep in intellectual touch with his age. Thus it is obvious that even the researches of the chemist or the achievements of the engineer come within his proper ken, and of all things most inexcusable in anyone pretending to write poetry are ignorance and unwillingness to learn.

Humorous and Comic Verse.

As to humorous and comic verse, there is little to say here. The ability to produce such is a gift that cannot be imparted.

Training may and should enable anyone to write correct metres, but no amount of technical instruction would teach a writer how to produce anything like the best efforts of the elder Hood. Still technics will be here to the full as helpful to the comic versifier as to those who aim at only the serious side of poetry. Hovering between the serious and the absolutely comic are those light society verses, of which Mortimer Collins gave some charming examples. These find ready acceptance, and the public taste for any trifles of this kind is likely to grow.

There is, in fact, a large public for poetry generally. The returns of only one firm of a year's sales of poetry gave the following results.—Byron, 2380 ; Burns, 2250 , Campbell, 207 ; Chaucer, 637 ; Cowper, 800 ; Hemans, 1900 ; Hood, 980 ; Leigh Hunt, 76 ; Keats, 40 ; L. E. L, 109 ; Longfellow, 6000 , Lowell, 307 ; Milton, 1850 ; Moore, 2276 , Poe, 310 ; Pope, 706 ; Rogers, 32 ; Scott, 3170 ; Shakespeare, 2700 ; Shelley, 500 , Southey, 267 , Spenser, 360.

These are hopeful figures ; and, as we know, the successive editions of Tennyson and Browning and some others go off quite as well as a popular novel. The age is ultra-scientific and materialistic, and poetry is the great corrective to its hardness, its want of generous enthusiasm, of high and noble impulse, and especially its dry rot of infidelity, veiled under a so-called scientific philosophy.

Poetry with a Purpose

Before closing this general survey of the field of poetry, it may be well to say a word on the subject of poetry with a purpose. I am here speaking, of course, of poetry worthy so to be called, and not merely verse and metre. There are, and ever will be, those who would wholly divorce poetry from purpose except in the pure æsthetic sense, as it is contended that the aim of poetry is to *please ;* but to me the answer seems to be that the question how far poetry is

affected by purpose depends on the nature of the purpose,
and according as that may be good or bad, so *pro tanto*
does the poetry wedded thereto gain or lose. Thus the
poetry of *Paradise Lost* is distinctly mated to a purpose,
but, as that purpose transcends the loftiest efforts of human
genius, the poetry gains proportionately; and, in like manner,
the epic of Virgil fills a lower sphere, since it concerns only
the building of an empire and the glorifying of a particular
people   Without refining too much, however, we may safely
conclude that, as a rule, the marriage of poetry to politics is
fatal to the former, and, obviously, since the politics are
necessarily subject to utter change, and the generation of
to-day may have no real sympathy with things that seemed
to its predecessors matters of life and death   As a rule, I
think poets who have thrown themselves heart and soul into
the cauldron of practical politics have by so much ruined
their fame as poets ; and, as an instance, we may take
Dryden, the whole of whose *political* poetry, splendid at the
time, is now a dead letter.   At the same time, there are, no
doubt, cases in which poets have by their political chantings
effected great changes for the better ; and possibly their true
greatness lies in the sacrifice of fame to patriotism.   As a
rule, however, pure poetry has little in common with a work-
a-day world, whence most of us seek to be removed by the
glamour of the singer, and probably few comparatively of
the many who have tried, have really effected much by
assaulting abuses of a serious kind with the artillery of
rhyme or the spear-points of satire.   One of the best examples of this type is that of Ebenezer Elliott, the famous
corn-law rhymer, whose fiery verses had, it is believed, much
to do with the repeal of the corn laws.   In our own days, we
have Dr. W. C. Bennett, who is in some respects the poet of
popular Liberalism ; and others might be cited.   It is probable that openings will be found by-and-by for much
metrical exercise in the *purpose* direction ; and, in truth, we

have this already on a small scale in the case of the verses admitted to the comic or satirical papers, much of which is poetry with a purpose quite as much as Hood's *Song of the Shirt*.

Some Practical Points.

Yet one word more on some practical points. "Poetry does not pay" is the cry of everybody. The exceptions of Tennyson, Browning, and one or two other living poets prove the rule; yet it is probable that the true reason lies in the fact that nearly all the so-called poetry offered for publication is either rubbish or simply an imitation or echo of some well-known poet past or present. Yet there is a great deal of verse used up by periodicals, some of which pay for verse, for the majority expect to have the right of printing verse for nothing. Verse is either good or bad; the latter ought never to be accepted, and the former, if accepted, ought certainly to be paid for at, at least, the same rate as prose. The fact that poetry, even when good, is rarely paid for by editors is due greatly to the eagerness of writers of verse to get into print. There is, however, a field for metrical writers, and in connection with floral Christmas, New Year, Easter and birthday cards and dainty little books, and there is a fair number of firms who pay fair prices for good verses. Then there is the more lucrative field of writing words for songs. This is far more difficult than is supposed by any except those who have tried the work; but there are numbers of popular composers of music who are entirely incapable of supplying the words required for the vocalisation of their melodies; and anyone possessing the gift of writing metres that can be sung is sure of well-remunerated employment.

The fact is, "poetry" would pay far better than it does if only it were generally more worthy of the name. Longfellow, who is not in any true sense a great poet, made money by his poems; and so have other American writers of verse. I fancy that anybody capable of writing *poetry*

adapted to the comprehension of the ordinary reader would
meet with quite as much success now as in the days when
Moore received £3000 for *Lalla Rookh*.

And now, lastly, as to a lower but more promising department in verse

There is doubtless an increasing demand for amusing
metres. There are many easily pleased and frivolous people
who prefer a parody to any poem. They want to be di-
verted, and to those who have the vein there is doubtless
ample encouragement in this direction. Few books—judged
by *sales*—have had such success as the *Ingoldsby Legends*.
To the metrical jester nothing comes amiss, and the faculty
can be cultivated for finding a jest in everything until it is
perfect. Liberties, too, can be taken with versification
absolutely inadmissible in any serious composition Thus
Mr Lewis Carroll says, or sings—

> Who would not give all else for two p-
> Ennyworth only of beautiful soup?

This division of a word, by the way, is absolutely wrong in
any serious form of verse, although some examples may
occasionally be seen in the collected poems of writers who
ought to know better than to indulge in such license. Of
course, there are verses and verses in the case of comic
or society compositions, or those blending satire with fun
and humour, as in Hood's famous and probably matchless
poem of *Miss Kilmansegg and her precious Leg*. Some of
Dr. Wendell Holmes's lighter poems are charming examples
of what such pieces should be, as in his arch lines on *Con-
tentment*, wherein, among other like remarks, he observes—

> Plain food is quite enough for me ;
>   Three courses are as good as ten ,
> If nature can subsist on three,
>   Thank Heaven for three—Amen.
> I always thought cold victuals nice—
> My *choice* would be vanilla ice.

It is not very difficult for those with some metrical talent to acquire a facility for this kind of light and graceful versification, and there is for such verses, brief, neat, polished, pointed and witty or satirical, a variety of paying openings on the staff of papers like *Punch*, *Judy*, *Fun*, *Moonshine*, *Funny Folks*, and many others.

There is now a decided bias in many quarters towards parody, as may be perceived by a glance at Mr. Walter Hamilton's excellent collection, but the young writer should beware how he commits himself to this perilous path in light literature. Writing on January 13, the *Daily Telegraph* most severely and properly criticised Mark Twain, who, in his sketch, *A Yankee at the Court of King Arthur*, has broadly caricatured the chivalry of the Round Table and made a jest of all the legends thereof, which resembles the coarse practical jest of the university student who puts a clay pipe into the mouth of Homer or Pericles. To make a jest of that which is held in reverence by others is very contemptible work indeed, and leads to moral sap and rottenness in any writer who indulges therein. The writer in the *Daily Telegraph* keenly retorts on Mark Twain, by observing—

"King Arthur swore each of his followers to 'reverence his conscience as his King, To ride abroad redressing human wrongs, To speak no slander, no, nor listen to it, To honour his own word as if his God's, To lead sweet lives in purest chastity, To love one maiden only, cleave to her, And worship her by years of noble deeds'. Such an oath presented to a modern Yankee would seem to convey in almost every phrase a covert insult to American institutions. In a land where commercial fraud and industrial adulteration are fine arts we had better omit appeals to 'conscience'. The United States are not likely to 'ride abroad redressing human wrongs'—as they never gave a dollar or a man to help Greece, Poland, Hungary, or Italy in their struggles to be free. 'To speak no slander, no, nor listen to it,' would utterly uproot America's free press—based to a great extent on scandalous personalities. Loving one maiden only, and cleaving to her, must seem too 'high toned' in the States, where there are so many facilities for ready divorce."

The fact is, burlesque, travesty, and parody are at the best miserable things, and it were well if every journal were to speak out as boldly and well as the *Daily Telegraph* has done here, although it must be said that some of the statements above are too sweeping, for in reality the work in question is mainly a satire on Protection, and it is certainly a clever production, the irreverence being more in seeming than in reality. At the same time, young writers should be warned against *imitations* of this kind of writing, whereto there is now far too great a tendency.

But this is digressive, although it has a very practical side too. In closing this section I would now remark that in ordinary prosework there is much room and scope for the exercise of an acquired metrical faculty. Many a time in ordinary work is it very convenient to make one's own quotations, to round off a period, or give a heading to a section, especially when away from one's books and references. In one case, when supplying a series of chapters in a work on Manufacturing Industries, with fit quotations for the various subjects, over a section relative to the Canning Industry—the special subject was Lobsters—the following was written—

> Most animals have bones within
> To keep in shape their flesh and skin,
> But the Crustacean tribe is known
> By having flesh inside its bone.

Over a chapter devoted to Leather Manufacture this appeared—

'Tis strange, indeed, that of one beast the hide
Enables man another beast to ride.

These are but trifles, but they illustrate the value of a thorough metrical training, as they run off the pen just when wanted, and any young student can soon acquire the knack by practice. It is essential, however, at the outset, to learn to versify *correctly*. I have already dwelt on this point, but a word more will be useful. I have before me a copy of *Brighton Society* for 1889, and in a Christmas "poem"—as I presume the writer imagines his imperfect rhymes to be—there are attempts to rhyme "water" with "shorter," "proportion" with "fortune," and "previous" with "grievous". This is as bad as a hymn in which "Saviour" is made to rhyme with "favour". Even in books similar blunders are found. In one of the old annuals I find a poem by the late Miss Strickland wherein one stanza is spoilt by rhyming "morn" to "storm". As I have said in more than one place in this book, poetry in these days must be altogether perfect. The rhyme—if rhyme there be—must be finished, and the verbal construction of the verse must be wrought up to the highest possible degree of metrical excellence.

Nothing will more help the student here than reading the best poems of the *best* poets, and bearing in mind that he must not admire any piece of verse simply because it is by Byron or Tennyson or any other duly canonized bard, but because by applying the general rule of criticism, he knows as well as feels it to be good. To show how far *verbal* excellence alone tells, the nice placing and judicious choice of words, take such a little gem as that of Oliver Wendell Holmes in the "Two Armies". The one army bears on its banner, in effect, the dreadful words, " Our glory is to slay," while on the banner of the anonymous, self-denying, patient, and fearless fighters against vice, want, and all forms of human suffering is the glorious line—" Our mission is to SAVE".

But the particular passages calling for note are these   In
the stanzas relative to war—and war is sometimes dreadfully
justifiable—the poet says—

> Though from the hero's bleeding breast
>   Her pulses Freedom drew,
> Though those white lilies in her crest
>   Sprang from that scarlet dew,

yet, in spite of all this, we are significantly reminded that—

> While Valour's haughty champions wait
>   Till *all* their scars are shown,
> Love walks unchallenged through the gate
>   To sit beside the Throne !

Now note the beautiful antithesis between the *white* lilies
and the *scarlet* dew—scarlet because *that* is the colour of
arterial blood, and means *life*.   Dr. Holmes has rarely written
anything better than this, which is in its way perfect.   Every
syllable goes straight to the mark, and metre, rhyme, and the
natural euphony of each word all blend finely together,
making music to the mind as well as to the ear, and calling
up two pictures of power, beauty, and rare sublimity.

The Technics of Verse Further Considered.

Yet one word more as to the technics of versification.

In the *technical* part of versification there is very much to
be observed that unfortunately rarely engages the thoughts,
as it should do, of the young writer whose inclination
prompts him to begin metrically.   Too often he forgets
entirely the precept of Pope, that

> The sound must seem an echo to the sense,

he takes no particular pains to let his accent fall on the best
words, so that the verse may *read itself*, and not require to
be artificially read.   Even great poets occasionally fall into
lapses.   In his generally-exquisite poem, the *Ode to a Skylark*, Shelley spoils one stanza by a strained pronunciation

of the word profūse, which, by the metrical construction of the line where it occurs, viz.—

In profūse strains of unpremeditated art,

has to be read profūse. Then, again, in rhyme it is very desirable to vary these as much as possible, and to have as many tones, or tunes, as can be given. Thus, a sequence of say "cloud," "loud," "bowed," "shroud," is bad; and, as far as practicable, the consonantal portion should be changed, as well, of course, as the vowel portion. Anything of a sing-song character should be avoided, and yet the rhyme where it is employed ought to be distinct and as musical as possible. The poet Keats tried some experiments with rhymes, by making them fall on unimportant words, but the effect was not happy; and blank verse is to be preferred to such a fantastic trick as that he attempted with very little success, spoiling thereby such a lovely passage (so far as the *thought* goes) as that in *Endymion*, so often quoted, commencing—

A thing of beauty is a joy for ever,

but awkwardly continuing—

Its loveliness increases, it will never
Pass into nothingness.

Byron, in spite of the splenetic and jealous attacks of Swinburne, who does not raise himself one poetic foot by trying to depress the author of *Childe Harold*, is a great master of the art of making the rhyme tell. Take a few random instances—

The cold in clime are cold in blood;
Their love can scarce deserve the name;
But mine was like the lava flood
That boils in Etna's breast of flame.

Here the stress of rhyme falls on all the leading words. So in Pope's exquisite hymn of *The Dying Christian*—

> Vital spark of heavenly flame,
> Quit, oh ! quit, this mortal frame ;

and throughout the whole piece, wherein the rhyme corresponds to, and harmonises with, the key-words of the poem.

My attention has been the more directed to these points inasmuch as I have had under my notice such vast quantities of verse from inexperienced, half-informed writers, who evince complete ineptitude as to the management of the telling words and the rhymes. In a recently-published volume of verses, called "poems," I find the following, taken quite at random as the volume opens—

> And he learnt that by message or sign, sight or sound,
> With Matilda he must not—the stern order ran—
> More communicate, under the king's strongest ban.

Who can read these lines and not perceive the awkwardness of the writer, and mark the feeble endeavour to accommodate grammar and metre? In good verse we do not often find any awkward inversions, and in real poetry never. The sense and sound and sequence of words are all *natural*, and flow forth song-like in music whose art is wholly concealed. Obviously there are many points that can only be properly learned by practice, and by the careful and thoughtful study of really good models. The young writer of metres, however, who once gets on the right track will soon find his view enlarged, and he will, after a time, instinctively feel what is right and what is wrong in metrical construction, just as the professional musician can detect the slightest fault in the most complicated piece of concerted harmony.

Many young versifiers, too, have a knack of beginning a piece in a certain form of verse, and then introducing quite conspicuously something different. There are, of course, cases when metre can and should be varied, and much effect can be gained thereby, but there must be a *reason*. If a rhymer begins, say, by using a four-lined stanza, with double rhymes for the first and third lines, and single rhymes for the second and fourth lines, we expect him to continue this form to the close of the piece. If in a subsequent stanza he drop the double rhyme, the natural inference is that he is careless, or that he had not skill enough to maintain his self-chosen form beyond the opening. Many otherwise good pieces in print are marred by gross inattention to these little points. A poem having faults of this kind is—if otherwise good—like a badly cut diamond, and the better its intrinsic merits the more glaring is the blemish due to careless, ignorant, or clumsy mechanical manipulation. My main object here is not so much to set lessons—for to meet all such cases would need literally thousands of examples—as to put the student in poetry on the right track for discerning blemishes as well as recognising beauty in standard poetry, and to suggest that *thought* is imperatively needed at every step in versifying if the result is to be something worthy to be called poetry, wherein we have glorious and radiant thought or intense feeling wedded to words of power and melody. Take nothing for granted because you see it in print, or even because it has the sanction of a name high up in literature. Read and examine for yourself He who cannot read critically will certainly never write correctly, and it is in intelligently understanding what is read that the first real steps are taken towards writing well. Here is an example from Scott, a passage from *Marmion*. Relative to the hero, we are told—

> His square-turned joints and strength of limb
> Showed him no carpet knight so trim,
> But in close fight a champion grim,
> In camps a leader sage

Here is a manifest blunder. No doubt Marmion's strength of limb might prove him a formidable man-at-arms, but could have nothing to do with his *sagacity* at the council board. These may seem trivial points, but they are not so in reality, and it may be depended on that the highest and best poetry is always entirely in harmony with sense in its most practical phases. The poetry that will not bear this test may be very pretty to the superficial and thoughtless, but it is not good *per se*, and probably when analysed, will be found to be little better than so much sweet-sounding rubbish.

III.—BLANK VERSE.

Blank verse is such an important form of metrical composition that I deem it desirable to devote a section thereto. According to Dr. Johnson, it is verse where the rhyme is "blanched," but, like most definitions, this does not really tell us very much about the matter. In the middle ages some attempts were made in the Latin countries of Europe to reject the Gothic system of rhyme and restore the blank verse metres of ancient Greece and Rome. The initial essay at blank verse in England was made by the Earl of Surrey. who translated the first and fourth books of Virgil's *Æneid* into blank verse in 1547. Blank verse, however, utterly failed to win any popularity at that time. Only those deeply tinctured with classical learning could appreciate its cadences and rhythm, and practically rhyme remained unaffected. The extreme fitness, however, of the new English metre for dramatic composition was soon perceived, and it came into general use before Shakespeare's advent, and possibly this was fortunate, as there is ample internal testimony in Shakespeare's plays to suggest that his natural tastes inclined to rhyme. Blank verse remained virtually confined to the drama, with but few exceptions, until 1667, when Milton's *Paradise Lost* demonstrated the power, richness, and wealth of harmony that lay latent in blank narrative verse for the poet who had the genius to develop these qualities. Not a little criticism was evoked. however,

by the daring experiment, and in a statement made in a re-
issue of the poem, Milton himself justified the absence of
rhyme, and declared it to be, not a neglect, but an example
in English versification of ancient liberty recovered to the
heroic poem from the troublesome bondage of rhyming
As we all know, since then blank verse has been used in
many forms for almost every kind of poetry, but its proper
original is the ten syllabled, five accented metre of *Paradise
Lost*, as shown in the opening lines—

> Of man's | first dis | obe | dience and | the fruit
> Of that | forbid | den tree | whose mor | tal taste
> Brought sin | into | the world | and all | our woe,
> With loss | of E | den till one great | er man
> Restore | us and | regain | the bliss | ful seat,
> Sing Heaven | ly Muse—

Obviously blank verse encumbers the poet less than rhyme,
and for really grand and sublime strains, and for the more
profound philosophic or intensely spiritual forms of poetry,
it possesses special advantages. Unfortunately it lends
itself also to baldness and has a tendency to run into prose,
measured and somewhat cadenced prose no doubt, but still
prose, and not by any means verse

Not only have Cowper and Wordsworth evinced the
power that resides in the compass of blank metres, but
Southey and Shelley have both evinced its capability to be
employed in metres essentially lyrical—a far harder task to
execute satisfactorily. Thus, in Southey's *Thalaba*—a poetic
narrative of faith and its victory, such as only a true Christian
poet could have sung, we have some splendid achievements
in blank verse metres, as in the fine passage beginning—

> How beautiful is night !
> A dewy freshness fills the silent air ;
> No mist obscures, nor cloud, nor speck, nor stain,
> Breaks the serene of Heaven ;
> In full orbed glory yonder moon divine
> Rolls through the dark full depths.

It is perilous, however, for the young and inexperienced writer of verse to attempt forms of this kind as he is likely to descend into prose or bathos. Blank verse, to be acceptable, must be very, very *good*. It is essential that it be really melodious, and that it be entirely removed even from the suspicion of being only measured prose cut into lengths. Let the young essayist in blank metres study such a poem as *Comus*, and mark well such a passage as that in which the lady, the heroine of the piece, when lost in the wood, exclaims—

> A thousand fantasies
> Begin to throng into my memory
> Of calling shapes and beckoning shadows dire,
> And airy tongues that syllable men's names
> On sands and shores, and desert wildernesses.

Then, recovering from her natural fears, she breaks forth into the splendid passage—

> These thoughts may startle well, but not astound
> The virtuous mind, that ever walks attended
> By a strong-siding champion conscience.
> O welcome pure-eyed faith, white-handed hope—

Then, after an interlude of song, alluding to the notes, Comus is made to say—

> How sweetly did they float upon the wings
> Of silence thro' the empty-vaulted night,
> At every fall smoothing the raven-down
> Of darkness till it smiled !

This, indeed, is one of the finest passages in English poetry, or, indeed, in that of the world. Then later occurs the exquisite passage—

> I was all ear,
> And took in strains that might create a soul
> Under the ribs of Death.

Here is matchless verbal music wedded to sublime ideas and the most perfect poetry, but compare much ordinary

narrative blank verse with the above, and the vast difference
will at once be seen.   Decidedly, blank verse used to convey
simply ordinary ideas or common descriptions of things, is
not nearly so good as honest, plain prose.   When Tennyson
tells us of

> The music of the moon
> Hid in the plain egg of the nightingale,

we feel at once that we are in the presence of a genuine
poet, and if to such a one rhyme would be here or there a
restraint, shutting out some of his finest thoughts or excluding his most subtle spiritualism from ready verbal expression, why, let him take blank metres for his vehicle.   At the
same time, we must not be blind to the fact that much
blank verse, even that written by real poets, is very little
removed from prose, and has really no true claim to be
reckoned as poetry.   Wordsworth, in his *Excursion*, frequently ambles along in a most prosaic way ; yet we may
forgive all this for the sake of the sublime passage in which
he boldly proclaims that the material world itself is but a shell
whence to the ear of Faith the voice of God is distinctly
audible.   This magnificent passage runs—

> I have seen
> A curious child, who dwelt upon a tract
> Of inland ground, applying to his ear
> The convolutions of a smooth-lipped shell,
> To which, in silence hushed, his very soul
> Listened intensely, and his countenance soon
> Brightened with joy, for murmurings from within
> Were heard, sonorous cadences ! whereby
> To his belief the monitor expressed
> Mysterious union with its native sea.

Now comes the crowning beauty of this fine passage—

> Even such a shell the universe itself
> Is to the ear of Faith.

How simple the language : plain, short, everyday words,

with but a single exception—universe—but how exquisite the art of their natural arrangement, and how sublime and overpowering the thought!

So again Pollok, in his blank verse epic, the *Course of Time*, a poem full of prosaic pauses, has a splendid out-burst of poetry and domestic happiness, wherein the closing line—

Gems leaping in the coronet of love—

is happy in its unexpected and novel turn.   Naturally enough much prejudice now popularly exists against blank verse, and the young versifier who chooses this form for his essays handicaps himself terribly, and should not attempt such a form unless he has not only something new to say, but something essentially so truly poetical, that it *must* win recognition from readers of culture and taste.

Now and then, it is true, a writer has succeeded in attracting attention by eccentricities in metre which astonished the ignorant in such matters, and by their daring won critics into astonishment, which was made to do duty for admiration There is such a case as that of Walt Whitman, who thought it clever to clip his Christian name into Walt, and being unable or unwilling to acquire the necessary mechanical metrical skill of the versifier, made a short cut, as he thought and thinks, and invented a sort of compromise between puffed-up, word-stuffed prose and the tumid, wordy style of very indifferent poets.   He adopted a sort of prose-run-mad style, and imagined that by printing lines of certain length, and using capitals at the beginning of each, he had actually composed verses   He has persevered, and as even he has flashes of sanity, and now and then a happy thought or sentiment a little above the average and the commonplace, he has won for himself a qualified place somewhere between prose and verse, not quite belonging to either, and is tolerated rather as a literary curiosity than as a genuine worker in poetic literature. Just at the opening of 1890 Mr. Whitman published the following *Welcome to Brazil*—

Welcome, Brazilian brother! thy ample place is ready;
A loving hand—a smile from the North—a sunny instant hail!
(Let the future care for itself, where it reveals its troubles, impedi-
   mentas,
Ours, ours the present throe, the democratic aim, the acceptance and
   the faith,)
To thee to-day our reaching arm, our turning neck—to thee from us
   the expectant eye,
Thou cluster free! thou brilliant, lustrous star! thou, learning
   well
The true lesson of a nation's light in the sky
(More shining than the Cross, more than the Crown),
The height to be superb humanity.

This is called an "ode". It is nothing of the kind. It is merely rhetorical prose, and may be taken as an example of what metre must come to when the writer determines to *begin* and not end with poetic license. In the above, metres are simply jumbled together anyhow, and there is an utter absence of any touch of original poetic thought.

It is Young, indeed, who says—

An undevout astronomer is mad;

and so, too, is the poet, or else he has allowed his soul to sink down into the mire of gross materialism. A great writer tells us—

All great lays . . .
Deal more or less with the Divine, and have
For end some good of mind or soul of man;
The mind is this world's, but the soul is God's.

Coleridge assures us that, to him, poetry was its own exceed-ing great reward, soothing and multiplying his enjoyments, and giving him the *habit* of wishing to discover the good and the beautiful in all that surrounded him.

13

IV.—THE DRAMA.

The drama is really one of the earliest forms of concrete literature. Born in Greece, and adopted by Rome, the play languished during the mediæval period, and led a wandering, vagrant, out-of-doors' existence, except where, in its sacred aspect, as dramatising portions of Holy Writ, it came under the sheltering wing of the Church. Tragedy essentially is of Greek origin ; and Greece, too, gave us the comedy and the farce. Rome alone adapted or adopted, and the Greek national stage stands alone, indeed, in its creative greatness.

In England, as everyone knows, the drama rose in the Elizabethan age, and Shakespeare's genius blazed forth and made a new epoch in the intellectual history of England. There came, too, with and after Shakespeare quite a concourse of great dramatists, such as no other age of the world ever showed before or since ; and, but for Shakespeare's transcendent greatness, many of these would now stand far higher in the literature of the world to which these Elizabethan worthies belong. Then followed a long succession of more or less great and brilliant writers for the stage Besides Ben Jonson, Beaumont and Fletcher, Massinger and John Ford, John Webster and others, there came later Dryden (who failed to establish a rhymed form of drama), Wycherley, Congreve, George Farquhar, Gay, Goldsmith, Sheridan, and many others. Yet, in the present day, it cannot be justly said that the contemporary stage possesses great attraction for the young writer. It is said that original work is not required : that adaptations, the work of those behind the scenes and possessing a practical acquaintance with the construction and arrangement of the stage, are alone acceptable. As someone has cynically remarked, engineers, carpenters, chemists, costumiers and upholsterers —to say nothing of ballet-masters and scene-painters—are the real producers of the contemporary drama : and where

is, then, the inducement for any young writer to turn to the
stage? Yet this is a fallacy It is all very well to affirm
that managers are deaf to the most impassioned dialogue,
and insensible to the exquisite play of conflicting wits ; but
the fact remains that the matter generally offered to theatres
is very bad indeed from a literary point of view The MS.
plays sent in are usually but imitative pieces, exhibiting
ignorance of all the first requirements of a good play It
may be depended on that any really *fine* and *original* imaginative conception that is dramatic in its spirit and general
intent will make a good and an acceptable piece; but then, too
often, when such a piece is composed, it is found to be impossible to be acted owing to the author knowing nothing about
the exigencies of the stage and other minor technical matters.
Sometimes it will be found that a play wretched as to dialogue
acts very well, from downright force of dramatic situation ;
while a splendid poem, like some of Robert Browning's,
fails utterly as a play, and is tolerated only on account of
its purely intellectual merits. The young writer who aims
at the stage may, however, do much to help his efforts by
studying the structure of the stage, reading *acting* plays,
noting the stage directions, and thinking out the practical
reasons for all that is done—and examining Shakespeare's
pieces in accordance with a stage manager's requirements.
The young dramatist in anticipation ought further to equip
himself mentally by a course of careful reading of the plays
of all nations and times. He ought also to be familiar with
such great masters of dramatic criticism as William Hazlitt
and Augustus William Schlegel. Thus may the young
writer obtain a good knowledge of the drama as it existed
in Greece, Rome, and subsequently in Italy, Spain, France,
and finally in England.

Certainly, for those who look to the theatre as a legitimate and wholesome place of intellectual recreation, it is
highly important that those who can produce intellectual

and poetic dramatic literature should be encouraged. Writers like Mr. A. W. Pinero, Mr. Sidney Grundy, Mr. W. S. Gilbert, Mr. Sims, and Mr. H Pettit surely indicate that intellectuality still lingers on the British stage, and that the property-man is not yet omnipotent there. Years ago, old playgoers protested against the substitution of splendid scenery and fine upholstery for intellect, wit, and poetry in the drama. An outcry was raised against Charles Kean, who ruined himself to mount Shakespearean plays with perfect historic and archæological accuracy. But Charles Kean never meant to *subordinate* the intellectual element, or to put the poetry of the visible before that of the invisible. In a word, decoration was not used then to conceal defects At present, there is certainly an unfortunate tendency to prefer a play because it is well put on the stage, and hence a writer remarked recently, dealing with this very subject "Now-a-days provincial theatres are filled with monkey imitations of the worst faults and mannerisms of modern amateurs, who have gained a London reputation What we want is a school of training and education, a home of instruction and practice. . . . Why should not the sister arts be trained, fostered, and educated alike?"

Take above all things, good models As in poetry, aim high. We always fall short of our ideals, of necessity. Among the best writers on the drama is, as stated above, beyond all question Schlegel. Those who cannot read German, should get Mr. John Black's fine translation. Schlegel indeed covers the whole dramatic ground thoroughly, and he is in all cases noteworthy for the depth and lucidity of his criticism

Shakespeare in particular is very fully dealt with, and very much may be learned from the masterly manner in which the great German analyses the whole of Shakespeare's plays. Even through the medium of translation much of Schlegel is remarkable for its beauty of expression, and as a sample, this excerpt from his exposition of *Romeo and Juliet* seems to me one of the most eloquent things of the kind in literature. The passage runs as follows—

"It was reserved for Shakespeare to join in one ideal picture purity of heart with warmth of imagination; sweetness and dignity of manners with passionate intensity of feeling. Under his handling it has become a glorious song of praise on that inexpressible feeling which ennobles the soul and gives to it its highest sublimity, and which elevates even the senses into soul, while at the same time it is a melancholy elegy on its inherent and imparted frailty; it is at once the apotheosis and the obsequies of love. . . . All that is most intoxicating in the odours of a Southern spring, all that is most languishing in the song of the nightingale, or voluptuous in the first opening of the rose, all alike breathe forth from this poem. . . The sweetest and the bitterest love and hatred, festive rejoicings and dark forebodings. tender embracings and sepulchral horrors, the fulness of life and self-annihilation, are all here brought close to each other; and yet these contrasts are so blended into a unity of impression that the echo which the whole leaves behind in the mind resembles a single but endless sigh."

I have not deemed it needful to attempt to epitomise the early history of the drama. Tragedy is its original, the *goat-song* as it is in Greek, derived from the well-known circumstance that the earliest players sacrificed a goat to Bacchus. But the young writer who feels a dramatic instinct stirring within him, should first of all make himself well acquainted with all the main facts connected with the gradual development of the play in its many forms. For the early, as well as the later and present period of the English drama, I can recommend as likely to be very useful a little book by Mr. Henry Grey, entitled *The Plots of some of the most Famous English Plays*. These begin with

Marlowe's *Tamburlain the Great*, 1588, *Doctor Faustus*, 1589, and include the principal plays of Jonson, T Dekker, Otway, Cibber, Addison, Rowe, Home (*Douglas*, with the familiar speech "My name is Norval"), Knowles (the *Hunchback*), and Lytton's *Lady of Lyons*. Shakespeare is not included

There is a great multiplying of theatres, and the social status of the actor is being much raised. Many signs are round us of an increasing disposition to a more liberal patronage of the drama on the part of a large section of the public. In its early days the stage was at once newspaper and novel to the multitude, and afforded the main avenue for the free expression of imaginative genius. It was so among the ancient and cultured Greeks, who sat in the open theatre during the summer afternoons of Attica listening to the finest utterances of some of the brightest and most powerful intellects of the age. It cannot be that the stage will ever again be Athenian or Elizabethan, but it will be vastly more extended, and will remain a great field for those who have dramatic ability to cultivate into something better than we have had of late years. Here, as in all departments of literary work, ability must be conjoined with industry, and the would-be dramatic writer must first become acquainted with what has been already accomplished. How much room there is for true genius—especially of the inventive type—is best shown in the fact that, as a rule, the pantomime is usually only a version of something old, while the comedy in its various forms is mostly derived from continental sources.

In conclusion, I cannot do better than transcribe here some remarks from that fine work previously referred to, Schlegel's *Dramatic Literature*, translated by Mr. John Black. The great German critic says: "The dramatic poet represents external events as real and present. In common with the lyric poet, he also claims our mental participation, but not in the same calm composedness; the feeling of joy and sorrow which the dramatist excites is more immediate and vehement. He calls forth all the emotions which the sight of similar deeds and fortunes of living men would elicit, and it is only by the total sum of the impressions which he produces that he ultimately resolves these conflicting emotions into a harmonious tone of feeling."

V.—THE NOVEL—ITS HISTORY, PLACE, AND FUNCTIONS.

It is said on good authority that, setting aside the special reading of professed students and scientific men, the only books now read popularly are novels This is a great fact, and one of which writers of fiction will take good heed. The public in immediate view for the successful writer of fiction is vaster than any novelist of old ever dreamed of, and then, beyond all doubt, it is the novel alone that rivals and will rival the newspaper in influence, popularity, and power.

What is fiction, how did it originate, what has been its development, and how should it be practised as an art? are all highly interesting and eminently practical questions, which it is the business of this section to attempt to answer. A great writer has said that fiction is not falsehood. If a writer puts abstract virtues into book-clothing, and sends them upon stilts into the world, he is a bad writer; if he classifies men, and attributes all virtue to one class and all vice to another, he is a false writer. During the last quarter of a century a very great change, indeed, has come over the whole spirit of fiction; its scope has been enormously widened, its character infinitely diversified, and the generally narrow limits of the novel, as understood in the first half of the nineteenth century, have been indefinitely enlarged. The novel has been lifted to a higher place, although, it must be confessed, it occupies some very low

ones now, and its importance has been very greatly increased
of late years   It was no small thing when, in the latter part
of 1889, the Bishop of Ripon bestowed quite a benediction
on novels and on novel reading, and went so far as to con-
fess that it had once been his ambition to write a novel.
Now, too, there are so many more classes of novel readers
than before, when the impossible romance or the fashionable
novel including an elopement, a duel, and a wedding at the
close formed the two principal sorts of fiction extant.   There
are now novel readers, for example, who take up fiction as
a department of English literature to be duly surveyed and
thoughtfully studied, and for these the historic, the political,
and the philosophic novel are in much demand   There are
those who turn to the novel for *actual information* as to
what is going on in the world around them ; and then there
is the vast and ever-increasing host of those who read for
amusement only.   Besides these forms of fiction, there is
the idealistic novel of the new social science school,
which embodies various schemes and theories for the
amelioration of the masses, and to cite but one instance,
just consider the practical effect of a book like Mr.
Besant's *All Sorts and Conditions of Men.*   Evidently
here at the outset of our inquiry we have ample encouragement to the young writer who possesses the faculty
of narration, and is willing to properly equip himself for the
work to be done.

Yes, there is *work* to be done here if great and good
results are to be attained, and let it be ever borne in mind
that if the work be greater now, the ultimate reward is far
greater than of old.

It is recorded that once the great Sir Walter remarked to
his friend Rogers, the banker poet, referring to the rise of
Byron, Shelley, Coleridge and others : " It's a lucky thing
we came before those fellows ! "   Obviously better work is
demanded now, and better work must be done if supreme

success be the object in view. For one thing only, style in writing must be better, not worse, as it so often is in first attempts in fiction, where, for example, a confused story, a complex plot and artificial, unnatural characterisation are all jumbled together in a style of presentment equally slovenly and obscure. Just listen to what that master of a fine narrative style, Gustave Flaubert, had to say on this very subject—

"Style, as I conceive it ; style as it will be realised some day—in ten years, or ten generations! It would be rhythmical as verse itself, precise as the language of science, and with undulations—a swelling of the violin—plumage of fire! A style which would enter into the idea like the point of a lancet ; when thought would travel over the smooth surfaces like a canoe with fair winds behind it. Prose is but of yesterday, it must be confessed. Verse is *par excellence* the form of the ancient literatures. All possible prosodic combinations have been already made ; those of prose are still to make."

Now, let us take two contrasts—one from a book, and the other from a newspaper. In the former we find the following—

"The dear green grass is very lovely; but the birds fly low—low. The sky is very grey ; and one is reminded daily, hourly almost, that the clouds are indeed the 'waters above the firmament'—even here in the south. How it goes with her? you ask. They tell me, aloud, my little wife improves slowly, they whisper that she is dying. She lies with a starry smile in her great eyes, and hands locked in pain. I have done with that mad wishing which men call Hope. Her birthday fell with the child's ; and she was twenty. How can death do it?"

I forbear, out of consideration to the writer, to give the title of this book, but even a tyro may perceive the utter hopelessness of the style and the profound unconsciousness of

the writer that both matter and manner are bad   Turning
now to the *Daily News* for December 17, 1889, we read in
an article, entitled "The Hush of Night," the following—

"No longer sounds the blackbird's vesper hymn.   By his
clamorous call-notes he is heard alone ere he settles to his
rest among the ivy.   The thrushes too are silent, save a bold-
hearted minstrel here and there, who, undaunted by the cold,
is singing still.   And when the colour has faded from the
west, when the moon is bright along a silver sea, and the
dark sky trembles with the glitter of the stars, hardly less
striking is the silence of the night.   There is no sound but
of the night wind as it stirs the withered reeds, the shiver of
dead leaves among dismantled boughs, or the ring of foot-
steps on the frozen road.   Hushed are the noises of the
summer night, unheard its ceaseless sounds of stirring life.
For nightfall then, though ever closing tired eyes in sleep,
still roused slaves of Nature from their rest, and in the hours
of darkness there was stillness but not silence.   Then even
before the sun was down were heard shrill voices, faint but
still audible, of bats that fluttered out upon their noiseless
wings.   Then in the dusk the beetle droned along the high-
way.   On the edge of every coppice rang loud the chirp of
crickets.   Along the bank of the river rose the hum of innumerable gnats.   Now, in the dark of cave and tower and
tree, the bats hang motionless.   The wings of the beetle
are folded in his winter sleep ; long since silent is the chorus
of the crickets.   Vanished is the vast array of gnats whose
unseen armies raised over the woods that mighty hum that
filled the summer air "

When newspapers publish such composition as this, it certainly is high time that the novelist looked to his style.   In
the same way, every fine and successful work of imagination
must necessarily raise the standard *pro tanto.*   And here yet
a word more as to style

It is not too much to assert that style is all-important to the young writer. Not one tentative piece of early MS. in a hundred has any style in it, and the sub-editor or publisher's reader before whom the offering comes is naturally prejudiced at the outset. The basis of style lies, of course, in real grammatical accuracy and a copious and judiciously used vocabulary. The arrangement of the parts or clauses of a sentence is a very determining thing in style In their structure the Romans aimed to keep the meaning, or at all events, the full meaning of each sentence in *suspense* until the conclusion was reached, and obviously such a style imparts unity to each period and gave a cameo-like finish. Thus, to take a poetic example from a modern writer, in his fine poem referring to the disaster of Flodden Field—disaster for Scotland—Professor Aytoun makes the survivor of those who rescued the royal banner, say on returning to Edinburgh—

> Take the banner that I bring you,
>   Guard it as a holy thing—
> For the stain you see upon it,
>   Is the life-blood of your king.

Many writers of the present day affect brevity, but brevity is not always force. Their paragraphs often want solidarity and there is looseness in their style, while the reader wearies at length of what has been not without reason, termed the "scrappy, snappy style". The study of really good models is a sure means for insensibly improving style, but the young writer must be careful to avoid *copying defects*, which is often very hard to prevent, as the young and inexperienced frequently mistake what are the *blemishes* in their favourite authors for *beauties*.

How many novels have come before a critic, novels that circulate for a season at the libraries and are, of course, forgotten soon after being read, wherein there is no more style, properly considered, than in a cookmaid's letters.

The writers manage to tell the story after a fashion, they put in dialogue which is very much as they have heard it, and they patch up the whole performance with scraps of French, German, and Italian, which, very imperfectly understood by the writer, and "hashed" by the cruel printer, only confuse and exasperate the reader of any real education or true culture.

Such a romance as the *Scottish Chiefs*, if it appeared now for the *first* time, would decidedly attract little if any notice, for Scott and Bulwer have lifted the historic standard for novels far above the level when Miss Porter put forth her romance of Sir William Wallace.

Fiction, as an art, is one of the oldest forms of literature, beginning in the shape of commemorative legend and song, and, simple enough in origin, it has grown at last to be the most complete of all man's intellectual achievements.

Prose fiction is usually said to have begun with the famous Milesian tales attributed to Aristides. These Milesians were Ionic Greeks who settled in Asia Minor, and were conquered by the Persians 494 B.C A few prose romances appeared in the time of Alexander, but the drama and the poem practically engrossed all the capable writers of imaginative literature, and we take a long leap to the time of Lucian, in the reign of Marcus Antoninus, who concealed his keen satire in the guise of story-telling. Then later came Heliodorus and others as romance writers. Heliodorus was, by the way, a Christian novelist, and his lives of *Theogenes and Charicleia* is said to be the oldest true story extant, for all the Milesian tales have utterly perished.

Longus, with a work called *Daphnis and Chloe*, imitated the pastoral tales, and this is the form of novel produced by Richardson in *Pamela*. A few names bridge long periods. What is notable in these early fictions is the absence of what is known now as *plot*, but incident abounds, although often it is not to us interesting, while to those for whose amusement these early romances were composed doubtless there was a feast of continual delight.

One work stands out distinct in the early classic period This is the *Golden Ass* of Appuleius, whence Boccaccio drew much material, and in which is found the lovely story of *Cupid and Psyche*, the purest and most finely-imaginative piece of romantic fiction probably that we have inherited from Pagan literature.

In Western Europe early romance was largely based on and greatly coloured by the Norse mythology and the complex legends from the Orient, which the breaking-up of the Roman Empire spread far and wide, as the Northmen came into contact with the more lively ardent races of the South, and then the Crusades gave a further impulse in the same direction. The Celtic people of Great Britain furnished much food for wild fiction. Then came the Arthurian myths, and in France Charlemagne and his Paladins gave rise to a variety of romantic legends, many of which are doubtless interwoven with much fact. One of the great romances working up much of this floating legend is the famous *Amadis de Gaul*. Later in the sixteenth century Raoul le Febre drew on classic fable, and presented astonishing Greek tales and myths in all the dress of chivalry. Italy was late in the field with prose fiction. In the thirteenth century there was the *Cento Novella Antiche*, and then came in due time that epochal work, the *Decameron*. From some of the cloisters there issued spiritual romances, often expressly designed by Churchmen as "improving literature," and among these was that splendid work, the *Golden Legend*.

With the sixteenth and seventeenth centuries fiction began to take more distinctive forms, and some of these forms, modified, of course, remain with us now. Rabelais gave forth the prototype of the comic romance, Sir Thomas More, in *Utopia*, prefigured the political novel, and Sir Philip Sidney, in *Arcadia*, gave us a pastoral romance. The eighteenth century produced Defoe and Samuel Richardson, but novelists were few and far between until the present century which is especially the era of novelists, and has brought the art of fiction to a pitch undreamed of by any previous generation of romancists.

It is curious that just as fiction began in fancy, so is it to be observed now that a strong tendency exists on the part of a large section of the reading public to indulge in *romance*. It has been well said that romance naturally falls into two divisions. To the one belong tales of adventure, to the other those of mere fancy. Thus, we have in phantasy the famous old story of *Peter Wilkins*, who found himself transported to a region where people were winged, and then there is *Frankenstein*, with its awful weird power, while in the present day Mr. Anstey has given us some of the wildest fancies in his charming *Vice Versa*. In the romance of adventure we have the fine novels of Marryat, Cooper, Lever, Maxwell, Ouida, Wilkie Collins, Blackmore, and many others, and it must be confessed that there is yet an ample field for this class of fiction, seeing what Mr. Rider Haggard, Mr. Louis Stevenson, and others have accomplished. As for the romance or novel of phantasy, *that* will ever be the special production of absolute and creative genius. There is, undoubtedly, however, not a little caprice and waywardness in the public taste for novels. In the *Scots' Observer* for December 14, 1889, there appeared an article on this subject wherein the writer said—

"There is fashion in books as in all else. To-day we stifle ourselves with French realism, to-morrow we excite ourselves over the tea-parties of the Boston School : each vagary has its turn. At present fashion permits us to go to sleep over one of two things—the book of adventures or the philosophical novel. The craving for tiger stories is almost satiated now ; but it seems that a long time may yet elapse before the young man ceases to be charmed with the agnostic who perverts the curate in twenty minutes, while the young woman surrenders her admiration for the curate who converts the agnostic in the last chapter   If the cry of a few generations back was 'Give us a haughty earl!' the cry of the readers of to-day is 'Give us the regulation agnostic!' If the regulation agnostic is not in stock, we are willing to accept a little mesmerism or thought-reading as a substitute."

This is very true, indeed, and in the January issue (1890) of *Merry England*, Mr. Gladstone, in an article on the religious novel by the late Lady Georgiana Fullerton, entitled *Ellen Middleton*, written in 1844, and recently republished, observes—

"Religion of late years has been driven back in great part from that acknowledged position of prominence and authorised power which it once used to occupy in ordinary life; although not absolutely 'relegated into obscure municipalities and rustic villages,' yet it cowers and skulks in society, and manifests not itself until, by some careful application of the touchstone, it has ascertained in what quarter sympathy exists. Or else, in minds more fearless, or less delicate, it projects upon the surface, not in its natural effluence, but according to some harsh and crude form, with effort and with assumption."

The religious novel has not been written out as yet, and it offers a wide field for those who could meet and defeat the agnostic and the evolutionist each on his own grounds.

It will be perceived from the above that the story teller has, of all writers, the widest field of action and the largest of possible publics before him   But it must be remembered, too, that those who essay to write a novel without informing themselves previously on all necessary points, are preparing for certain failure, so far as success worth naming is concerned   Even genius, that of the most imaginative kind, combined with a fine fancy, must gain enormously by studying technical details

Be it remembered, too, for the comfort of those not endowed by nature with commanding ability, that in these days there are very many separate reading circles and many a writer can find fame and fortune inside one of these, who, strive as he may, is never able to occupy that position which enchains the attention of the whole reading world.   I believe that the writer who works and thinks, and above all *takes pains*, he who avails himself of every aid and of all the borrowed experience within reach, and who resolves to do whatever he undertakes just as well as he can, is sure ultimately of success.   It may not be at all of the supreme kind, but it will be adequate if the exertions made to achieve it have been honest and *un*interrupted, for the great secret of successful work is found in two things, concentration and continuity, and it is just here that genius so frequently fails.

Painstaking is all in all.   Macaulay as a writer is a great example, and Gibbon too.   In ordinary fiction, of course, such elaboration of work is not essential, but all who have succeeded greatly have been students of style, most careful workers in what may be called word-mosaic, and especially particular in putting the last finishing touch to all work before permitting it to pass forth to the public.   In illustration of this, Mr. Charles Dickens, the younger, writing in the *English Illustrated Magazine*, referring to the literary labours of the elder Dickens, says—

"Beyond my father's early and brief connection with *Bentley's Miscellany*, a very great part of the work of the twenty busy years from 1850 to 1870 was devoted first to *Household Words*, and then to *All the Year Round*, and nothing better illustrated his indomitable energy, and the boundless capacity for taking pains which distinguished him, than the strenuous manner in which the editorial duties of those journals were discharged ".

He continues as follows—

"Everything that could maintain the high standard which he had set up was done. Nothing was considered too small, no detail too petty, for his own personal attention. The utmost pains were given to the consideration of every manuscript that came into the office, no matter whether its owner bore a name honoured in literature or was only a raw recruit in the great army of writers. An amount of time and labour was devoted to the polishing and finishing other people's work in proof which would surprise many occupants of editorial chairs, and which, there is no doubt, very considerably astonished some of the contributors whose work required the greatest quantity of excision and 'writing-up'."

And yet with all this fine sense of what is really essential to supreme literary success, Dickens himself could blunder sometimes, like all of us, and not long since a correspondent of *Notes and Queries* wrote in reference to *Dombey and Son*, as follows—

"The edition known to me is the original one, as it came out in parts, and I am unable to say whether the mistake, which is as follows, has been corrected since. Dr. Blimber, who, notwithstanding his pomposity, etc., is, I presume, intended to be a scholar, not an ignoramus like Squeers, imposes it as a penalty on the boy Johnson to repeat by heart from the Greek Testament St Paul's first Epistle to the Ephesians. Could Dickens have been ignorant that there is only one Epistle to the Ephesians in the New Testament?"

This surely suggests very forcibly what frightful errors *must* result when a writer is careless, and refuses to take due pains to revise his work.

14

VI.—FICTION AS AN ART.

It may be well *in limine* to say a word as to Imagination and Fancy, two things often confounded together. First of all Imagination concerns itself with realities. It is entirely concrete. The imagination of a new continent would necessarily comprehend sky, horizon, forests, and plains, hills and valleys, lakes and rivers. With imagination, which can never work on abstract lines without investing them with definite and individualising peculiarities or attributes, is connected the faculty of conception, or the power to call correctly to mind the form and details of something we have read of or seen. Let it not be rashly assumed, however, that imagination is only a reproductive power, a form of memory in fact. It is the error of mistaking memory for imagination that often leads the young writer into serious faults, especially those of servile imitation, to say nothing of unconscious plagiarism True imagination combines with itself a most important faculty designed for modifying and reducing to co-ordinated harmonies and right proportions the gatherings of the imagination, and this naturally leads as the result to the active development of what may be called a creative faculty, which is absolutely essential to every true artist, whether he work in pigments or in words. Thus it will be perceived that the true functions of a genuine imagination, not a mere memory or observing power only—are to re-combine, and where desirable, add to exact impressions of life in any or all of its forms, and it is on the way wherein this is done that all depends, if a successful result is to ensue. Fancy is quite different. It may, perhaps, be likened with some reason to imagination broken loose from all restraints, and indulging in everything that is impossible, grotesque, or altogether beyond reasonable expectation or actual experience. Fancy is derived from the Greek *fantasia*, and admits of the wildest and most disordered conceptions, although, even then, some canons must be observed, and especially must good taste be preserved intact, otherwise the resultant license will descend to absurdity, foolery or worse. As an example of imagination we may take the late Lord Lytton's *Harold* wherein facts of all kinds relative to the period have been brought together and blended with a consummate art. Such a work as Mr. Anstey's *Vice Versâ* is the product of *fancy* only. Thus to illustrate this further a bust of Byron might evince fine imagination on the part of the sculptor in giving full expression to his conception of how the author of *Childe Harold* should look in marble, but a statue of the Prince of Darkness belongs to the realms of *fancy*. Dickens was richly endowed with both imagination and fancy. Let the young writer beware of copying. Some freak of nature, some eccentricity in man or woman, some abnormal incident being observed, these are straightway copied into words, and the whole presented abruptly, crudely, and probably quite irrelevantly to the matter in which they are set. It is in the *combining* of the facts observed in harmony with other facts, and in making new and consistent wholes, so to speak, out of many parts that the art of the imaginative writer consists. Mere *imitative* work will not live.

It is very important therefore that the worker in fiction who means to succeed, should avoid all *copying*. Let him carefully abstain from producing, as so many do, faint adumbrations of other writers' characters. Be original. Look at and listen to all that passes around, and draw thence materials to be worked up anew by the imagination. The only things that may be wrought up in imaginative fiction from books or newspapers, are facts relative to things illustrative of the kind of story that is being written, and these must always be subordinated to and helpful of the main *motif* of the work. Charles Reade "worked up" an immense mass of fact in this way, but he had a shaping and powerful imagination, and his characters were always original. With the fictionist there must be constant recourse to the great and ever-growing literature of knowledge, for even more than the poet, perhaps, should the novelist endeavour to be and to know all things after a fashion. It may be well, perhaps, to say a word here as to the two great literatures extant. There is first, says De Quincey, "The literature of *knowledge*, and secondly the literature of *power*. The function of the first is to *teach*, and the function of the second is to *move*. The very highest work that ever existed in the literature of knowledge is but provisional. . . . A book upon trial and sufferance. . . . For instance, the *Principia* of Sir Isaac Newton was a book militant on earth from the first . . . as soon as a La Place builds higher upon the foundations laid by this book, he effectually throws it out of the sunshine into decay and darkness. . . . Now on the contrary, the *Iliad*, the *Prometheus* of Æschylus, the *Othello*, or *King Lear*, the *Hamlet* or *Macbeth*, and the *Paradise Lost* are not militant, but triumphant powers as long as the language exists in which they speak, or can be taught to speak. . . . The literature of knowledge builds only ground nests that are swept away by floods . . . but the literature of power builds in aerial altitudes of temples sacred from violation " Facts are all important, but the writer of fiction must learn how to employ and group his materials and how to make it a part in all cases of a *new* whole. This is, of course, art, and some may ask can novel writing then be really reduced to an exact science, or can it be taught like perspective, or the disposition of lights in painting? It can up to a certain point, granting in the student a decided faculty for fiction to begin with, and, curiously enough, some years ago, a leader appeared in the *Times* on novels, wherein occurred the following passage : " Is there an art of fiction? Can we, if we please, found an

academy, institute lectures, receive pupils and teach them how
to tell stories? It is claimed by one who is himself a story-
teller, that it is as possible to teach fiction as to teach painting;
that both arts are governed by certain laws and rules which
may be taught; that there is a *technique* which may be
taught; that there are models which may be studied, masters whose methods may be learned and imitated, general
elementary rules which may be laid down; in fact, so far as
any art can be taught, fiction may be taught, and so far as it
is desirable to have art schools, it is desirable to teach the
art of fiction. On the other hand, it is not contended that
every one *can* be taught to write a novel; nor, indeed, can
every one be taught to paint a portrait, or to carve a group
in marble. But, provided that one is born with the story-
telling faculty, the art of fiction may be taught, it is urged,
with as much certainty and quickness as any other art. It
is argued that people learn this art without instructors,
professors, or course of lectures; the reply is, that if they
had previously gone through such a 'mill' as is provided
for students in painting, they would have learned how to
write novels without the disastrous failures which too often
attend early efforts, without the waste of that valuable
material which is never so fresh and good as when the
novelist first begins, and without the acquisition of faults
and tricks which are never corrected and become incurable
defects of style. It is from the want of some recognised
school that beginners rush into print with manuscripts which
ought never to see the light, crude and hasty daubs without
perspective, drawing, colour, or grouping; without in fact,
the perception of the elementary principles of their art."
The same writer went on to say: "As soon as people have
once grasped the fact that fiction is a real art, an academy
for the purpose of teaching it would produce almost immediate results . . novelists . . . would take more pains,
they would learn that what is easily written is hard to read;

they would consider their situations and their character;
they would try to give epigram and point to their dialogue;
they would realise the meaning of style which, to some who
write novels, seems at present a word absolutely without
meaning; in a word, they would acquire the first principles
of their art, and endeavour by every means in their power
to be correct ".

There is much sound sense here. No doubt some fairly
successful novels do appear by writers who manage to combine great ignorance with great talents; but, *pro tanto*,
writer and book are the worse, and day by day a higher
standard is being erected, and, in the midst of such excessive
literary competition as that of the present day, the writer
cannot know too much or be too well equipped with the
technics of his art. There is a right and a wrong way of
doing everything, and story-telling is certainly included here.
Want of a good technical knowledge, correct taste, and a
just idea of proportion has utterly ruined the chance of some
young writers of real ability from obtaining any recognition,
and it has equally marred some of the most splendid efforts
of nineteenth century genius. Look at Victor Hugo, for
example. He was a man of very high poetic genius, full of
original ideas, possessing a rich and most vivid imagination.
Yet some of his fiction is about as bad as it can well be,
viewed as story-telling or narrative *art*. *Les Miserables*, for
example, abounds in glaring faults, and is at times utterly
provoking on account of long digressions and historic essays
and philosophical dissertations inserted at the wrong place!
If these things were seen in a *drawing* or a painting everyone
would utterly condemn them. I have had a novel before
me with very little story, and less plot, but with the narrative
correctly proportioned in its episodes, and every dialogue
going to the mark intended and helping on the movement
of the tale, and really elucidating the characters represented.
All was skilful and apposite. The book was one of no

special merit, but then it was the work of an experienced writer, one who had been through "the mill," and knew and obeyed the canons of correct taste. I have had another work emanating from one possessing great gifts of language and power of expressing passion and pathos, and endowed with ample invention, but in this case half-a-dozen stories and as many plots were all jumbled up together anyhow. The scenes shifted as in a pantomime, and the whole work was simply grotesque. Need I say which of these stories won its way into print? The former, a book of little real worth, was virtually faultless, and gave no trouble to the reader, who recognised on the first few pages the impress of an experienced literary hand. The latter was a nightmare, a vision of all sorts of things, the results, indeed, of "the poet's eye in a fine frenzy rolling," difficult to read with patience, and impossible to print. A wealth of poetic similes was lavished on this work, which contained material enough to serve a professional writer for at least three novels; but the whole thing had to be rejected, although with real regret to see so much intellectual power expended in vain.

There is much art, of course, in beginning a novel effectively. It is best to have beforehand an outline of the main story, with its principal episodes and incidents, which ought to be cumulative, and then begin at a point of real interest, even if this should necessitate making a retrospective section to "explain" matters. The faults that prevail with young and inexperienced writers are numerous enough, but one in particular is not knowing how to *indicate* portions of the action of a narrative which are essential thereto, but not of interest *per se*. I have had a very great experience with early efforts, and have repeatedly been amazed at the ineptitude of writers who seem helpless to get their hero or their heroine out of one situation into another of interest without writing pages of absolute twaddle between, which naturally spoils everything, and effectually prevents the book from being

"accepted" anywhere In one novel in particular, I remember
that the writer, when one of her characters rang for a servant,
and this, let it be marked well, was at a *critical* point in a
sensational story, must needs tell the reader how the servant
heard the summons in the lower regions, and what the
Buttons said, and how she puffed her way up, and how she
ejaculated certain things to herself, leaving a litter of " h's "
on the stairs.   All this is thoroughly bad, and to be utterly
condemned.   It is entirely destructive of effect, and irritates
the reader beyond measure.   The waves of action must flow
one way, and roll on, like a full tide, with an ever-accumula-
tive power.   Then, in description.   It is a great mistake and
an exhibition of weakness to be continually likening one
thing to another.   Some writers have this fault in a very
pronounced form.   They cannot trust themselves, but must
rely on some well-worn simile or metaphor.   In the opening
pages of a novel I recently read in MS. I find a proud old
widower father, a landed proprietor of the present day, described as "a Viking"! It is not thus that Dickens, Scott,
Thackeray, Lytton, George Eliot, and Charles Reade describe
their characters.   We want to know what things *are*, not what
they most resemble.   Some writers cannot refrain from comparing their heroine to a lily or a rose, the swan or the dove,
and so completely do they envelop their characters in similes,
that all direct interest in the personality is lost, and every
touch of realism that might have been is lost, and we find
but a faded copy of familiar things that have served their
purpose long ago in fiction and poetry, and are in truth but
literary lumber.

Never on any account copy or adapt or in any way
appropriate things, great or small, from any imaginative
work.   You may draw freely on history, science, philosophy, voyage and travel, theology, physics, antiquities,
archæology, books of topography, naval and military works,
and the like.   The groundwork of a story should be

original, likewise the plot and the order, and consequential effect, or influences of the main episodes. Having thus a complete skeleton of the story, you may and should enrich it all you can by lavishing on the detail all the stores of rich reading and close observation, if you only observe the rule to add something of your own to all you adapt from books or from your own eye or ear notes. If you take gems from your reading to adorn certain places in your own work, recut, repolish and reset them. Do not show *raw* material anywhere. Charles Reade, in a work like *The Cloister and the Hearth* (his finest by far), drew liberally on a vast number of mediæval words and books, but then he *absorbed all the material first* into his own imagination before reproducing it as a setting, a *mise-en-scène* or a sequence of incidents to serve the purpose of his fascinating and always exciting story In one word, the imaginative faculty is to be the *solvent* of all that is gathered up, and then the resultant material can be run afresh into new matrices and made to serve new purposes. Scott, it is said, sat down to write novels without in most cases a pre-arranged plan, and the genius may do this, but it is perilous work for the writer who is not a genius. Wilkie Collins, Reade, Miss Braddon, and a score of others, are very careful as to the *planning* of their plots. These are the foundations of novels, and deserve the utmost care and study. The story-teller aims at verisimilitude, and before he can properly narrate a tale, *he* ought to *know it himself.* In a word, the best plan is to construct a plot, then to fit in the characters with incidents appropriate to each, and so managed as to illustrate each point. Then we have a true narrative, as it were, which should impress the writer as a reality, and thus facilitate its verbal delivery on paper. This is the best course practically considered. It is wonderful how if a tale be conceived on these lines, after a while, it will inform the mind of the author like a reality,

and the characters will grow into living beings, and in a
manner clothe themselves with all befitting attributes.
Remember that what is vivid enough to the writer must be
less vivid to the reader, and you must feel much yourself to
make others feel a little. Never attempt delineations of
things, persons or places, quite unknown to yourself, and
such as transcend your own experiences. Do not try to
write in a dialect, unless you know it thoroughly, and do not
interlard your text with scraps of foreign languages which,
probably, you very imperfectly understand, and which only
annoy the reader for amusement, and are the scorn of the
reviewer. Strive with all your might to be original, in the
sense mentioned above in the passages relating to *imagination*. I have had in a batch of books for review three or
four novels, all turning on foolish young men entangled
with a concealed marriage, and then meeting, when too late,
the very woman they *could* cleave to. The step-mother,
the fascinating governess, the village genius, and many
other familiar types will occur to the reader, and all these
should be avoided by the young writer. Mr. Andrew Lang,
one of the most graceful writers of the day, gave in 1889, a
lecture at South Kensington, London, on " How to fail in
Literature," wherein there is much that is exceedingly apposite and pointed, and much that is in general harmony with
many of the principles laid down in this work. For one
thing, Mr. Andrew Lang remarked, " He who would fail
could not begin too early to neglect his education, and
must on no account observe life and literature. To
cultivate a bad handwriting was an elementary precaution
often overlooked. Those who would court disaster should
be as ignorant and as reckless as possible. As a matter of
style, they should always place adverbs after the word 'to,'
as 'Hubert was determined to energetically refuse to
entangle himself with such'; and should use more adjec-
tives than words of all other denominations put together.

They should also hunt for odd terms, as 'a beetling nose,' and should have startling descriptions, as 'the sun sank in a cauldron of deathly chaos'. Unusual terms should be put where they would cause the reader the most surprise—as, for instance, trees round a man's house might be called his 'domestic boscage'. 'Fictional,' for 'fictitious,' was to be distinctly recommended; 'all the time' might be employed for 'always,' 'back of' for 'behind,' and 'do like he did' for 'do as he did'. Reversing the advice of Cæsar, it might be said that he who would fail must avoid simplicity like a sunken reef. Then there was the Wardour Street style, constructed out of Malory, Browne, Urquhart, and others, and producing a result like nothing so much as the Book of Mormon."

Then, too, Mr. Lang went on to observe that it was an excellent plan to notice nothing, to go through the world with eyes and ears shut, and then to embody the results in a novel. Further, Mr. Lang gave a good many other pieces of advice to authors how not to get their books published, and then, going on in the same vein of light pleasantry, he instructed them how not to get reviewed One plan was to write to a critic to endeavour to induce him to give a favourable and an unfair judgment, by reminding him that the author once met him somewhere , young authors would not believe in the honesty of critics, but, while holding that everything in reviewing was done by bribery and corruption, they never offered the critics a *quid pro quo*. A writer who wished to fail with an editor should always insist on seeing him and wasting his time—a thing that an editor most hated, unless his visitor was young and beautiful. In conclusion, Mr. Lang said that if writers really wished to succeed they might turn his advice outside in, and give the same attention to literature that was required for success in other arts.

These are all noteworthy points, and fully correspond with

the general views advanced in this Manual.   The writer who
would *not* fail in literature should cultivate his various
faculties carefully, and train each to its proper work.   They
ought each and all to go to the mark.   Wherever the writer
finds himself, in whatever place, and in whatever company, his
material lies around, and should be instinctively stored up in
memory, to be crystallised there for future use.   Let there
be a good mental organisation, and let each class of ideas
be kept distinct from the rest.   Especially cultivate the most
useful habit of mental composition.   Do not, like Victor
Hugo, or Balzac, compose on paper, or worse still, on oft-
corrected proofs.   No one ought to take up the pen before
he is ready to write.   Scott wrote rapidly, and his manuscript
exhibits but few alterations.   Let it not be supposed that he
composed when he wrote, in the usual sense, for he has himself confessed that he often lay in bed with his work
" simmering " in his head, and then when he got to pen and
paper it somehow wrote itself out !   Correct in this fair copy
as much as seems fit, but do not begin to write, as some, to
find the whole thing has to be done over again.   This kind
of work begets a loose, slovenly habit of thought, and is
more or less fatal to a logical order of mind.   Prepare
" copy " carefully for press or for the ordeal of the publisher's
reader.   All publishers, with very few exceptions, pass on
offered manuscripts to a professional reader and adviser.
He is always a practical man, and he is sure to be favourably
impressed at the outset if the work coming under his notice
is in good order and clearly written.   Recollect that MS.
reading and judging is hard and most responsible work.
Yours is not the only work that comes before the " reader ";
he has a drawerful or more at a time, perhaps even a load
enough to make a donkey stagger, and he is sure of necessity
to be more or less biassed against the slovenly MS. which
is obscurely written, unpunctuated and unparagraphed, and
perhaps full of solecisms which his hawk's eye detects

instantaneously on merely turning the pages. Such things may seem trivialities to the mind of the self-conscious genius who feels an afflatus, and says, " Ah, if only they come to *that* part of the story, if only they catch hold of the great episode in the third volume, success is certain ". Unfortunately " they do not," as a rule, " get so far," and the MS. goes back marked " unsuited," which it most certainly is, and the author, after a cold fit of despair, sends it forth again unaltered, and again receives it back with the same result How should it be otherwise ? A reader of MSS. without end has no time to write his reasons, and, indeed, it would not pay him to do so. He knows the wisdom of withholding reasons, and unless special arrangements are made, the author of the rejected MS. usually is entirely ignorant of the real reasons prompting the repeated rejection of work which is possibly good in matter, but hopelessly wrong in manner.

In closing, something should be said here on the subject of literary collaboration. Of late years, there appears a decided disposition towards this method of literary production. The case of Rice and Besant—the modern Beaumont and Fletcher, is well known, and on the continent we had Erckmann-Chatrian. Mr. Stevenson recently wrote a novel —by no means one of his best—in collaboration, and Messrs. Philips and Wills have written in conjunction *Sybil Ross's Marriage.* I am much inclined to think that this division of literary labour will be a feature before long of much work in fiction and it may lead to new openings and new forms of work for young writers. It has occurred to me, in fact, that it is not unlikely that in the search for novelty, it may occur to some organising mind engaged on imaginative literature to produce novels as periodicals are produced, viz., as the combined result of many individual efforts. Suppose just for the sake of argument that the chief writer, acting as general editor, constructed the plot and

assigned to, say half a-dozen writers, each his appointed
task By giving each writer only that to do in which his
strength lay, a book should result of extraordinary merit.
The detail of working could easily be arranged, and the
editor or novelist-in-chief would simply have to harmonise
and fit in the various portions of the narrative Thus the
finest descriptive writing, the best and wittiest dialogue, the
most intense passion, the driest humour, the most poetic
flights might all be harmoniously combined, and in this way
a true epic novel of the times, embracing whatever concerns
men and women, might be produced. This is but a crude
idea as thrown out here, but it may in some degree be
worked out by-and-by, and at any rate it is probable that
work may be found before long for bright young writers in
imaginative to " fill in " for successful authors who have
more commissions from publishers and editors than they
can well execute. After all, this is to do in literature
what is often done in painting and in sculpture,
where the "carver" frequently has more to do with
the finish of the design in the marble than the sculptor
himself.

And now as to the solid returns that may be expected
from successful fiction. One firm prints, it is said, in
round numbers quite six million volumes of fiction a-year,
and the following are said to be the sales of *one* year of what
may be called standard works in imaginative fiction. Lord
Lytton's novels, 80,000; Scott's, 30,000; Marryat's, 60,000;
Robinson Crusoe, 40,000 (18 months' sales); *Gulliver's
Travels*, 2480; *Innocents Abroad*. 5575; *Tom Jones*, 8200.
All these were in the popular sixpenny editions. Of the
late Lord Lytton's novels in the higher priced editions, there
were sold in one year of *Night and Morning*, 1170 copies;
the *Last of the Barons*, 1440; the *Last Days of Pompeii*,
1470; *Alice*, 980; *The Caxtons*, 880; *A Strange Story*, 740;
What will he do with it? 1604.

Going lower down in the scale of merit, far lower down, indeed, we find that Harrison Ainsworth's romances sold as follows:—*Windsor Castle*, 10,170; the *Tower of London*, 11,750; *Rookwood*, 9256; *Old St. Paul's*, 10,000; and others from 8000 to 5000.

Turning to Cooper, a far better novelist, and one of much higher tone, morally and intellectually, we find the following statistics:—*The Deer Slayer*, 3290; *The Bravo*, 1550; *The Borderers*, 2030; *The Last of the Mohicans*, 4360; *The Pathfinder*, 3636; *The Pilot*, 3575; and then we find that the translation of *Monte Cristo* sold in one year 40,000 copies; and the returns of Dickens range from 4000 to 7000, being high numbers, remembering how many homes already possessed the works of the great novelist.

In more recent times, very long numbers have sold of successful fictions. *The Mystery of a Hansom Cab*, a strong but in a literary sense by no means marvellous work of Australian origin, ran up to a quarter of a million; *Called Back* sold in enormous editions, and one of Mr. Farjeon's stories, published in 1889, ran up over 30,000 before the close of that year! Figures are dry reading and these need not be multiplied here. It may suffice to say that a *successful* story once well published sells by thousands, and as the reading circle is ever widening, the circulation of good fiction will undoubtedly increase.

What is the remuneration to the author likely to be? Lord Beaconsfield had £10,000 for *Lothair*—a very indifferent work as literature, but in that case special reasons enhanced the value. *Romola*—one of George Eliot's finest works—earned for the writer only £7000. Dickens received for *Our Mutual Friend* £24,000. The late Lord Lytton made £80,000, and Anthony Trollope £75,000, by novel writing; while, if we descend to comparatively minor authors of fiction, we may safely say that the returns are much in excess of what could be made proportionately in any of the recognised professions or vocations of life. A novel, at all saleable, should return from £100 to £500, and a good writer can produce at least two fictions in a year. Then there is the growing practice of running serial fiction through provincial papers, whereby much money may be made, the author retaining full rights, and having the advantage of seeing his work in print before finally committing it to the book form. There is an increasing disposition on the part of newspapers of all kinds, provincial and London too, to publish fiction, and these form first-rate arenas wherein writers can try their powers. It must, of course, be observed that some works of fiction are manifestly altogether unsuited for effective serial publication, and such as these should certainly be submitted to the judgment of the "publisher's reader". Very many authors, too, could not write effectively for periodical publication, but, no doubt, some of those who do, gain thereby in many ways. Still, in the case of good book-work, the ordeal of the "publisher's reader" is unquestionably a true test. It has been my lot to go through vast quantities of work of the most hopeless character regarded as wholes, and yet, in many cases, including much which was good and fresh, and would have pleased readers, had the writer only known the way to write. Some idea of what is here meant may be gathered from the fact that in one case of accepted work, it was my painful and thankless task to reduce the whole by *two-thirds*, *i.e.*, to take away two out of every three pages! All this would have been avoided by the writer of the work in question, had he only duly "qualified" himself for fiction by going through a course of literary technics like those here prescribed. It may be useful and suggestive to inquire into the question, What is the popular fiction of to-day? This is an exceedingly difficult problem to solve. Many books like *Robert Elsmere* attain to an immense circulation from special causes, for able and clever as that book is, no one can justly pronounce it to be a very entertaining or *interesting* novel, apart from the momentous issues it raises in theology. Some faint idea, however, of the popular side of the question may be gleaned from the Free Library Returns of fiction taken out, and those for Birmingham give the following. The figures denote the number of times that the undermentioned works were issued :—*Pickwick*, 389 ; *Bleak House*, 361 ; *David Copperfield*, 303 ; *Robinson Crusoe*, 294 ; *Oliver Twist*, 278 ; *Martin Chuzzlewit*, 224 ; *The Mill on the Floss*, 217 ; *The Arabian Nights*, 211 ; *Ivanhoe*, 200 ; *Vanity Fair*, 195 ; *East Lynne*, 188 ; *Adam Bede*, 181 , *The Channings*, 143 ; *Westward Ho !* 139 ; *My Novel*, 137 ; *It is never too late to Mend*, 121 ; and in poetry, Tennyson's *Poems*, 135.

These statistics are of some indicative value, and they evince among the lower middle class and the upper industrial classes a thoroughly healthful taste for what is good and pure in fiction.

It may be interesting to add the number of books published in 1889, which will thus faintly indicate the literary activity of the times. The gross total then was 8078 :— 828 belonged to fiction, 816 to children's books, and 473 to annuals and serials ; religion and theology claimed 571, and educational of all kinds another 600. London, as usual, headed the list as a publishing centre, the number of books turned out being 6774, Edinburgh coming next with 336 ; the total for Ireland being 63, and for Scotland 500.

One word in conclusion in regard to a humble and yet lucrative department in fiction. I allude to novelettes, wherein there is much scope for good work. In his excellent book on *Practical Journalism*, Mr. John Dawson speaks of a friend of his who has been at such work for over five years, and adds that although " he may never, as a 'penny novelist,'

achieve fame, he earns about ten times the income he did
as an actor, and finds the employment of a congenial
character ". The prices given vary from one, two, or three
guineas up to ten when very good, and pay the practised
producer well, and many a writer who now wastes his
powers on huge novels which every publisher's reader rejects
might do something in the way of earning money at once, if
only he would adapt his pen to what *is* required, and this is
not really so difficult as, if able to write at all and possessed
of observation, the careful study of a few successful penny
novelettes should soon show him " how it is done ".

System here is all-important as in most departments of
the real business of life. Every literary worker will naturally
have his own ways, but yet there are some general things
that should be useful and common to all. In my own case
I arrange in convenient places quite within reach groups of
books bearing on such subjects as art, amusement, and
pastime, out and in doors, topography and descriptive works
of scenery, as many being well illustrated as I can get.
These suggest, if they do not supply, settings for ordinary
fiction, and may be regarded as *disjecta membra* of the filling-
in portion of a story. Often they relate to places one knows
personally, and then they help all the more by reviving faded
impressions and setting one's thoughts back until one can
imagine very fully the place in question. The references to
technical books on art, sport, etc., keep one from falling into
errors which are so frequent in this lower plane of imaginative work and arise out of hasty guesses and dashes at
things imperfectly understood. Thus as one thing leads to
another, the outlines of a story are created, and then it
remains only to fill in the detail and supply the requisite
local colouring. It is best decidedly to form a general plan
first, next to let it expand into something like a sequence of
incidents marching on each by its own road to some pre-
conceived *denouement*, and, when thus far advanced, read

and observe and reflect to clothe the outline with as much realism and naturalism as lie within the scope of your power. Then when the whole is mentally wrought out it should be to you as a reality, like a story read, and sitting down, the writing ought to proceed easily enough as you are simply emptying your brain of what is already there. This is better than writing as you go. It is said that Scott did this, and if you happen to possess genius, you will not come to me or any one else for advice, but for those who have to supply the absence of genius by industry, patience, and thoughtful arts, the plan mentioned above is a long way the best. Even in Scott's case it is a question whether he might not have done better had he worked more on a plan, for many of his splendid romances are faulty enough in the arrangement, and Victor Hugo, for example, seems to have written his magnificent fiction constructively speaking "anyhow," following out some central idea, but otherwise jumbling up the most incongruous things and making digression his rule and not as it should be, the exception. I have seen very much of the evil consequences to art-work in fiction, arising solely out of the absence in many novelists of any right ideas as to construction. If, in fact, many stories could be represented to the eye by equivalent drawings, they would be found out of all perspective and out of all drawing, and full of such monstrous violations of all laws of symmetry that their very authors would be the first to utterly condemn the hideous caricatures of what a true work of art should always be.

VI.—LITERATURE FOR THE YOUNG.

Nothing has struck me more of late than the vastness and variety of the field opened up by writers for the young. The department of books for boys and girls of all ages is, too, one of great national importance and of high educa-

tional and moral import.   As a reviewer for many years of
books for young readers, I have had very unusual facilities
for comparison and general examination of such productions,
and of late years, as observed above, it has become obvious
that here is a really fine field for the young writer who can
readily adapt himself to the requirements of this type of
literature   The two poles of this form of literature are
found in work like that of Lewis Carroll's *Alice in Wonder-
land*, and in the tales of Jules Verne, wherein the latter
writer has worked out entirely unsuspected veins of interest
happily combined with practical lessons of science popularised.   The origin of books for the young carries us no
farther back than to the days of Perrault and the Comtesse
d'Aulnoy, and in reality, excepting such works as those old
favourites, *Evenings at Home, Sandford and Merton*, and a
few more of the same kind, it is not until we are well into
the Victorian age that we find any mass of books exclusively
written for the young.   With the close of the last decade
but one of the century, we saw a marvellous activity in this
department of literary work, and quite a regiment of writers
have now partly occupied what is perhaps one of the largest
future fields for the writer of literature partly imaginative
and partly matter of fact, partly instructive, and at its best
wholly entertaining.   Dealing with this subject, a writer in
the *Daily Telegraph* of December 31, 1889, remarked in
reference to books expressly composed for the young, we
have "faithful and devoted followers of Marryat, whose
style has a strong flavour of 'the briny,' and whose larking,
high-spirited, semi-disciplined 'middies' have done more to
recruit our navy with young officers than all the collective
inducements of the Admiralty.   And the school of Ballan-
tyne, who first brought boys in contact with the charms of
the frozen seas of 'Ungava,' and told them all about Kazaks
and Eskimos, seals and blubber, snow-houses, and sledges,
and dogs, and generally introduced them into Arctic circles,

yet flourishes apace; while, in the realm of romance of the fantastic order, have we not still with us the authors of *Treasure Island* and *King Solomon's Mines?*"

The same writer complains, however, that many of our books for boys are "too often dull, domestic, and didactic," and then, after alluding to Dean Swift and Gulliver's Travels, not exactly intended for boys and girls, he continues—

"From such considerations we get by an easy process of thought to the idea that 'Books for Boys' can be made temptingly instructive, appealing to the fresh young receptive intellect and reason through the imagination. A boy, for instance, who gets hold of Jules Verne's most recent fantasy will of necessity be induced to learn, if not exactly all, certainly something about the obliquity of the earth to the ecliptic, and the rate at which we are all whirling through space governed by forces Indeed, it is not unlikely that he would take with avidity to the finding out of what is meant by parallax, or the precession of the equinoxes, or the first point of Aries, or nutation, or 'great circles,' or the phenomenon of the 'harvest moon'; and such things as solstices and sun-spots, and celestial colures and coronas and the like would become keenly attractive to him. The 'right ascension' and 'declination' of a star would no longer be ugly problems in a dry astronomical treatise, but very vivid and valuable subjects of close personal interest. No such boy would ever dream of committing the sin spoken of by Sydney Smith of 'speaking disrespectfully of the equator'; quite the contrary, to him latitude and longitude would be lovable things, and the calculations they involve of the nature of games. The fact is that it is uninteresting tutors who make dull boys, and wise are those teachers who, consciously or unconsciously, get at and stimulate the reasoning faculty by sending forth their ideas on wings of fancy."

There is very much that is suggestive here. Much, very

much remains yet for the pens of writers for the young to conquer. There are worlds of romance and incident to be occupied, past, present, and future, and in the innumerable fairy tales of science there may be found themes without end on which good stories can be based. Geographically, enormous regions yet remain to the writer for the young. Then, it has long struck me that much might be done in working up geology into imaginative matrices of action, after the manner of Jules Verne. French art has done much to depict man on broad canvases during the very early periods of history, and there is ample scope for instruction and entertainment in calling back to life, say, the early lake-dwellers in Switzerland. To those whose taste, inclination, and general genius incline them in this direction there is surely an ample store of ready-made material ; and then, again, there is the opening presented for depicting ancient life in India, China, and Japan, say at a period anterior to the introduction of Christianity. Old histories, old collections of voyages and travels can be laid under contribution for the facts. *Maundeville's* travels and similar works can be read up, and all kinds of myths, legends, and old-world romances. Then, to the *fanciful* mind there is an endless vista of possible work, both amusing and instructive, in diving, say, into the arcana of chemistry, and perhaps endowing some of the atoms and molecules with human attributes, and making scientific truths plain to the young through the agency of some story made to fit in with the special qualities of different elements. Thus, all *food* comes remotely from a few simple elements, gases, etc. A well-laid, well-cooked dinner can be traced back to sundry gases and metals, which by nature's chemistry and the cookery of the sun, far more marvellous than aught in man's most elaborate *cuisine*, has been converted into living tissue, vegetable or animal. The interest of the young reader might be profitably excited by a writer possessing the requisite genius to vivify the elements with thought and design, and to show the connection between a gas and a fruit, a piece of metal and a morsel of meat. This is but a crude and random suggestion, but it will serve to indicate one direction wherein invention may move in this department of literature Just to particularise more closely, however, the kind of matter or material that can be worked up, take the account given at the close of 1889 by an explorer at a meeting of the Geographical Society in Berlin of the Kaiser-Wilhelm-Land. In the course of his descriptive sketch much information was conveyed which would serve well for the substratum of many a romantic tale of adventure and wonder. Take the following summary of some of the main points adduced—

There are, we are assured, "active volcanoes. As to its zoology, there is a want of mammalia. Game is represented by wild pigs, the 'walebe,' the 'flying dog,' 'flying squirrel,' and a bush rat. Pigs and small spotted dogs, which howl like dingos and are kept to be eaten, are the domestic animals. Birds are numerous. Three kinds of paradise-birds, cassowaries, crown doves, and forty varieties of pigeons, parrots, and the rhinoceros-bird may be named. Among the reptiles are crocodiles, tortoises, turtles, small (not poisonous) snakes, and a few frogs. There is plenty of sea and river fish, and vegetation is extremely luxuriant and varied. All sorts of palms and woods are to be found. There are quantities of climbing plants, parasites, orchids, etc The woods are almost impenetrable even on the hills, which are thickly covered with forests, so that no view can be obtained from the summits."

Thus much for the physical geography, the *flora*, and the *fauna*. The "impenetrable woods" immediately suggest to the professional writer of "tales, adventure, and wonder" a practically unlimited ground for the play of imaginative fancy. Then, coming to the ethnology, we learn that "the inhabitants vary both in form and feature. The women are smaller and more delicate than the men. All the young and more pleasant-looking girls are carefully hidden, and Europeans only get to see the ugly old women."

Here is ample scope for imagining some Venus of these virgin woods resembling an antique carving of yellow ivory, and then the summary proceeds as under—"The forts are remarkable, in which, during war with a neighbour, the women and children are kept in safety They are made in the tops of trees, some 120 to 160 feet high, and are reached by very shaky steps or ladders." Surely in this last brief statement is the text for more than one tale of peril, of horror, and, perhaps, of devotion unto death. I roughly sketch here simply outlines of what may be done. It is not intended that these suggestions should be copied; it is simply meant that they should suggest to the young writer the sort of notes he should make in his reading and the kind of fact-foundation that may serve for him to rear up a structure out of his own fanciful imaginings. Those who *have* a faculty for narrative will, I am sure, find many useful hints here, and those who do not may conclude thence that as yet, at all events, tales of adventure are not exactly in their literary way.

Finally, as to children in fiction, a writer in the *Nottingham Daily Express*, after pointing out that the earlier novelists did not trouble about children, goes on to observe that after Dickens, with his wonderful and often touching delineations of childhood, we must not forget Thackeray. He has, it is true, "fewer memorable children, but with what exquisite tenderness he writes of the neglected little son of sinful Becky, gently leading his father to a purer existence; how marvellous is his picture of Amelia, waking to life and love again after her great sorrow ' to clasp a little boy, as beautiful as a cherub, with George's eyes '. Only one woman, or perhaps two, have ever approached Dickens and Thackeray when they wrote of children, but even they never surpassed the matchless creations of George Eliot. A child—the baby waif found by the old weaver, Silas Marner—is the heroine of the most artistically perfect of all her books. The miser forgets his lost gold as his hand steals over the small head 'sunning over with curls'. That gold, restored in the after years, is as dross in his eyes, compared to the girl he loves as a daughter. *The Mill on the Floss* is another example; the story of the brother and sister roaming beside the sunny river will be read and remembered when the very names of the popular authors of the moment are forgotten. It might seem as if a wide chasm of difference separated Mrs. Ewing's short simple stories from those of the marvellous woman who gave an astonished world *Romola* and *Middlemarch*, but the quiet lady whose busy silver pen has only been laid down for a little while, and whose fame was of the most restricted kind, produced work of rare and delicate quality—work perfect after its own modest fashion. The vanished hand, whose sympathetic touch drew 'Jackanapes,' has left few successors to inherit its cunning. Mrs. Ewing left a vacant place that will not easily be filled." Among other writers is L. T. Meade, whose exquisite *Daddy's Boy* is a masterpiece, and then *Little Lord Fauntleroy* suggests of itself a new avenue for writers of books for the young. Altogether the outlook here is one full of encouragement to the writer who decides to take up child life as his staple theme.

VII.—ON READING AND THE USE OF BOOKS.

In several sections of this manual much stress is laid on the absolute necessity there is for the young writer being well read. Literature increases so rapidly, the claims of life are of many, heavy and exacting, that unless a good foundation of general reading is laid early, it will be found practically

impossible to make up for arrears of necessary reading
in later life.   Read much, read thoughtfully, read early—
sums up the best practical advice to the young writer, and
with all this, there must be not only the retentive and orderly
memory, but the ceaseless cultivation of all the observant
faculties, and especially the larger reading of the *things* all
around us.   Many persons have good memories *per se*, but
there is no *method* in the storage.   The things are there,
indeed, but placed anyhow, and are not readily available.
How often do we find fairly clever persons *after* an interview of importance or a social gathering regretfully dwelling
on all the fine things that they *could* have said had they
only thought of them at the right time!   Now the right
time is equivalent to the right place in writing, and the
writer should have his accumulating faculties so nicely
disciplined as to act harmoniously with the distributing
powers, so as to give the best of his reading and his own
observation exactly when and where it is wanted, and he
should have, finally, the faculty of expression for giving
due verbal form to his stores of things remembered in the
most effective way possible   That is, summed up, the whole
art and mystery of good composition.

But reading on a large scale is an essential part of the
foundation, whereon a writer must rely, and this is just
a thing likely to be neglected in these superficial days
of haste and shams.

For myself, I owe an incalculable debt of gratitude to
early reading.   Before settling on any determinate course
in life, it happened that after having, as a youth, had
uncommon faculties for reading, I found myself free of the
London Library with its hundred thousand volumes, and
during a period of some years, I really did nothing very
particular beyond visiting the library, generally daily, early
in the morning—often waiting eagerly for the doors to open
— and having read much at the shelves all over the building,

I carried away a dozen works or so, many of which were returned in a day or two, and this reading at one period filled up all the day and evening too, and in the fine weather I read much on the way to and fro, so that I think it is not too much to assert that I really read as much as *could* be read in the time, and as that was a period of several years, the quantity must have been immense, as, indeed, may be seen by the entries in the Library Books. Much that was thus read was superfluous in a sense, for books supersede books, and sometimes one late volume may represent effectively the practical essence of a hundred, or even more, earlier works.   Let not the young student be dismayed at the prospect held out here, as one too vast for him to survey with patience, for it will be found that I give later on a much reduced and practical outline of what it is necessary to read, but I still say that although mine was an extreme case, the young writer will benefit greatly by reading early, when the assimilative faculty of the brain is in its freshness and power, and the material thus stored up will *fructify*, take new forms, often fresh and unexpected avenues of thoughts and inquiry, and suggest very much that will *never* come to the writer who has read little and trusts to his talent or his genius.   I read, certainly, with the direct object of becoming a writer.   I always felt that to pour out one should first pour in.   There must be material to shake up in the kaleidoscope of imagination, to produce forms of beauty, and fancies largely come out of facts.   I read for one thing, as a means for attaining to a wider vocabulary, an approximation to a true *copia fandi*, all the poetry I could find, that is, all British, from Cædmon to Tennyson, and I read, through the medium of translation, all the poets of the East, of Greece, Rome, and modern Europe, and finally, of America.   The novelists of all ages and countries were devoured, and then history, theology, philosophy, industrial records, science, and everything that could be read.   It is true enough that something good or useful may be learned out of almost *any* book   Many books do not require a quarter-of-an-hour's study in a course of reading like this —and with a system it is simply amazing how much work can be got through in a single day.   Constant practice, too, of this kind, begets a readiness of mental grasp of a book that is equivalent to the physical dexterity and rapidity of the gymnast who, by practice, can do in an instant what others could not accomplish in a year, or, indeed, at all. Then one book is often the key to another, and as know-ledge of books accumulates, one gets to recognise common characteristics, types, and classes.   The mental appre-hension is quickened, and rendered more luminous.   It is, as in the case of the connoisseur in painting, who, after a time, can judge much by simply one rapid searching look. Many recommend note taking and common-place books. They are very good, indeed, in their way, but if the student can dispense therewith, it is better, certainly for general literature, that he should carry what he knows first in his own mind.   Scott, for example, could sit down and write in general out of his mental stores, and when this is done, the effect will usually be finer, as there is a crudity and a rawness about the deliberated insertion of cut and dried excerpts into literary work.   It is a patching of what ought to be a seamless garment woven complete from the loom of the writer's brain !

Notes and memorandum books are great encumbrances too, and occupy much time that may often be turned to better account   The necessity one is under, when notes are dispensed with, to be accurate is a gain in itself.   Of course, reference books or excerpts can, and must, be used often. Few have made more use of such than I, but I do not think there is material gain in continually hindering a student's reading as some recommend, by obliging him to stop perpetually to make written extracts.   I know the result frequently is, simply, that the "notes" are all the work that is ever done. There may be, and often is, far too great an elaboration in the preliminary stages and thus practical work is never done.

Taking what may be termed fairly current literature and as suggestive of the kind of books likely to be most useful to a general writer, I note the following—

Religious: *Mistranslated Passages in our Bible*, by the Rev. J. H. Murray; *Classified Bible*, by Dr. J. Eadie, Cassell's *Bible Dictionary; The Bible and the Newspaper*, C. H. Spurgeon. In Ecclesiastical History. Neander's *History of Christianity and the Church*, Archdeacon Farrar's *Life of Christ; Legends of the Monastic Orders*, by Mrs. Jameson; Professor Ranke's *History of the Popes;* Dr. Wylie's *History of Protestantism; The Church and the Churches*, by Dr Dollinger; *Compendium Theologicum*, by the Rev. O. Adolphus. In Judaism: Ewald's *Antiquities of Israel.* For Mythology and Folk-lore there is the *Manual of Mythology*, by Sir G. W. Cox; then we have Keightley's *Fairy Mythology of various Countries;* Chambers's *Book of Days* and the *Folk-lore of Shakespeare*, by Thistelton Dyer.

The following will be found very useful books in their respective departments: Bohn's *Hand-book of Proverbs; History of English Thought in 18th Century*, by Leslie Stephen; *Kant's Critique of Pure Reason*, by Professor Mahaffy; *Comte's Philosophy of the Sciences*, by Lewes; *English Positivism*, Taine; and *Schopenhauer, his Life and Philosophy*, by Helen Zimmern. A very good work, too, has just appeared, entitled *Ready Reference, the Universal Cyclopædia containing everything that everybody wants to know*, compiled by William Ralston Balch. This work is quite a treasury in its way, and it is the very book for a writer to take with him when away from home, as it really contains the essence of hundreds of works of reference, and is conveniently arranged.

Among miscellaneous and decidedly useful books, I should suggest the following—

Leger's *History of Austro-Hungary*, from the earliest time to 1889, translated by Professor Freeman; Canon Malcolm Maccoll's *Christianity in Relation to Science and Morals;* Keatley's *Selections from Pliny,* Ashley's *English Economic History,* and the Rev. J. Frank Bright's *Growth of Democracy.* These are all solid books, not likely to be read by the mass and such as should breed ideas in the thoughtful reader. Carl Lumholtz's fine work, *Among Cannibals,* is a fund of fact-information on the *fauna* and *flora* of North-east Australia. Such a book as Gilbert's *Calendar of Ancient Records of Dublin* opens up another field and suggests sources for historic bases to stories of the past whereto it is desired to give an archaic flavour and an historic matrice.

Mr. Nevill's fine work, *Old Cottage and Domestic Architecture in South-West Surrey,* also suggests a type of work whereto the writer of story localised specifically may resort to freshen up and supplement what he knows already of the locality. Then, again, much may be gleaned from such a treasury of information on the subject as *Musical Instruments and their Homes*, by Mary and W. Brown, which is copious and trustworthy, and out of the common way. In a tale introducing musical matters facts thus derived would " work up " effectively, and please and surprise the reader who likes to be easily informed in recreative reading, and rarely objects to be instructed, provided the instruction helps on and does not hinder the flow of the story.

In the ancient drama, the *Attic Theatre*, by A. E. Haigh, is likely to be useful, and Dr. A. Weismann's *Essays on Heredity* may come in useful in working out the psychological part of an introspective tale. Various collections of proverbs and anything that can be obtained on folk-lore are likely to be of great service, and for information as to the modern Continental drama, Arsène Houssaye's *Behind the Scenes of the Comedie Française* contains much valuable information. Dr. Doran's book about *Court Fools and Players* should be read, and then there is the fine recent work, *Acrobats and Mountebanks*, by H. Le Roux and Jules Garnier, which might well set up a story-writer with facts for any acrobatic episodes he desired to work up.

It is to be observed that I simply throw these remarks out as *hints* and *suggestions* of the general way in which books should be employed. Among old books, I should glance at Ashton's *Curious Creatures in Zoology*, which includes some old travellers' tales of very singular animals. All Bohn's antiquarian library should be examined, and in such a work as Borlase's *Natural History of Cornwall* will be found quite enough to furnish an apt writer with all the background for a Cornish story. This might be supplemented by Downing's *Architectural Relics in Cornwall. Finger-Ring Lore*, by W. Jones, is likely to suggest turns for many a paragraph, and so, too, would *Folk-lore of the Punjab and Kashmir*, a collection of popular legends, and such as could be well wrought up into the tissue of reflective or conversational pieces in ordinary fiction. Another grand book is Major-General Forlong's *Rivers of Life*, wherein will be found 339 engravings of the rudest, as well as the most elaborate, symbolisms of early religions. In *Magyar Ornaments*, by Dr. Carl von Pulsky, will be found much which gives to the eye a good idea of domestic life in Ancient Hungary, a land little used as a ground for story-telling by English writers; and then there are numerous works on the history, the *fauna* and *flora* of all the countries of the world, which will, each in their several turns, serve to supply pith for the general literary matter of imaginative work. Certain books of reference are naturally more or less indispensable to the general writer. An *Encyclopædia* is necessary, and more than one if practicable, as every encyclopædia has its peculiarities, and what one lacks another supplies. *Many Thoughts of Many Minds—both Series* are very useful. I believe the author, Mr. Henry Southgate, has left more of his gleanings from all kinds of books, and a further series would be highly useful to literary workers. Dictionaries of Quotations, a Concordance to the Bible and to Shakespeare are highly desirable, and as many of the standard poets as possible. Collections are very serviceable, too, of year-books of all kinds, works of industrial, financial, and commercial reference, and economic and social statistics. Many books have come before me in imaginative literature wherein the writer has failed miserably in the *groundwork* of his production through not going to easily accessible sources for facts, and foolishly drawing on his fancy where he ought to have gone direct to recorded facts and figures In these days neglect of this kind is un-pardonable, and it is expected that when a writer affects to reproduce in fiction the *actual*, that he should take the requisite pains to render that *actual* on a base of well-verified fact.

And now to go into detail as to what may be called a general foundation in English literature.

With the literature of his own country the young writer *must* possess a good working acquaintance, and the more he knows of it the better. He should systematise these studies in his own mind and map out his general knowledge into, roughly, the following divisions :—Old English. This will introduce him to Cædmon, the first real English poet ; to the Venerable Bede ; to Ælfric, who translated, like Bede, a part of the Holy Bible ; and to Alfred himself, whose works should be read. The Saxon Chronicle should be studied, and the careful student will perceive the use that the late Lord Lytton made thereof for his fine romance, *Harold.*

From old English the student should pass to early English. He will become acquainted then with the works of Layamon, said to be the first writer of English after the Conquest—the *Brut*, an alliterative metrical chronicle of noble deeds done by Englishmen being his chief work. Orm should be noted, author of the *Ormulum*, a series of versified devotional studies, and then the chroniclers, Geoffrey of Monmouth and Robert of Gloucester, and some others should be consulted.

We now pass to the middle English period, say from 1250 to about 1480. Langland, the author of the famous *Vision of Piers, the Ploughman*, must be read as a pioneer of didactic writers seeking an ideal life after the pattern of Heavenly Truth and Love; and John Gower must be included with his famous *Confessions of a Lover*. Chaucer comes in here, and in prose we have "Maundeville the Traveller".

Next in order comes the pre-Elizabethan period. Sir John Fortesque must be noted with his work on *The Difference between Absolute and Limited Monarchy*, a forerunner of the militant political writers who were destined to overturn the monarchy itself. Sir Thomas More and his works should be carefully studied. The *Utopia* is simply a masterpiece, and stands at the very head of literature of its class. Something should be learned of William Tyndale, the martyr, and the father of our English Bible, and likewise of Foxe, whose *Chronicle of the Martyrs* can be bought now for a few pence. Skelton is another notable name. He satirised Wolsey, and composed much verse. Hawes was another didactic writer, while Wyatt and Surrey introduced respectively the sonnet and blank verse into English poetry. This brings us to the Elizabethan period, that splendid sunburst of English poetry. Shakespeare I presume to be a *sine qua non* subject of study, and, therefore, for brevity's sake, need not refer to him further here. Adopting a generally chronological order, we note George Gascoigne, who scourged the vices of that time in a strange old poem called *Steele Glas*, and contemporary with him was Thomas Sackville (Earl of Dorset), who wrote the *Mirrour for Magistrates*. Sackville wrote, too. in conjunction with Thomas Norton, a blank verse tragedy called *Ferrex and Porrex* and subsequently entitled *Gorboduc* Roger Ascham produced the *Schoolmaster*, dealing with education, and Sir Philip Sidney gave two permanent and beautiful contributions to English literature in his *Arcadia* and his *Defence of Poesy*. Spenser and his works must be studied carefully. The *Fairy Queen* is in itself a species of poetic literature, and has created many poets since, and well furnished their minds with themes for many beautiful efforts in painting and imaginative art generally. In the Elizabethan drama we have many illustrious names besides that supreme master of the drama, Shakespeare. George Peele wrote several fine plays, and so did Robert Greene, whose *Triumph of Time* suggested to Shakespeare the groundwork of the *Winter's Tale*. Thomas Nash and John Lyly should be read too. The latter wrote *Euphues, or the Anatomy of Wit*. Christopher Marlowe must be included too. His chief plays are *Dr. Faustus, Edward II.*, and the *Jew of Malta*, the last-named being a tissue of absurdity and bombast. Indeed Marlowe, notwithstanding Mr Swinburne's singular infatuation as to his merit, is much overrated. Ben Jonson, Beaumont and Fletcher, Massinger, John Ford, and John Webster. and some others should also be read.

Among the prose writers of the Elizabethan age, Bacon occupies a considerable space. It is necessary to read his *Essays* , and some acquaintance should be made with the writings of Sir Walter Raleigh, John Stow, Holinshed, and John Speed, who wrote a *History of Britain*. Then there is Richard Hooker, whose *Ecclesiastical Polity* is one of the great monuments of English literature.

We come now to a group of poets of a very different order, men for the most part inspired by a profound belief in the Christian as a divinely revealed religion, and devoting their lives to metaphysical poetry designed specially to make men better, more devout, and purer in their thought and lives. The following are the greatest and best among these: George Herbert, Richard Crashaw, who wrote the ever memorable line on the miracle at the marriage feast at Cana, which Englished, runs—

The conscious water saw its God and blushed,

but is infinitely finer in the original Latin ; Henry Vaughan, George Wither, and Francis Quarles, the author of the *Divine Emblems.*

Among poets on a lower moral plane I would cite Love-lace, Herrick, Sir John Suckling, Waller, and Sir John Denham, whose fine poem, *Cooper's Hill*, lives still as a piece of very good descriptive work Then there is Cowley, of many metres and little or no poetry.

The Commonwealth epoch is full of the glory of John Milton, whose soul, as Wordsworth tells us—

Was like a star and dwelt apart ,

And whose voice—

Was like the sea,
Pure as the naked heavens, majestic, free.

It is requisite to be acquainted with Thomas Fuller, who wrote the *History of the Worthies of England*, and especially with Sir Thomas Browne, the famous author of *Urn-burial* and the memorable *Religio Medici ;* the *Holy Living* and the *Holy Dying* of Jeremy Taylor, and the *Saints' Rest* of Richard Baxter must be taken account of, as also John Bunyan's *Pilgrim's Progress*, while some attention ought to be given to George Fox, William Penn, Isaac Walton, Lord Clarendon (*History of the Great Rebellion*), John Evelyn, and Samuel Pepys, whose diaries contain much curious and suggestive matter

Our next period extends from the Restoration to the reign

of Queen Anne One of the most considerable figures is John Dryden, whose prose is well worth reading; his poems—dramatic, narrative, and lyrical—together with his translation of Virgil should be studied. Butler must be remembered too, with his *Hudibras*, that wonderful burlesque epical poem ridiculing the Puritans, and forming quite a treasury for quotation purposes The greatest poet of the age, omitting Dryden, was Pope, whose *Essay on Criticism* is quite a manual of instruction in metrical composition. The famous poem, the *Rape of the Lock*, is a kind of fashionable novelette in exquisitely smooth rhymed verses, sparkling with wit, while the *Essay on Man*—inspired as to the argument by Bolingbroke—is a splendid didactic poem, although some of its principles are not at all in accordance with pure Christian truth Pope translated *Homer* and wrote, among other things, that matchless poem, *The Dying Christian to his Soul*—one of the few quite perfect poems extant.

Many other writers of this period remain for study. Wycherley, Congreve, Farquhar, Sir John Vanbrugh, and Colley Cibber must be glanced at as dramatists Among philosophers we find John Locke, who wrote the well-known *Essay on the Conduct of the Understanding*, the great Sir Isaac Newton—true type and example for all time of what a Christian man of science should be; and then there are the eminent divines, Isaac Barrow, John Tillotson, Robert South, and some others.

Among poets, too, we must not pass over Edward Young. the writer of the *Night Thoughts*, a didactic poem in blank verse, possessing amid much false taste, some rare beauties of true poetic thought; and as minor writers of verse we have John Gay, Thomas Parnell, and Matthew Prior.

The great essay writers of this period require to be studied too. Swift wrote besides *Gulliver's Travels*—that trenchant satire—the *Tale of a Tub*, written in defence of the Church of England. Defoe, better known as the earliest of our true novelists, was a prolific essayist, while Joseph Addison and Richard Steele require to be carefully read.

As we advance in the eighteenth century, our task grows heavier. Oliver Goldsmith, Dr Johnson, Edmund Burke, each with a specially fine work—the poem of the *Deserted Village*, the romance, *Rasselas*, and the *Essay on the Sublime and Beautiful*, respectively—are probably familiar to the reader. Laurence Sterne with *Tristram Shandy*, Samuel Richardson with *Clarissa Harlowe*, Fielding with *Tom Jones*, Smollett with *Roderick Random*, and a few more *must* be read. Among historians, we have the philosophic Hume, Robertson, and the magnificent Gibbon, whose *Decline and Fall of the Roman Empire* is a sort of education in itself to read deliberately and with due reflection.

Adam Smith, with his *Wealth of Nations*, and Sir William Blackstone, with his *Commentaries on the Laws of England*, must be read, and so, too, should Paley (*Evidences of Christianity*, *Horæ Paulinæ*, and *Natural Theology*), and Bishop Butler, whose *Analogy of Religion* has been a chief bulwark of Christianity for more than a century. Bishop Berkeley must be read, too. He wrote against the materialistic tendencies of his times.

Macaulay, Hallam, Arnold, and Froude must be studied among later historians. Amid eminent divines are Thomas Chalmers and Archbishop Whately. Some knowledge is requisite of Hugh Miller, who wrote so much that is good on geology, and John Stuart Mill must be studied, and also Herbert Spencer, Sydney Smith, De Quincey, Charles Lamb, John Wilson (Christopher North), and especially Thomas Carlyle and John Ruskin. Ruskin, in particular, *must* be read. He is all in all the most finished master of poetic prose in the language. Among great

novelists with whom the young student must be acquainted
are Walter Scott, Jane Austen, Charlotte Bronte, Thackeray,
Dickens, Bulwer Lytton, and George Eliot.

With English poetry in its many progressive phases from
say, 1700, the student must be well acquainted. The
principal poets are James Thomson (*The Seasons, Castle of
Indolence*, etc.), Collins (*Ode to the Passions*), Thomas Gray
(*Elegy in a Country Churchyard*, etc.), William Shenstone
(*The Schoolmistress*, etc.), Thomas Chatterton (*The Poems
of Rowley*), George Crabbe (*The Village*, etc.), Cowper
(*The Task*, etc.), Burns (*Tam o' Shanter, The Cottar's Satur-
day Night*, etc.), Beattie (*The Minstrel*), Falconer (*The
Shipwreck*), Henry Kirke White (miscellaneous verses),
Hannah More (many good sacred pieces), Sheridan (*Plays*),
Samuel Rogers (*The Pleasures of Memory*), Keats (*Endy-
mion*, etc.), Shelley (*Ode to the Skylark*, etc.), Byron
(*Childe Harold*, etc.), Robert Pollok (*The Course of Time*),
Scott (*Marmion*, etc.) Coleridge (*The Ancient Mariner*),
Hemans (exquisite lyrics on domestic life), Southey (*The
Curse of Kehama*, etc.), Campbell (*The Pleasures of Hope*,
etc.), Wordsworth (*The Excursion*, and sonnets), the two
Brownings, Keble (*The Christian Year*), Robert Bloomfield
(*The Farmer's Boy*), Heber (*Palestine*, etc.), Moore (*The
Irish Melodies*), Hogg (*The Queen's Wake*, etc.), Thomas
Hood (*The Bridge of Sighs, The Song of the Shirt*), James
Montgomery (*The World Before the Flood*, etc.), Leigh Hunt
(*The Story of Rimini*), and others, including, of course,
Tennyson, Swinburne, and other living poets. It must be
observed that if some in the brief list given above are
scarcely poets in the emphatic sense of the word, they
remain among the immortals on account of some special
work and some special circumstances attending them
and that work. To show what I mean, take a single instance,
that of Robert Bloomfield and his poem *The Farmer's Boy*.
Bloomfield was a poor boy, who taught himself nearly all he

ever knew, and became a working shoemaker. His *Farmer's Boy* appeared in 1800, and, taking into account his circumstances, was a wonderful production. The following is one of the best passages—

> Say ye that know, ye who have felt and seen
> Spring's morning smiles and soul-enlivening green,
> Say, did you give the thrilling transport way,
> Did your eye brighten when young lambs at play
> Leaped o'er your path with animated pride,
> Or grazed in merry clusters at your side ?

There are many who might now turn out verses like these and yet find them fall absolutely flat on both the public and the critics. Those, in fact, who simply *imitate* past successes due to special conditions will find that they have all *but* those conditions, and the matter alone can only land them in disappointment and neglect. Besides the poets enumerated above, there are many others wherewith the student should become acquainted. Thus, taking them alphabetically, we should supplement those given above by Akenside (*The Pleasures of the Imagination*), Joanna Baillie (*The Plays on the Passions*), Blair (*The Grave*), Bowles (the predecessor of the natural school of modern poetry), Elliott (the famous Corn Law rhymer), Hurdis (*The God of Nature*), Marvell (*The Emigrant's Song*, etc.), Southwell (a noble poem on *Conscience*), Waller (love verses, etc.), Wither (religious pieces of the seventeenth century), and yet a few more, which will naturally arise out of reading those actually named, for such writers open avenues of thought and interest to others often greater than they, and thus the student is led on insensibly to acquire stores of knowledge that would have simply dismayed him had he been at first shown the aggregated mass of what he thus acquires step by step with little apparent effort.

In reading poetry for the purposes of study it is highly

needful to note what may be conveniently termed epoch-marking or epoch-making writers. To illustrate this by a few examples. How many of our young people, even those of culture, know aught of Bowles?   Yet a knowledge of him and his work is really necessary to explicate properly the rise and development of nineteenth century song, so true is it that it is not always the greatest poet who makes the greatest epoch in poetry.   William Lisle Bowles, born as long ago as 1762 (he died as recently as 1850), distinctly gave the impetus to the romantic school of English poetry which marks the fusion of the eighteenth century mode of dealing poetically with persons, places, and things, with the nineteenth century metaphysical and yet often realistic manner. It was Bowles who in a sense really inaugurated the new era of poetry, which has culminated in Tennyson, and then, be it borne in mind, his long life began only three years after Burns was born, and ended when the Victorian era was well advanced.   It was, in truth. a case of showing the way, and the veteran poet lived to see the setting of Southey, Coleridge, Wordsworth, Shelley, Byron, and the rise of their successors, and, although he himself never gained the ear of the people, he might well say that he had been the initial motor to the latent development of poetry, and to its complete divorce from the narrow limits of the eighteenth century.

Yet although Bowles was all this, let no young rhymer imitate him.   He is a standard poet, but if he began to write *now*, and gave us the same strains as he did a century since or so, none would read and none would praise him, and he would go down, dismally down, amid the crowd of small poets of the day, of whom we may remark with Mr. Toots, in *Dombey and Son*, what they say or sing is of " no consequence".   To prove this take the closing lines of Bowles on Shakespeare in a " grand " poem he composed on the greatest of poets—

O Sovereign Master! at whose command
  We start with terror, or with pity weep;
Oh, where is now thy all-creating wand?
  Buried ten thousand thousand fathoms deep!
The staff is broke, the powerful spell is fled,
And never earthly great shall in thy circle tread.

Nothing pretending to be verse and metre could well be poorer than this. There is nothing new in the whole, and it is not even very musical. Isa Craig, in her centenary ode on Burns, produced in one passage more actual *original poetic substance* than can be found in all that Bowles composed—so far as *invention* goes—in the following—

As lamps high set,
Upon some earthly eminence,
Unto the gazer thence,
Seem brighter than the spherelights that they float,
Dwindle in distance and die out,
While no star waneth yet,
So through the Past's far-reaching night
The *star-souls only keep their* light.

Bowles, however, is only to be imitated by bardlings of the day with certainty of utter failure, and should be remembered principally as one who showed the way distinctly to infinitely better issues than he ever dreamed of, and he lived to see many an immortal blaze of starry song whereto he had himself supplied the tiny but original spark.

It must often be, too, in days like these, that the young reviewer will have to deal with various forms of sceptical literature. Those who wish to be able to meet and vanquish the enemy should be acquainted with the method and arguments of Paley in the works already named, as well as with those of such later writers as Lightfoot, Westcott, Sandays, Wace, and Row, and with the very popular work of Professor Drummond, *Natural Law in the Spiritual World,* an attempt to reconcile science with theology.

For meeting the arguments of later opponents of revealed religion, however, few books are better than the very admirable *Present Day Tracts on Man in Relation to the Bible and Christianity*, dealing with every aspect of their questions by learned writers, all of them specialists in these particular subjects. Finally, I would recommend a good Bible dictionary as a highly necessary companion when writing on religious subjects.

Pari passu with all this reading a general idea of language should be acquired. It is not at all necessary that the young writer should be a linguist; rather, perhaps, the reverse, but then he must possess some acquaintance, and the more the better, with the history of language. He should know, for example, that the ancient tongues include Hebrew, Syriac, Arabic, Coptic (the ancient Egyptian), Ethiopian, Indian, Phœnician, Punic, Scythian, Celtic, Gothic, Runic, Gaelic. He ought to know something of Greek and more of Latin, and he ought to obtain, at all events through the medium of good translations, a working knowledge of the principal classics and of the great master-pieces of modern European literature.

The following may be taken as a brief sketch of such a course of reading in general Continental literature as should form a sufficient groundwork for the writer in general fiction or poetry :—First he must have some knowledge of the letters of the Arabians, of the genesis of the Provençal literature which formed the foundation of modern romance, and thence we turn to Italy, when Dante, Petrarch, Boccaccio, Politiano, Pulci, Boiardo, Tasso, and Ariosto must be duly read, or, at all events, studied through excerpts, commentaries, and the like. It is desirable to know something, too, of Italian comedy, and Goldoni and Alfieri should be included. Turning to Spain, we have the romance of the Cid, Cervantes, the romantic drama as represented by Lope de Vega Carpio. Quevedo and Calderon must be duly noted, and in Portugal we have Camoens. For Germany, we must turn to Klopstock, Lessing, Wieland, Schiller, Goethe, Korner, De la Motte Fouque (*Undine*), Richter, and Uhland. These for imaginative literature. In metaphysics, it would be well to know something of Kant, Fichte, Schelling, and Hegel, while in history we have Schlegel, Humboldt, Bunsen, Ranke, Niebuhr, and Mommsen. In Russian literature it is highly desirable to know something of the principal writers. A good text-book of Russian literature has been translated into English by Cox (Oxford). Russia is a coming factor in European thought, and will in due time exercise great influence thereon. In regard to Russian literature, which will reward the student therein, I note that Mr. Charles Edward Turner, a Professor in the St. Petersburg University, has written a useful little manual entitled *The Modern Novelists of Russia*, whence much may be learned highly useful to the practical student of European fiction. The novelists dealt with are Goncharoff, Tourgénieff, Dostoievski, Tolstoi, Garshine, and Korolenko. Very much may be learned therein regarding the inner life of the Russian people. Modern Russia, according to Mr. Turner, can be understood only through its novelists. That literature seems to be almost a native product; it owes little to the classics of any age or any country. Let it be ever remembered that it was Tourgénieff with his fine work, *Stories from a Sportsman's Notebook*, who moved Alexander II. to complete the emancipation of the serfs. Altogether there is a great deal to be gained by an intelligent study of Muscovite fiction. It will, for one thing, most certainly enlarge the young writer's views of life and of men and women, and a vast nation like that of Russia cannot be put aside by the writer of fiction, who is essentially one studying mankind in all its developmental racial phases.

Thus much for languages.

A word here, however, is in place as to the future of our

own tongue, on which the coming destinies of the whole
human race must very greatly depend.

The question what will be, or, as some careful speculators
would prefer to put it, what can be the language of the
future, is absolutely one of very great importance to all
writers, and readers too.   No doubt a pasigraphy, or system
of universal writing has ever been a desideratum to the
philosophic mind, and probably Leibnitz, who is accredited
with the origin of such an idea, was by no means the first to
conceive such a thing ; for it is certain that from the first
systematic culture of languages, the foremost exponents of
each were intensely anxious that their several tongues should
prevail in the competitive struggle,   and as the Greeks
carried their beautiful, flexible, forcible language as far as
they could, so the Romans, with far greater success, being,
indeed, the more practical people, impressed Latin on the
greater part of the old world, in a way that has made, as
we know, an absolutely indelible impression on almost all
Western European tongues.

Then again there is a decided ethical side to the problem
in the fact that, as Humboldt puts it, language should not
be considered as a dead but as a living thing ; for it is ever
creative (he speaks, of course, of languages in actual use), and
he adds, " human thought elaborates itself with the progress
of intelligence ".   This is profoundly true.   The way in which
words while expressing ideas often *react* on our minds, and
lead to the evolution of new ideas, shows in an emphatic
way that language is a *creative*, as well as an intellectually
organising force.   That language, too, has a strong tendency
to assimilate *or be assimilated* is indisputable, and verbally,
as we all know, language is in a constant state of flux, one
tongue borrowing from another, so that were it not for the
difficulties of pronunciation and the peculiarities of grammatical construction, we might very well anticipate a time,
when in the natural course of things, all languages would be

as it were fused together. We have been told of the "ancient Hebrew" clad in mysteries, the "learned Greek," the "eloquent Roman," the "Tuscan grave," the "braving Spanish," and the "smooth-tongued French"; and not to weary the reader, it may be at once said that every language is more or less indebted to other languages for some, if not for many, of its salient qualities.

The world has of late been more amused than really interested, by the absurd efforts of certain Continental savants to compose a universal language, a thing that may result from natural processes, but which cannot, I believe, be artificially brought about. There have been already a great many books written on the subject of the language of the future. In 1847, Mr. James Bradshaw brought out his "scheme for making the English language the international language of the world"; some three years later there was published a treatise on the *Probable future position of the English Language.* Then, in the third volume of the *Quarterly Journal of Science,* 2nd series, is a very important paper on the subject by Mr. William E. A. Axon, and in a current volume of his, entitled *Stray Chapters on Literature, Folk-lore and Histology,* a remarkable paper entitled *English—the dominant Language of the Future.* After reverting to the time when Latin was a kind of universal language among the educated, and when subsequently Spanish enterprise in colonial sentiment bid fair to make Spanish the language of the New World, Mr. Axon collates a variety of highly interesting and elucidatory matter in reference to the probable prospects of the English language. Max Müller, we are reminded, reckons the number of living languages and dialects at nine hundred in round numbers; and we do not know what may be the latent power of Russian, which is spoken by a population now rapidly increasing. It is certain, however, that Oriental tongues do not make progress; and although when, in 1783, Rivarol

gained the prize of the Berlin Academy for his dissertation
on the universality of the French language, two mighty factors have since come into powerful and accelerative operation
which very clearly point to the predominance of a language
which is at once the strongest and the most flexible and the
most assimilative of all tongues—viz., the English. It has
been well said that English unites the Romance and Teutonic
stocks, nay, it is far more, for as a language it has assimilated
to itself and still assimilates more copiously from all the
other tongues of the world, than any other European tongue.
In 1883 Mr. Barham Zincke calculated the progress of the
English language thus. He stated that in 1880 the statistics
stood as follows : United Kingdom, 35,000,000 speakers of
English ; United States, 50,000,000 ; Canada, 4,000,000 ;
Australia, 3,000,000 ; and South Africa, etc., 1,000,000.
Taking the ascertained rate of increase in these populations
as constant, Mr Zincke concluded that in 1980, only one
century later, the account would stand thus : United Kingdom, 70,000,000 ; United States, 800,000,000 ; Canada,
64,000,000 ; Australia, 48,000,000 ; South Africa, etc.,
16,000,000 ; bringing up a grand total to about a thousand
millions. Against this there is the competition of the seven
principal European languages ; but it must be remembered that no one of these is in the least likely to absorb
the others, and the expansiveness in point of population can
hardly be equal to that of America, Australasia, and South
Africa. It is pretty certain that the time is not far distant
when the states of Mexico will be absorbed into the great
American Union, giving a fresh impetus to the English
language over an extensive region, and as New Zealand
grows to be the dominant commercial power of the whole
Pacific, and probably the possessor of most of the Islands
of Polynesia, there will be a proportionate extension of the
English language operating on the Spanish littoral of South
America. I have myself no doubt, that supposing things

continue much as they are, during the century to come, the population of Australasia may be very much greater than the 48,000,000 assigned by Mr. Zincke. It will be nearer a hundred millions, and probably, by then, a considerable number of English-speaking settlers will be in New Guinea, of which the highlands are healthy and fertile, while many other islands of the Malayan Archipelago will be in all probability successfully colonised by men of British blood. It is probable, however, that owing to the settlement of Australasia by English-speaking people, the English language will, in another generation, if represented by red, say, on a philological map of the world, spread a broad prevailing band from the British Isles right across the whole of the North American Continent, including Cuba, which is sure, sooner or later, to add one more star to the banner of George Washington, across the Pacific, covering all Polynesia, Australasia, most of the islands up to Burmah and India, while by then, the tongue of the Anglo-Saxon will doubtless be quite familiar far north of the Zambesi in Africa. We may fairly assume, too, that English will, by the ever accelerative process of constant literary assimilation and absorption have then taken to itself a still larger proportion of the best words of the principal European languages. If we could summon up, in illustration of this continual process of adaptation, a series of practical printers for, say, the past two centuries, engaged in English printing offices, we should then see how ceaseless has been the process of appropriation of foreign words, and how those words which for a certain time have been "set up" as foreign, gradually lose their inverted commas, their distinctive italics or continental spelling, and are finally accepted by compositor and press-reader—good, if rough and unscholarly, judges in such things—as veritable English at last!

It is a long while since Spenser told us that Dan Chaucer was "a well of English undefiled," but ever since the

Pilgrim Fathers first approached the storm-beaten shore of Massachusetts, the destiny of the English language as the dominant tongue of the future world was fixed, and the settlement of Australia by England confirmed this destiny, humanly speaking, beyond all revocation.

To the writer of the future, and the not very distant future either, this ceaseless expansiveness, assimilation, and general enrichment of English holds out a truly splendid prospect. For one thing it offers to those who can reach it, the very largest *contemporary* audience that writer can possibly have, one infinitely larger than any of the whole past of human history, and infinitely greater than can be attained to by any three of the competing tongues, if any tongues really *do* compete with English, and thus it follows that the commanding masterpieces of the English literature to come will circulate beyond anything of the past. Let us trust that the men and women who have this unbounded influence will use it only to good and pure and lofty ends, and that they will ever be informed by the spirit which moved Words-worth to exclaim—

> We must be free or die, who speak the tongue
> Which Shakespeare spake; the faith and morals hold
> Which Milton held

VIII.—PUNCTUATION AND PROOF-READING.

Success in any pursuit is no trifling matter, and yet, if carefully analysed, success will often be found to be an aggregation of trifles One of the details that authors should not neglect is punctuation. This is a thing neglected to an extraordinary and often disastrous degree. Writing should be good and clear in every MS, spelling correct, and punctuation ought to be carefully attended to. It is far too much a custom to rely on compositors and printers' readers, but it is not their duty to punctuate, and often they have not the capacity. It is said that Lord Byron could not punctuate, which means that he would not take the trouble to learn. He knew what he intended to convey to his readers, and punctuation is only a means to that end. Jeffrey, the famous editor of the *Edinburgh Review*, was particularly clever at punctuation, and so is Dr. O. W. Holmes. The importance of punctuation is often very great. Most of us have heard of the unfortunate clergyman who, through a manifest error in the placing of a comma, was reported as saying—

"Why only last Sabbath, in this holy house, a woman fell from one of those seats while I was preaching the gospel in a state of beastly intoxication".

Of course this blunder was due to the putting the comma after house instead of after gospel, although attention to punctuation here would have suggested, as it so often does, the advantage of altering a sentence open to such awkward misconstruction, and making it read thus—

"Why only last Sabbath, in this holy house, while I was preaching the gospel, a woman fell from one of those seats in a state of beastly intoxication".

It is true that careful punctuation may remove an ambiguity, but it is better far in such cases to alter the construction. Often and often have I in proof-correcting had to point out to careless writers that the only way to make their matter read properly was to *recast* some portions. I have seen much time and thought fruitlessly wasted on an awkward sentence which really required casting afresh.

It may not be generally known, perhaps, that the contract for lighting Liverpool was made void (1819) by misplacing a comma in the advertisement, which ran—

"The lamps at present are about 4050, and have in general two spouts each, composed of not less than twenty threads of cotton". The comma followed instead of *preceding* the word *each*, and so seriously altered the meaning.

17

In the well-known instance, "The prisoner said the witness was a convicted thief," we have an example of how easily a newspaper reporter may slip into libel quite innocently. The sentence is right enough when punctuated properly, thus: "The prisoner, said the witness, was a convicted thief".

Punctuation is simply division of writing into sentences, and of these into members and clauses, in order to render the *meaning* clear. The ancients, it is well known, had but little acquaintance with points, or employed them only, when used at all, for rhetorical effect.

It is said that punctuation according to sense was invented by the Alexandrine Aristophanes, a famous grammarian. The art, however, somehow fell into utter neglect, and it was not restored until the time of Charlemagne, who appointed Alcuin and Warnefried to undertake the work. At first only a point called stigma was employed, and sometimes a line. The present system is very nearly that introduced by the great Venetian printer, Marentius, in the latter part of the sixteenth century.

The chief marks are the comma (,), the semicolon (,), the colon (:) (not very much used), the period or full stop (.), the dash (—), the note of exclamation (!), and that of interrogation (?).

The comma is the shortest pause, and is a cut-off, as in such a sentence as, "It was bright, yet obscure in some parts". The comma serves for parentheses, as, "This man, considered simply as a soldier, was worthy of all praise". The comma marks also phrases of an adjectival, adverbial, or participial kind. The semicolon is a longer pause, and properly indicates a half member of a sentence, thus: "The ships were in extreme peril; for the river was low, and the only navigable channel ran very near the left bank". In truth the writers, of whom there are many now, who indulge in short sentences, do so at the cost of semicolons, putting a period where other writers would use the semicolon, and commencing a new sentence. The colon is very little used now. The full stop ends a sentence. The dash marks an unexpected turn in a sentence, or an unlooked-for interruption, and the note of exclamation is used after an outburst of any emotion or to denote extreme surprise. The interrogation is used to ask a question.

Two very good text-books on the subject are Mr. A. Arthur Reade's practical treatise on English composition, entitled *How to write English*, and a more elaborate work by Henry Beadnell, entitled *Spelling and Punctuation*, and going most thoroughly into the whole details of correct punctuation.

In proof-correcting, practice is everything, but the learner will find the printer, if he can have access to him, will show him "how it is done" better than a book. If a word or words should be left out, write the omitted word or words in the margin and draw a line to the place where you wish the insertion to be made. Take care not to draw the line *over*, but make it go *between* the lines. Mark the place with the caret ∧. Should you wish to omit some word or words, draw a line through them and make a "*d*" in the margin, or write the full word "delete". Should you afterwards find that something marked out ought to remain, place a line of dots underneath and write in the margin "stet,"— "let it stand". If a letter is upside down—a common thing—make a little ┿ at the place, and in the margin a kind of curly ℮ upside down. Should two words be too close to each other, or a part of one word be attached to another, make a mark at the place and in the margin draw a figure like the cross-trees of a ship's mast ♯ To draw two letters together that have become separated, place the marks ⊃ in the margin opposite the place. Italics are marked with one line under, thus <u>italic</u>, small capitals *two* lines, and large capitals *three* lines. A new paragraph is marked [and the letters N. P. should be placed in the margin. If you wish to suppress a division into paragraphs and to make it read as one, write in the margin the words "run on," and draw a line from the last word in the first to the first word in the second paragraph. If it be desired to shift the position of a word or words, surround the word or words with a loop, and draw the tail to the place where the new insertion is to be made. Write in the margin "*trs.*" which means "transpose". Sometimes one letter is larger than the rest through the type being mixed accidentally with that of a larger letter. This is indicated in the proof by writing against it "*w f.*," which means "wrong fount". When it is desired to change a capital into ordinary letters, draw a line through the capital and write in the margin "*l. c.*" meaning "lower case," this being the tray of type nearest to the compositor; the "upper case" containing the capitals which not being in such constant use are farther from his easy reach. These are the principal forms of corrections

There are numerous other points which arise in extensive proof-reading, and some of these are too technical to be understood properly through the medium of a book. Those cited above are quite enough for the young author's purpose at first, and should enable him to correct an ordinary proof fairly well. Errors are divided into those known as "printer's" and those as "author's" errors. The latter ought to be few indeed, the less the better, and the gain in all ways of only sending clean, correctly paragraphed, and punctuated MS. or "copy" to the printers is exceedingly great. Many living writers are much to be commended for their carefulness in this respect. Miss Braddon writes beautifully clear "copy," but some preserve the foolish old notion that it is a sign of superiority to scrawl and write as nearly illegibly as practicable. Dean Stanley was a dreadfully bad writer, and the famous Paley wrote a fearful hand. He never crossed a "t" nor dotted an "i," his "e's," "a's," and "o's," "n's," "u's," and "w's," were identical, and

usually his " h's " were like his " n's " ! It is said that some
manuscript of his is extant, which is believed to be
absolutely illegible ! Do *all* just as well as you can. I cannot too emphatically express that as the best advice that
can be given to the young aspirant. As to " copy " or
manuscript, never *roll* it. Let it be flat, and, if possible,
unfolded. It will be better reading for editor, publisher's
reader, and compositor. Nothing is so exasperating as a
curly manuscript that requires to be forcibly flattened, and
on the least relaxation of pressure closes like a spring. It
makes everybody who has to deal with it thoroughly *cross*,
and let me remind the young writer that it is much to his
disadvantage to begin by making an editor cross ! Use
envelopes if possible large enough to hold the sheets of your
MS. *unfolded.* They will then lie nice and inviting before
the eye of the editor or the publisher's reader and adviser,
and in all probability will give an initial pleasure, and this
is no small thing Remember that your work goes before a
stranger who is working in all probability for his living. His
time to him is money, and he does not want to waste it in
flattening out curly, snake-like coils of MS. which, perhaps,
may prove to be hopeless rubbish when reduced to a legible
level. Use black ink on white paper. Blue paper is
abominable to the reader, and is sure to annoy. Leave space
between the lines ; paper is cheap, and everything that you
can do technically to make matters easy and agreeable to
your arbiter and judge is helpful to *you,* and *pro tanto* increases your chance of finding acceptance. Avoid all
affectation. Be simple, plain, and direct. Do not pretend
that you have only " dashed " this tale off as the inspiration
came, or that you send a trifle of a poem which you think—
although unworthy, etc.—may fill a corner. Write briefly,
and to the purpose. If you want to be paid, say so. You
are appealing to business men. There is no sentiment in
this part of the literary life. It is exactly like a transaction

in Mincing Lane produce You send your goods in sample or in bulk, and the recipients test them by rough and ready rules to see if they are suited to the special requirements of that particular literary market. Do not be discouraged by failure. Try again, and do *something better* That is the certain way to succeed. Keep your rejected manuscripts. They may come in at a future time, or they may "work up," or be capable of being added to something better. If later, by the light of experience and more sense, you find them rubbish, you can easily burn them, and, at all events, have the satisfaction of knowing that they have aided you in attaining to a higher level of literary excellence.

Exercise care and judgment in sending matter to publishers and editors. A manuscript that might please the reader of one publisher would perhaps fail to obtain the approval of another firm It is useless sending stories to any kind of business or class publication, unless they specially include recreative columns, and efforts to place Christmas literature should be made by the end of the summer. Note well the terms of rejection. Sometimes it is plain that rejection is due not to the want of merit in the matter offered, but from other reasons. Many of the magazines are practically supplied with good literature for from a year to two years in advance. A certain writer once sent a tale to a certain quarter, and had it returned in due course, but on it was written " A very powerful story ". That encouraged him to " try again," and eventually that manuscript found its way into print. Time, place, and fitness are all important factors. Your manuscript may go where there is a plethora of much better stuff with prior claims for acceptance, and another quarter remain untried where an opening exists. Try— try—try is the only thing to be done in the face of refusal. Accentuate and strengthen your efforts by *improving* the quality of your work, and, by dint of repetition, you must succeed at last.

IX—MAKING A NAME IN LITERATURE.

How to make a name in literature is undoubtedly a very fascinating subject of inquiry. The desire for the *digito monstrari*, the hankering after the bubble reputation, is at the bottom of most of the literary ambition of the young. It is not strange. There is a singular fascination in thus proving the might of the pen, and suddenly emerging out of complete obscurity into the fulness of intellectual glory *in excelsis*. This desire, so far as it really stimulates the young to do good work and to enrich the mind with noble and refining studies, is most strongly to be commended, and although the anticipated fame may never come, something hereafter to be recognised as a thing far better may be gained. Is it not Schiller who says—

> What shall I do to be for ever known ?
>   Thy duty ever—

and then he adds significantly—

> Think'st thou, perchance, that they remain unknown
>   Whom *thou* knowest not !
> By angel trumps in heaven their praise is blown ;
>   Divine their lot !

But to drop down to the practical, often the great, question of how to make a name in literature resolves into how to make a name that shall render the matter that goes forth under it marketable. Mr. Edmund Gosse, who is certainly well qualified to speak on points like these, writing in the *New York Forum*, very justly remarks that the " circumstances under which all the various degrees of fame are reached are closely analogous, and what is true of the local celebrity is true, relatively, of a Victor Hugo or of a Tennyson. The importance of the reputation is shown by the expanse of the area it covers, not by the curve of its advance. The circle of a great man's fame is extremely wide, but it only repeats on a vast scale the phenomena attending on the fame of a small man."

This is very true. It is also true that fame and monetary success do not invariably go hand in hand. Look at Mr. Herbert Spencer. He ranks very high in any list of English writers remarkable for originality of thought, but the *sales* of his books have never been large. Mr. Gosse goes on to observe—"To take only a few of the most illustrious Englishmen of letters, it is matter of common notoriety that the sale of the books of, say, Mr. Swinburne and Mr. Leslie Stephen, the Bishop of Oxford (Dr. Stubbs) and Mr. Lecky, by no means responds to the lofty rank which each of these authors takes in the esteem of educated people throughout the Anglo-Saxon world ".

Then there is the other side of the picture. Martin Tupper was once more popular than Tennyson, and Eliza Cook sold infinitely better than Robert Browning! The fact is, popularity and absolute literary merit are not exactly one and the same thing. He who would write for the many must necessarily reap the largest *immediate* reward. As a rule, that which wins instant recognition loses it as rapidly. A splendid blaze of fireworks will bring numbers of people into the street who would not stir a yard to see

> The Pleiads rising through the mellow shade
> Glitter like a swarm of fire-flies tangled in a silver braid

Which of the two would win the biggest audience in the Park—Punch and Judy or a recitation from the *Fairy Queen?*

Mr. Gosse goes on to say—" In literature, at least as much as in other professions, the race is not to the swift, although the battle must eventually be to the strong. There is a blossoming, like that of forced annuals, which pays for its fulness and richness by a plague of early sterility. What the young writer of wholesome ambition should pray for is, not to flash like a meteor on the astonished world of fashion, but by solid and admirable writing slowly to win a place which has a firm and wide basis."

This is quite correct. At the same time it is not all who can afford to wait and toil on unrecognised, doing only solid but hardly appreciated work for the " fit few " rather than the fickle and superficial many, and thence much work of the pot-boiling kind must be done. Even this type of work may be well or ill done, like many other things of the kind, and here those who are destined to rise hereafter will surely show the mettle of which they are made. The main thing is to observe the truly golden rule of doing that which lies nearest to your literary hand first, and doing it as well as ever you can. If you have but a thin tale to produce, pivoting on a well-worn incident, and ordered, perhaps, to utilise old blocks, you can at least put in good effective writing. Remember the example by the late Lord Lytton of Leonard Fairfield, in *My Novel*, the village genius, who, when he has to write for bread, and anonymously too, still puts into the taskwork assigned to him of his best. Be generous in pouring out good measure. It may be depended on that "saving oneself for a fitter occasion" has been the ruin of many a young writer. " Oh," I have known such a one say, " I cannot write my best under such conditions as those. I'm not going to make such a rag as that paper." It is likely enough that this young gentleman had not in him the making of any " rag " of a paper, but the spirit prompting the remark exists in many, and it is an element against success. Be loyal to whoever employs your pen. Once that is engaged, exert your utmost powers, and oft it will be found that in pouring out what you fondly thought your best you have but laid bare within ores of unsuspected richness that you may work for something better I have a firm belief that in matters literary reaping close makes good future crops. If it does not, why then the vocation should be abandoned A weakling, capable of only a spasm or two, will never do for the long and strenuous fight that has to be fought in these days to win a front place in the army of the world's competitive writers.

It was a firm knowledge of this that caused Carlyle to dictate in his old age what, superficially considered, seems a rather unkind letter. It appears that a young gentleman who proposed to adopt literature as a profession asked Carlyle for his advice on the subject, and received the following note dictated by the Chelsea sage to his niece—

" Dear Sir,—Mr. Carlyle bids me say that he has never in his life heard a madder proposal than the one you have just made to him. He would advise you by no means to quit your present employment. He thinks it would only be a degree less foolish to throw yourself from the top of the Monument in the hope of flying.—I am, dear sir, yours truly, MARY CARLYLE AITKEN."

We can almost hear the old sage chuckle over this missive, which I must observe, was just a little unfeeling. Mr. G. H. Lewes gave—I believe, to the same applicant—a very different reply. He wrote—

" My advice is by all means not to throw yourself on literature for a living. Very splendid talents and wide knowledge are often incompetent to secure bread and cheese, and except in the department of journalism there is but a perilous outlook for anyone who has not already proved that his talents are commercially valuable. Now, it seems to me on this question you can decide for yourself. Assuming that your present employment is intolerable to you, and that you have a strong bent towards literature, I would urge you to ascertain decisively whether editors and publishers are willing and eager to pay you for your writing. If they are, you can form some estimate of your probable success when you devote your whole energies to literature. Meanwhile, you can do what hundreds of others are doing— namely, cultivate literature in your leisure hours, and try by

your productions to increase your income, and find a foot-
ing for yourself on the shifting sands of periodicals. To
give up any honourable employment on the vague chance of
success in literature is what all rational men would advise
against. You must not confound your hopes and wishes
with the conditions of success It is for you a question of
pounds, shillings, and pence, not of literary activity, and
that question, you, like everyone else, have the means of
settling by simply offering editors and publishers what you
have written. Believe me, both editors and publishers are,
for their own sakes, eager to accept and pay for whatever
promises to be commercially valuable, and no one will
accept work that does not seem to promise such commercial
advantage.—Yours truly, G. H. LEWES "

There is much sound sense in this advice. The aspirant
in literature can do what is not practicable in other vocations, he can *try* his powers fully without actually
committing himself to the calling of a man of letters before
he is *quite* sure of his fitness therefor Or he can ground
himself upon journalism as so many have done, and wait,
watch, and work for his opportunity to emerge thence some
day into the more tempting domains of book-land

A high authority declares that he who purposes to be an
author should first be a *student*, and another deep thinker
says, never write on a subject without having first read
yourself full on it, and never read on a subject till you have
thought yourself hungry on it. These two excerpts fully
justify, I think, all the main contentions I have made
throughout this manual. Of course the *reading* requisite to
writing on any subject need not be that of *books*. It is
better far when it is the reading of *things*. You visit, say a
manufactory, and *read* there—the expression is rightly
enough employed—the information furnished by the various
machines and apparatus there, and you listen to the explana-
tions offered. You *read* the out-door aspects of nature

Gaze up, perhaps, at the sky, which as Ruskin tells us truly enough is so strangely neglected, although it is just that part of creation in which nature has done more to *please* man than in any other of her works. The thought less vacant minded just see that the sky is clear or clouded as the case may be. The poet glances up and gathers thence a thought and tells us that he saw—

> The blue sky
> So cloudless, clear, and purely beautiful
> That God alone was to be seen in Heaven.

That is reading nature's face to some purpose. In like manner you should, if a writer, read the various aspects of all forms of still life. Learn from *direct* observation to distinguish the different trees like the old English poet who sings of—

> The gloomy pine, the poplar blue,
> The yellow beech, the sombre yew,
> The slender fir that taper grows,
> The sturdy oak with broad spread boughs.

Or take, read over, and meditate on this exquisite metrical monograph on trees from the *Fairy Queen*—

> Much can they praise the trees so straight and high—
> The sailing pine, the cedar proud and tall,
> The vine prop elm, the poplar never dry;
> The builder oak, sole king of forest all;
> The aspen, good for staves; the cypress funeral;
> The laurel, mead of mighty conquerors
> And poets sage; the fir that weepeth still;
> The willow, worn of forlorn paramours;
> The yew, obedient to the bender's will;
> The birch for shafts, the sallow for the mill;
> The myrrh, sweet bleeding in the bitter wound,
> The warlike beech, the ash for nothing ill;
> The fruitful olive, and the plaintane round,
> The carverholme, the maple seldom inward sound.

Study the aspects of the sea, the river, the lake, and the flowers of the field. Then read what Ruskin writes on such themes as the common grass or a stray pebble.   Watch well those you meet at home and abroad and in the street. Try and note all mannerisms, personal peculiarities, and distinct traits   When once the habit is thoroughly formed of looking for these things, the faculty for taking mental notes to be stored up in the memory begins to grow, and, strengthened by use, may be relied on after a while to work almost automatically.   You will acquire the same sort of observing power that resides in the eye of the painter, and you will learn to discriminate nice shades of difference in persons just as surely as the skilled musician discriminates between the most soft and refined passages in melody.   This habit, first of watching for and then detecting peculiarities of any kind, and finally of noting them mentally, is really nothing but a sort of reading, and it is obviously the best of all kinds for the writer, as the results are really *his*   In a word, it means originality.   This is what Goethe had in mind when he wrote, " People are always talking about originality ; but what do they mean ?   As soon as we are born the world begins to work upon us, and this goes on to the end."   Exactly so, but the best writer is the one who reads more clearly and quickly the aspect and phases, great and small, of *all* his physical environment, and who makes the happiest guesses at the moral and spiritual truths hidden beneath, and often peeping half through.

New openings for bookwork in the future are likely to appear   For one thing, I am confident that before the dawn of the twentieth century a Copyright Convention will be established with the United States, and that vast field for authorship will be in a small part open for English writers. Then Australia is rapidly advancing in population, and has a high percentage of readers, while even Canada and South Africa and other regions where the English language prevails will form new outlets for the books yet to be written.   In America it is not difficult to see the day when the population will be a hundred millions of English-speaking men and women—a prodigious audience—and, indeed, much as authors have multiplied of late, and much as they are multiplying now, it appears as though *readers* must multiply still faster. The multitudinous demands of highly-civilised life, with its business and pleasures, its enormous claims on time, and its tremendous competitions, will on the whole, I think, render the training necessary to make a professional writer too exacting to be taken up by any but the fit, and as the general disposition towards material ease and increased recreation increases, the vast majority of the well-to-do community will infinitely prefer the pleasures of reading to the toils of authorship.

It may be well, perhaps, to inquire briefly what is the most popular fiction in the United States? This is no easy question with such a vast country, but at all events, we can answer the question so far as the Empire city goes. A writer in the U. S. A. *Independent*, dealing with fiction in New York, says—

" *Uncle Tom's Cabin* was the book most in demand in 1887, last year (1888), *Ben Hur;* next to that the greatest demand is for *Monte Cristo*. The circulation of complete editions and separate plays of Shakespeare is, however, usually as large as any work of fiction. Of the separate plays the *Merchant of Venice, Romeo and Juliet,* and *Richard III.* are the most popular. The works of Charles Dickens are in great demand, *Pickwick* heading the list, while *Oliver Twist* and *David Copperfield* are great favourites. Jules Verne's *Mysterious Island* and *Twenty Thousand Leagues under the Sea* come usually next. The other novel-writers mostly in demand are Thackeray, Scott, Mrs. Craik, Sue (*The Wandering Jew*), Charlotte Brontë, Black, Mrs. Holmes, Hawthorne, Samuel Lover, Ebers, Charles Reade, Wilkie Collins, Marryat, and Bulwer."

This certainly evinces a very catholic, healthy, and highly

commendable taste.   As to the American novel itself, that
is unique in some respects.   A writer in the *Saturday
Review* remarks—

"With the rapidity of development which characterises
the century, American fiction has, in certain directions,
taken on the infirmities of old age before it has over-
passed the crudities of youth.   Or, perhaps, one might
fancy it has borrowed the corruption of older communities
before it has had time to attain its own richest maturity.
Some new American writers of novels betray ominous
tokens of the influence of the French realistic school.
We say ominous, because any young and growing art
injures itself by borrowing modes and methods alien to
its original nature.   Better its own awkwardnesses of
immature youth than the brilliant improprieties stolen
from France, which sit uncomfortably on unaccustomed
limbs "

This is rather a one-sided view, however   It has been
more aptly said that the difference in quality and effect of
the American and English novel of to-day is like the
difference between two fires, one of which has been lit but
lately, the other has burnt for long.   It is certain that the
contemporary novelist is rich in his intellectual methods,
and at his best, he studies, analyses, and sets forth the
minds and hearts of his characters more than the average
English novelist usually does.   He, the American fictionist,
is certainly distinguished by the firm grasp he has of
character, and this imparts great vitality to his work.   Let
American novelists only keep clear of the corruption of the
French method of dealing with realities in fiction, and their
novels to come will be marked with high qualities and
probably help to still further uplift the art of the contemporary novelist.   Anyway there is a rich heritage awaiting
the future novelists who shall write for the millions of
readers of the new world which appears so fully to justify

Bishop Berkeley's prophetic line penned several generations. ago, asserting that

Westward the course of Empire takes its way.

An Empire, indeed, but emphatically an Empire of the English-speaking peoples.   And now, a word as to the main theme of the novels to be.

De Quincey it is, who says that a false ridicule has settled on novels and on young ladies as readers of novels.   He goes on to vindicate the contention that after all, the great commanding event, the one sole revolution in a woman's life is marriage.   This was written more than sixty years ago, and much has happened since then.   Novelists have been of late discussing what are called the limits of English fiction —that is, three novelists of reputation, Mrs. Lynn Linton, who "deplores" what she deems unwarrantable restrictions; Mr. Besant, who very properly vindicates the sacredness of the family; and Mr. Thomas Hardy, who seems somewhat of Mrs Linton's way of thinking.   In reality, it seems to the impartial on-looker that very few restrictions do exist now, and the present tendency is decidedly towards a licence which is very much to be regretted   I quite think that Mr. Besant is right in the main, but it has ever seemed to me, judging by the vast number of novels that practically end with matrimony, that a fine field exists for those writers who will deal with their hero and heroine during married life and take the reader completely into the confidence of home life from its most interior stand-point.   There are so many obvious openings here for action and for introspective work and for showing, as an example, how some people as they grow older, develop entirely new and unsuspected phases of character which could not possibly be anticipated by either   Here, and in like directions, lie new and promising strata of incident and possibly the germs of a. somewhat new type of domestic novel.

Then, as hinted already, in the section devoted to the drama, there is probably a very increasing opening in the direction of the stage, for those who possess a dramatic genius. It is true that at present the public seem very apathetic towards the purely literary side of the drama, and just as the novel has killed the narrative poem, so has the novel in a manner killed the literary drama. A writer in the periodical *East and West*, says—

" There is no denying the fact that prose fiction in the form of novels has taken the place of dramatic fiction in the favour of the reading public. The result of this has been that what used to give literary quality to our dramas now goes to give dramatic power to our novels ; and our most capable writers of fiction no longer attempt to give it to us in dramatic dress. The natural consequence is to be found in the present state of affairs, in which our most successful playwrights are not men of such literary attainments as to be capable of producing plays of a quality to enrich our dramatic literature , while, as a further corollary, the public has from forced desuetude lost its taste for reading plays Thus we are brought round again lamentably to our starting point. ' Nobody writes plays worth reading ! ' cries the one side. ' Nobody would read them if we did ! ' retorts the other How are they to be reconciled ? Two facts there are upon which we can lay hold. The one, which must be accepted and made the best of, is that novels have at present taken the place of plays for reading purposes. The other is that our men of letters who attempt dramatic writing are too apt to ignore the necessity of a thorough acquaintance with the *technique* of the stage, which they must have if they are to produce plays which will be effective in representation—and it seems very unlikely that plays will nowadays stand any chance of being read unless they can satisfy this last condition."

In point of fact there *is* a public who reads good dramatic literature, and enjoys it too. Numbers of readers are multiplying so rapidly, that groups of persons of special tastes formerly to be counted by the score, now number hundreds and even thousands.   There is, in one word, more of everything.   The writer cited above goes on to say—

" There are many signs that recognition would more often be made of the intrinsic qualities of plays did they more often deserve it, and I cannot but think that any efforts to render them more deserving of it would be appreciated and welcomed.   To take at random one or two dramatists who have made some attempt to render their work a little worthy of a place in literature :—W. S. Gilbert has published his plays, and the care he has taken to produce really creditable work has been recognised ; Wills' *Olivia* admittedly possesses great merit, although his *Faust* was not calculated to raise his literary reputation ; Robert Buchanan's *Sophia* and *Joseph's Sweetheart* are a good pair of adaptations, in which the spirit of the original has on the whole been preserved with considerable literary feeling, in spite of certain liberties ; Alfred Calmour's *Amber Heart* was also an effort in the right direction , and more recently we have again had an opportunity of enjoying excellent work in *The Ballad-Monger*, the immediate success of which was a gratifying proof that the public can discern what is good."

My own impression is that there is a public ready to appreciate good *literary* dramatic work both on and off the stage, so to express it, for are there not many people who have a variety of objections to going to the theatre, and who yet greatly relish all the intellectualities and passions of a fine play ?   I know some who will not go to the theatre because they want a play to make them *think* and *feel,* and few of the current new pieces put on the stage nowadays do either.   Some will not go unless they can do so easily—*i.e.,* in a carriage and to a numbered seat—and this is far too costly a pleasure for many who can readily give five shillings for a fine poetic or philosophic drama like *Don Carlos* or

Wallenstein. This is but tentative Still I incline to the belief that for real dramatic ability writing for the stage is not by any means so hopeless as some seem to think it is.

There is, too, the humbler walk of writing plays for the drawing-room, for school entertainments, and the like. Of late not a few of these have appeared, and though they cannot be reasonably expected to win much reputation or to bring much pecuniary gain, they are not to be altogether despised as a means whereby the young dramatic writer may try and train his powers, and at the same time earn a little money.

How to push a work of any kind when once launched is a problem to many. Primarily one would say it must depend on merit, but by no means altogether. Merit has its season as well as fruit, and may appear at the wrong time, when no one has any appetite left. *Some* sort of merit there must be in aught that succeeds greatly, but it does not follow by any means that where there is no success there is no merit. Time and circumstance, a happy fitness with some passing whim of the public, may determine the success of a work. A letter from a popular statesman in the newspapers, " drawn " by some clever arrangement, may make a work, and throw into the shade another of equal or greater merit. Unless a book has real *intrinsic* worth it cannot be *sustained* as a success, but it may be puffed up long enough for paying purposes, which are, after all, the main ends of publishers, and perhaps of most authors Advertisement has much to do with success, but a publisher of much experience once drew my attention to the way in which all really phenomenal successes seem to run on quite irrespective of advertisements or of reviews. Indeed, it may well be said that in *great* successes the reviewers are oft-times little else than a chorus or an echo, and look on rather than aid in the movement. " But," said my friend the publisher, " what I *do* believe in is the recommendation of readers." He then went on to remark that, in his opinion, all marked successes were due to *readers* finding a book so good, useful, or interesting, that they could not help asking those whom they knew to read the book too.　There is much truth in this　If a book is once out and pleases readers, it is almost sure to sell.　But to attain this it must be above the average, and possess some special and salient features　Private recommendation is of great value in the case of books, but while some young writers shrink from asking this of their friends, it often happens that friends have a kind of distaste to recommend a book unless it is the work of a stranger !

X —General Advice.

Other things equal, a novel not too short, well conceived and properly executed, has perhaps the best chance with enterprising publishers.　Do not be disheartened by failure. Think how often some of her MS. came back to Charlotte Bronte.　By the way, it is curious that the successful story, *Mr. Barnes of New York*, according to the *New York Critic*, was rejected by so many publishers that at last its author seeing works he knew to be inferior circulating well, issued his story himself and had the satisfaction of seeing the sale go up to a hundred and fifty thousand copies.

Authors often owe much to their publishers.　As a writer in the *Daily Telegraph* aptly observed, the relations between publishers and authors have not always been so strained and perverse as some facile critics have supposed.　It is true that Campbell praised the First Napoleon because he had ordered a publisher to be shot, and that Byron, or some equally cynical writer, once declared that Barabbas must have been in the book trade.　In contrast, however, to the story of that Osborne whom Johnson knocked down with a folio, saying, " Lie there, thou lump of lead," there are many instances of real friendship between the men of genius and those who made their works known to the world—notably

Elmsley, whom Gibbon honoured as one of the most instructive of friends and companions. In the days of Charles Rivington, who first established his business under the sign of "The Bible and the Crown," there was a poor vicar in a country parish who was anxious to have some sermons which had pleased his simple congregation produced in a more permanent form. When the publisher asked him the number of copies which he thought advisable, the vicar proceeded to enumerate the parishes in Great Britain which might be supposed to be hungering for his words of wisdom. "There are ten thousand parishes in the kingdom," said the clergyman, "and I think we might safely produce thirty-five thousand copies of my sermon." Charles Rivington humourously assented, and shortly afterwards sent him in a bill which stated that, while the number demanded entailed an expense of seven hundred and eighty-five pounds, the sermons sold had realised exactly one pound five shillings and sixpence. He afterwards explained to the worthy vicar that in reality he had only printed one hundred copies, as he knew better than the author the probable extent of the sale. A somewhat similar tale of kindness is told of Thomas Longman in 1728. He had published Ephraim Chambers' *Cyclopædia*, which was not only the parent of all our English dictionaries of universal knowledge, but also the direct cause of the *Encyclopédie* of Diderot and the French philosophers. When the author was ill, Mr Longman left jellies and other refreshments at every spot where the absent-minded man could least avoid seeing them, and paid him five hundred pounds over and above the stipulated price of his work. Then there is the well-known instance of true kindness in the history of *Lalla Rookh*. Moore employed the editor of the *Morning Chronicle*, Mr. Perry, to arrange terms with Thomas Longman. The ambassador delivered his opinion that Moore ought to receive for the future poem the largest price that had been given for such work at that time. "That," rejoined Longman, "was three thousand pounds." And no smaller sum, as a matter of fact, was paid to the Irish melodist for that composition which we now know by the name of *Lalla Rookh*. It ought also to be added that, though a previous perusal was demanded by the publisher, the price was paid before a line of the poem was written, and that Thomas Moore, commenting on the proceedings, delivered his opinion that "there has seldom occurred any transaction in which trade and poetry have shone so satisfactorily in each other's eyes".

The matter offered should always be in correspondence with the known character of the medium fixed on, and it is not unadvisable to write and ask if an opening exists for such and such a thing, assuming that it should be found quite of the required standard of excellence. Write briefly and to the purpose. Never attempt to interest strangers in the story of your aspirations, your early struggles, or how you have been impelled to write. Long letters are the terror of business men, and create an initial prejudice. You must be content to play an impersonal part at first. You, individually, are to those addressed less by far than the postman who carries your precious packet. How can you really expect that strangers, exceedingly busy and loaded with all kind of business cares, will take any special interest in you because you are possessed with a belief that you can write? They would simply say—if they said aught at all—better not by far, we have too many writers already; and obviously under such circumstances as these the best way is to write a business-like letter, pithy and to the purpose, and *then* you may perhaps awaken a little interest and even some touch of sympathy, as being held to be one who has not lost his senses on discovering or fancying that he has discovered in himself the existence of latent literary ability. Write like this — the more laconic the better — only be civil and courteous, and perfectly explicit. Do not employ fine words. I have known foolish young writers put out-of-the-way words in their letters to strangers simply to indicate that they knew the meaning of certain hard words! I need not say that such arts as these have a directly contrary effect to that intended, and only create disgust and cause annoyance. The work you can *do* is the thing and nothing else. All must depend on that. Publishers are among the busiest men of the times, the most hard working, and generally the most discerning of men. And they are as a body quite as honourable as any other commercial class. It is said they fleece many authors, but authors do not often comprehend the risk the publisher runs when he buys the MS. of a writer whose name is not such as to command large sales. A good book may not sell, or at all events not for a long time, and no man, however clever, can exactly tell beforehand with certainty what is, and what is not, likely to sell among matter of excellence. I am not speaking here of rubbish which is sure to be rejected. It is exceedingly difficult to say why, of a batch of meritorious books, there are often only one or two that "pay". A publisher would soon be ruined if he bought all the good things offered him. There is much, too, that reviewers will praise, and the public will not read What of Walter Savage Landor and his fine classic poetry and his still finer classic prose?— does it sell? Cases might be multiplied, and the publisher who buys only to sell again has to be ever vigilant that he does not hamper himself with heaps of works for which the actual reading world cares nothing.

At the outset, the magazines afford a good opening for purely literary work. Many book publishers issue these magazines, and after a young writer has had a few essays, or it may be tales, inserted in a popular periodical, he is in a far better position to propose something more ambitious to the publisher thereof, who may then recognise him as a professional writer. I have always found it best to send proposed subject and method of treatment first to the periodical in question. Very often the reply will be that the subject has been already done, or that it is already in other hands, for what *you* have thought of may well strike another writer. The essence of success in getting on thus far is to be vigilant and prompt. A writer taking up a weekly periodical noted that a lady writer was contributing a series on Scottish female poets. He instantly wrote to the editor, and stated that if arrangements had not been made for Scottish poets, he would be glad to contribute a series thereon, and this resulted in a request for a specimen, and subsequently the appearance of a series of six papers. The same writer gleaned some particulars of a Colonial friend of a sea-side place he had been staying at in Victoria—a place not then known—being a settler's house enlarged into a huge boarding establishment, on the sea coast. He sat down and wrote forthwith an account of a new Australian watering-place. He expatiated on all the beauties of the fern-tree gullies which went down to the shore, on the picnics on the sands, and on all the features that had been furnished by one who had stayed in what is a lovely spot, and the paper was accepted at once by a monthly magazine It was founded on fact illumined by fancy. This is only suggestive of how to seize on opportunities as they arise.

Keep a record of all you get printed, and be contented to rise slowly step by step. It is not one in a thousand who can succeed on the *per saltum* principle, and those who rise rapidly sometimes fall as quickly. Always be ready to help others. They may help you in unexpected ways. Do not spare pains. When you get an article accepted, always try and improve it if time permits. Do not regard the remuneration then, and say, " Oh, an article *bringing in only* a few shillings need not be very good ". Your work cannot be too good. Is it not a part of yourself? Let all of it whether signed or anonymous be honest and thorough, and *then* you may smile at fortune. Honesty ought not to be practised *because* it is the best policy, which it most assuredly is, but for its own sake, and, truly, to be honest is the easiest thing in the issue, just as an upright posture is easier than a stooping one. Finally, I would add, have no affectations of any kind either in yourself or in your work. Do not pretend that you cannot write unless under certain conditions. If it really be so, keep the fact to yourself, whom it concerns alone. Discerning persons will think less of you for all your talk of how here or there you had an inspiration, and you will really do yourself much harm, and perhaps injure your prospects of advancement. Remember that with true merit we nearly always find modesty, and it has been beautifully said that modesty gives to talent the same charm which chastity adds to beauty.

XI.—TITLES, INDEXING, ETC.

Titles, whether of books, essays, or brief articles, are matters of considerable importance, and require often much thought and care. It may not, perhaps, be generally known that in the fifteenth century books appeared without any title page at all, and until within the last two centuries, it was quite a conventional thing for an enterprising publisher to put as an "attraction" on his title pages, the name of some eminent man who had never contributed a line of the matter within!

Of old titles many were exceedingly curious and often of inordinate length. Thus, to cull but a few examples. In the seventeenth century, a book appeared, entitled "An antidote to the epidemical disorders of the times". The title was further wrought out as "Stand still; or a bridle for the times : a discourse tending to still the murmuring, settle the wavering, stay the wandering, strengthen the fainting".

Jeremy Taylor wrote a book, called "The Golden Grove, or choice manual, containing what is to be believed, practised, and desired, or prayed for". Another work, called "Milk and Honey," is a collection of Christian experiences. These are but samples of many. Some of the Puritan divines indited curious titles, indeed, such as this—"Eggs of Charity, layed by the chickens of the Covenant and boiled by the water of Divine Love". The added sub-title is quaint, and runs—"Take ye and eat". As most people know, Sir Walter Scott preferred titles that revealed as little as possible of the book they referred to, and all his titles are of the more or less uncommunicative kind. This was, by the way, the method of our early novelists. De Foe adopted brief titles—*Colonel Jack, Moll Flanders;* Richardson ran on short titles having in themselves no particular meaning, such as *Pamela, Clarissa Harlowe;* and the great Fielding gives us *Tom Jones, Joseph Andrews,* and more briefly still, *Amelia.* Dickens himself rather inclined to this laconic description of the contents of a book, but many writers have elected to ticket their work in as descriptive and informatory a way as possible. Cooper's *Spy, Prairie,* and the late Lord Lytton's *Harold, the last of the Saxon Kings,* or *Rienzi, the last of the Roman Tribunes,* sufficiently declare the general nature of the contents of the works, and undoubtedly are meant to raise expectations in the reader. Many titles are of an enigmatical character. Among contemporary examples may be cited such as these— *Skill wins Favour, Where the Dew falls in London, What might have been expected, Alas! The Blood White Rose,* and very many more of the same kind. Charles Reade indulged in some strange sensational titles, such as *Hard Cash, It is never too late to Mend,* while Wilkie Collins followed much in the same line.

No doubt a difficulty exists in many cases in title choosing, consequent on the variety of appropriated titles and the difficulty of steering clear of what has been already used.

For my own part, I am inclined to think that books make titles, and that titles in themselves are not of such great moment as some imagine.   Of course, some titles are radically bad, and of these I should say that the one cited above, *Skill Wins Favour*, is a silly title enough, and long-winded interludes such as " A brief and authentic account of the surprising adventures and experiences of " is a kind of thing to be carefully avoided.   Simplicity, combined with good taste, will generally best guide a writer as to titles Look at such a title as *Jane Eyre*. 'Tis but a name, yet what a fame has grown out of that simple name?   *My Novel* is an example of the eccentrically simple, and has likewise had a happy fate.   Truly, for the novel proper the difficulty of finding good titles is increasing.   The number of separate works of fiction is amazing, and so far must be *pro tanto* very encouraging to the young writer.   Many magazines are now appearing devoted to novels, great or small, and nothing else, and numerous serials now appear containing a complete novel in each issue.   It would be impossible to simply entitle all these merely by the names of their respective heroes and heroines, and hence we get such titles as *In the Wild March Morning*, the *House on the Marsh*, and a multitude of others. Broadly speaking, I should say the best title is a quiet announcement of the nature or purpose of the work.   Of course, there are exceptional cases where a title of a different type may be desirable, and a very sensational work must have a corresponding title, as in the case of *A Strange Manuscript found in a Copper Cylinder*, or the *Wreck of a World*, or *Dead Man's Rock*, or the *Treasure Tree ;* but in general I fancy quite as much is lost as is gained by what may be called the screaming-shrieking title now affected by some publishers   The thing is being much overdone, and too often expectations are thus raised, especially where the work is illustrated outside, which are hardly borne out by the text. Spasms of literature may well amuse for a moment, but they have no lasting force, and soon fade out of recollection. In choosing a title it is well for the inexperienced to seek advice of some one who has practical skill in such matters, and it is useful, too, as the young writer is very apt to hit on titles already appropriated. The registers at Stationers' Hall not being indexed, it is almost useless to apply there for information on this head. The title is the inscription at the very threshold of the book, the invitation for the reader to come in and settle down to be interested, entertained, edified, or instructed, as the case may be, and not unfrequently to be thoroughly bored, or even exasperated, by the miserable fare set before him. The regular arrangement, mechanically or technically speaking, of a book, is this —half-title, full title, dedication (if any), preface (if any), table of contents, the text itself, and finally an index, although this is often omitted. And here let me say a word as to indices. These are too often wanting. Many authors are unwilling and others are unable to compile them; but in general works, especially works of reference, the index is very important. Index-making is an art, but it is not exactly a mystery. The best way to compile a simple index is to cut up paper into slips about two inches by three inches, and write on each the subject of reference. Put the clue word first. Thus, suppose you wished to index " The best way to compile a simple index," as mentioned above, you would write on the slip of paper, " Index, how to compile an," and place after it the folio of the page. You proceed thus until you have exhausted all the subjects, and then sort out the slips alphabetically, placing them in order. When you have, say, all commencing with " A " together, you sort them out into alphabetical order, working up to three letters. Thus, suppose you find " Arabian," " Arrow," " Army," " Art," you would sort these " Arabian, Army, Arrow, Art ". By working thus you will sort all the slips into alphabetical packs, and these must be numbered in one corner to guide the printer as to the sequence. Take care to cut off the number of the slip by a distinct parenthetical mark from the reference figure to the folio. There are many other details in indexing which will soon be learned in actual practice. Elaborate indexes are compiled on a cross reference principle. Thus, in such a passage as this, "Chasing lions in Africa," we should have three entries, as "Lions, chasing in Africa," " Chasing lions in Africa," and " Africa, chasing lions in ".

Index-making is not badly paid in connection with the more important books of history, travel and science, but it is most laborious and time-consuming work, and it must be perfectly done. An index must be positively without any errors. It is a kind of discipline in accuracy for the young writer, and may, and occasionally does, introduce him to something better, and if a publisher has nothing better to offer a young aspirant than indexing, let him take it and do it well. Rousseau himself, with all his eloquence, spent many tedious hours copying music, and he who does well in the little things of literature, may when he least expects it be promoted to something infinitely better. Anyway, indexing is honest literary work, and it is far better than pestering editors and others to insert articles or matter of little or no worth for nothing but the gratification to the vain writer of seeing himself in print. Alas! that is a very barren joy in itself. It is said that Dickens, when first he saw his work in type cried with joy and pride, but the tyro who ultimately succeeds is pretty sure to look back at last with amusement at the idea of there being any special glory in getting into print. One thing I am sure of, and that is, that the young writer should above all things, stoutly resist working for nothing. If his "copy" is worth printing, it is worth paying for. The scale may be low, but *some* payment should be insisted on, and that as a matter of principle and of justice to those who write for actual bread. In conclusion, I would say a parting word on the contemporary novel and its influences. Fiction is very obviously drawing within its charmed focus most of the best intellectual activities and forces of the times, and the novel is a kind of crucible wherein theories of life, morals, and of government, principles of all kinds, and almost everything that greatly engages the thoughts or attention of men and women is being cast and brought forth thence to be *tried* by the consensus of the vast and ever-increasing body of novel readers. Then again, be it well borne in mind that an overwhelming proportion of the best—and unhappily, all the worst—sentimental and æsthetic forces of the day now find expression, not by submitting to the trammels of metre or rhyme, but simply by being expressed in the novel, which has thus come to be to some extent, a sort of newspaper folded and bound in book form, of the spiritual yearnings, the mental aspirations, and especially of the mental pessimism and discontent of the age.

It has been said that if Shakespeare lived in these days he himself would have chosen the novel as his favourite vehicle of thought, and, however this may be, no one now disputes the enormous power that the contemporary novel exercises upon all or most of us. We know very well that the novel is little less than omnipotent in the home, where it operates as a subtle but determining force in more or less educating our wives, daughters, and sisters, and in thus moulding women the novelist naturally very powerfully influences men, too, and thus very greatly affects the ultimate destinies of the whole nation for good or evil. I can very well imagine that an observant foreigner taking notes among us might, on gaining a complete knowledge of the ordinary home-life of the normal British family, declare that in England the novel was very much what the priest used to be in France before the present era of hard rationalism and deadly animal luxury set in—and he would be very correct.

It is, I think, the average rather than the extraordinary novel—the novel easy to read and easy to understand, the novel that amuses and demands little or nothing of mental effort on the part of the reader—that exercises perhaps the most determining influence in the aggregate. I am fully aware that the intellectual oligarchy of each age is moved chiefly by works of absolute genius informed by certain definite purposes, but the greatest effects of contemporary fiction must be looked for among the Million, and we are now face to face with a coming democracy which unhappily prefers quantity to quality, and will pay little heed to the culture of the intellectual oligarchies unless that culture happens to be pleasing to the ideas of the many. The Million, in one word, now evinces unmistakably a most intense passion for fiction. Now the power of the novel that circulates freely among *average* girls and women of the day—those who have in themselves little or no substratum of culture, or even of principle—must of necessity produce there its very greatest effects ethically. Readers of this type insensibly form such characters as they ultimately acquire from their favourite fiction. Yet they rarely, if ever, have the least suspicion that in their novel-reading they are really and truly passing a crucial and determining course of self-education in opinion, sentiment, principle, and general moral character.

It must be remembered that to very many among us a novel is a kind of play-at-home, a play without external theatre or any of the visible circumstance of the stage, but a play whose subject is human life all the same. Precisely the same intense desire for some " new thing " that sent Athenians to listen in their out-door theatre to the last *jeu d'esprit* of Aristophanes now urges the British maid or matron as often as she possibly can to turn to a novel.

Opening the book is like drawing up the drop-curtain, and the reader silently revels in the drama played out with a multitude of pleasing details by the puppets of the novelist.

Pause and consider a moment what all this really means. Suppose we could, by some superhuman agency divest some of our novel readers of *all* they have acquired from their studies in the pages of fiction. Think what utterly empty-headed, vapid, soulless creatures many would then become. Some, indeed, would be found quite destitute of all general information beyond what was conveyed directly to them by the eye and ear—teachings of their circumscribed, monotonous existence. It would then appear plain enough that in these days of highly organised life, elaborately sub-divided and much differentiated, that, *minus* fiction, many persons would be absolutely stupid, and utterly uninformed in any high intellectual sense, and would simply move in narrow grooves, quite ignorant of, and indifferent to, all beyond. It is, in fact, through the *borrowed experiences derived* from the pages of fiction, that the great majority of the nation is educated mentally and morally. In an infinitely less complex civilisation, our forefathers as a body lived fuller lives, and had very much more personal knowledge of and regard for each other than is the case now among corresponding classes. Isolation as now known in our huge and utterly unneighbourly towns and cities did not exist, and as there was practically with the vast majority no time at all devoted to reading, very much more time was devoted than now to converse one with another, and thence to actual *personal* and so, *sympathetic* experiences of life. All is changed now. The word "neighbour" has little or no meaning, and sympathies have to be invented for us by our novelists, who thus in a sense supply what is so terribly wanting in our average, conventional, monotonous existence. Circumstance and experience in the pages of the novelist give to thousands illusory or vicarious interests in life, and supply a sequence of metaphysical emotions which operate powerfully on the formation of character. Thus it has come about that fiction now does to a great extent what fact formerly did in moulding the minds of the masses.

Who does not know orderly, well-kept, middle class homes, where life, but for the blessed distractions of fiction, would be but a monotonous round of meals, dressing, and visiting, and of strictly ceremonious parties with regulation music, and absolutely conventional conversation? Homes where, but for the imaginings and creations of fiction, the heart would never know one generous throb, or the mind evolve one heroic thought—homes where enthusiasm or impulse are unknown, and all is congealed into what is correct and decorous. But for fiction, I say, such homes would be simply the abode of a dull, stupid, intellectual and spiritual atrophy.

Shakespeare it is who tells us that—

Home-keeping youths have ever homely wits—

and doubtless in his days the timid or simple soul who clung tenaciously to the narrow limits of his little village had "homely wits," but now how great a change has been effected by the magic of the novelist's wondrous art. Let an individual be bound, as so many thousands are, to the Ixion wheel of a monotonous and an exacting toil—one, perhaps, admitting of no variety, and precluding by its very nature the full experiences and ripe results of a larger life— and see what fiction can do for him or her. In the sweet hour of well-earned leisure the wand of the novelist is waved, and up goes the dull, grey, dismal curtain of monotony as the first page of the book is turned. The toil-worn, jaded worker, all vapid in mind and worn out in body, is at once transported into new and surprising scenes of delightful activity and life impossible for the reader ever to enter in reality, and verily all the more charming on that account.

Characters crowd on the stage thus created, and for a while the tired, world worn and weary soul revels in a realm of fairyland, where, however, the fairies are wondrously real, and where the scenes delineated are so presented as to constitute the mere reading of fiction the nearest approach to a life of *personal* experience that the wit and ingenuity of man can possibly devise.

This is, however, but a faint and feeble picture of what contemporary fiction really is in its influential effects on the nation generally. In the pages of this manual I have shown through a series of sketches of all phases of literature, from the newspaper paragraph to the book, that, after all, the novel is that form of literature which constitutes *the* literary power of the age I have tried to lay down some principles and rules for the guidance and information of the young, and knowing how potent a spell fiction exercises over the vast majority of literary aspirants, I would earnestly ask all who take up the pen of the story-teller to recognise the great responsibility which rests upon them as makers, in some sense, of human character through the novels they write.

ADVERTISEMENT.

INDEX.

INDEX.

THE END.

London   DIGBY & LONG, 18 Bouverie Street, Fleet Street, E.C.

18 BOUVERIE STREET,
FLEET STREET,
LONDON, E.C.

THE NEWCASTLE DAILY CHRONICLE (the great Newspaper of the North), in speaking of good and wholesome fiction, refers to the "*high reputation that Messrs. DIGBY & LONG enjoy for the publication of first-class novels*".

A Selection from the List of Books

PUBLISHED BY

Messrs. DIGBY & LONG.

NOVELS.

A Modern Milkmaid. By the author of "Commonplace Sinners". In 3 vols., crown 8vo, cloth extra, 31s. 6d.

Wildwater Terrace. By REGINALD E. SALWEY. In 2 vols., crown 8vo, cloth extra, 21s.

"We strongly advise novel-readers to make the acquaintance of 'Wildwater Terrace'. An eminently readable and interesting book."—*Court Circular.*

"A powerful story, with some peculiarly dramatic situations and a good deal of descriptive skill."—*Literary World.*

John Bolt, Indian Civil Servant: A Tale of Old Haileybury and India. By R. W. LODWICK, late Bombay Civil Service. In 2 vols., crown 8vo, cloth extra, 21s.

Mrs. Danby Kaufman of Bayswater. By Mrs. MARK HERBERT. Crown 8vo, cloth extra, price 6s. Postage, 4½d.

"Is cleverly written."—*Vanity Fair.*

"We found ourselves reading it from beginning to end without any failure of interest."—*Spectator.*

"Exhibits considerable originality of conception." *Lead* .

Novels (*Continued*).

Beneath Your Very Boots (Second Edition)   By C. J.
HYNE.   Crown 8vo, cloth extra, price 6s.   Postage, 4½d

"By no means miss reading 'Beneath Your Very Boots'. The story is absolutely new and cleverly worked out "—*Athenæum*

"A capital story capitally told is our verdict on this novel   . The present tale is full of briskness and go from cover to cover, nor does the plot lack skill."—*People.*

"Mr. Hyne's story is distinctly entertaining, because it is both original and sprightly."—*Yorkshire Post*

Leslie.   By the Author of "A Modern Milkmaid," "Common-
place Sinners," &c.   Crown 8vo, cloth extra, price 6s. Postage, 4½d.

The Kisses of an Enemy.   By MARY SMITH.   Crown 8vo,
cloth extra, price 6s.   Postage, 4½d

Mrs. Lincoln's Niece.   By ANN LUPTON, author of "Whis-
pers from the Hearth".   Crown 8vo, cloth extra, price 6s. Postage, 4½d.

The Belvidere ; or, The Warning Maiden.   By WILLIAM
DWARRIS   Crown 8vo, cloth extra, price 6s.   Postage, 4½d.

"A well-written and really powerful story "—*Newcastle Daily Chronicle*

"   . The interesting adventures of this light-hearted heroine "—*Athenæum*

"There is plenty of incident in this story . .   and no little sensational excitement "—*Bookseller*

Bairnie.   By L. LOBENHOFFER, author of "Fritz of the Tower,"
"Theodor Winthrop,' &c.   Crown 8vo, cloth extra, price 6s. Postage, 4½d.

"Is in point of style and workmanship above the average of many more pretentious works   The characters very well drawn   . So distinct and true to life "—*Standard.*

"Gracefully written, and the sketches of north country character are sympathetic and amusing   . A decidedly clever story, while the end is as peaceful and pleasant as the entire tale ought to have been, so as to have main-tained throughout its idyllic tone."—*Graphic.*

Eric Rotherham.   By Mrs. WILLIAM D HALL, author of
"Marie".   Crown 8vo, cloth extra, price 6s.   Postage, 4½d

"It is a story which can be read and enjoyed   It is graced with some pretty groupings, many pleasing incidents, and not a few well-drawn word pictures and character sketches "—*Liverpool Mercury.*

Three Friends.   By YRLA.   Crown 8vo, cloth extra, price 6s
Postage, 4½d.

"The author may be congratulated on his success in producing a very readable story "—*The Times.*

"The friends of the title are three Prussian officers during the time of the wars with Napoleon early in the century, and they go through a number of surprising adventures, which are certainly told with spirit."—*Queen*

Novels (*Continued*).

The Sandcliff Mystery. By SCOTT GRAHAM, author of "The Golden Milestone" and "A Bolt from the Blue". Crown 8vo, cloth extra, price 6s. Postage, 4½d.

"The tale has some decidedly good things in it in the way of strong situations and epigrammatic comments "—*Athenæum.*

"There is plenty of literary ability distributed over 'The Sandcliff Mystery'. . . Its author, indeed, commands an easy style, as 'The Golden Milestone' proved clearly enough, and has rather a turn for sarcasm."—*Academy.*

Lord Allanroe ; or, Marriage not a Failure. A Novel with a Purpose. By B. E. T. A. DEDICATED BY SPECIAL PERMISSION TO THE RIGHT HON. W. E. and MRS. GLADSTONE. Crown 8vo, cloth extra, price 6s. Postage, 4d.

"We earnestly wish all novel writers would rise to the height of their responsibilities as the author of 'Lord Allanroe' has done Throughout its spirit is pure and healthy. No one can rise from the perusal of the book and still hold that Christian marriage entered on and lived through with knowledge of its duties, and the will to discharge them, is a failure One of the charms of the book lies in this, that while the general plan is full of romance, the details breathe of actuality . . . books such as this, which combines strength with delicacy, reality with romance, high theory with humble practice."—*Freeman's Journal.*

Paul Creighton. By GERTRUDE CARR DAVISON. Crown 8vo, cloth extra, price 6s. Postage, 4½d

Two Daughters of One Race. By C. H. DOUGLAS Crown 8vo, cloth extra, price 3s. 6d. Postage, 3d.

"The author of this book has produced an interesting story The quiet, natural style of the writer is a refreshing change from some of the feverish literature of the day."—*Publishers' Circular.*

Saved by a Looking Glass. By EDGAR H WELLS. Crown 8vo, cloth extra, price 3s. 6d. Postage, 3d.

"The tale is certainly cleverly planned, and the incident of the looking glass is highly ingenious."—*Literary World.*

"A story of a highly sensational crime developed with considerable skill "—*Leeds Mercury.*

Hidden in the Light. By EUGÈNE STRACEY. Crown 8vo, picture boards, price 2s. ; cloth extra, 3s. 6d.

The Mystery of Askdale. By EDITH HERAUD. Crown 8vo, cloth extra, price 3s. 6d. Postage, 3d.

"Must be ranked as sensational, is refined in style, graphic in portraiture, and dramatic in effect This last is to a great extent produced by the mystery of an alleged ghost, a mystery which is very ingeniously contrived and very satisfactorily cleared up "—*Morning Post.*

"The theme has been skilfully treated by the authoress. The reader will find in this tale interesting occupation."—*Illustrated London News.*

Novels (*Continued*).

Where Have You Been? By KATE THOMPSON. DEDI-
CATED TO HARRY NICHOLLS, THE ACTOR. A work wherein
the conjunction "and" does not once appear. Crown 8vo,
cloth extra, price 3s. 6d. Postage, 3d.

"Clever."—*National Observer.*

"An amusing story."—*Academy.*

Within an Ace. A Story of Russia and Nihilism By MARK
EASTWOOD. Crown 8vo, picture boards, price 2s.; cloth
extra, 3s. 6d. Postage, 4½d.

"Is an exciting and well written story by one who evidently knows Russia
and Russian ways. . Most interesting, and we recommend the book as one
of the best of its class we have recently come across. The author can tell a
story, and he knows his ground so well that his characters and scenes are true
to life and nature."—*Pictorial World*

"Briskly told, full of adventurous incidents."—*Saturday Review.*

The Mysteries of Deepdene Manor. By FRANK MAU-
DUIT. Crown 8vo, cloth extra, price 3s. 6d. Postage, 3d.

"This is one of the best written and most interesting romances we have
had before us for a long time."—*Perthshire Advertiser.*

"It is full of incident, plot and counter plot, and the harmonies are well
preserved. The work is written in a firm style."—*St. Stephen's Review.*

The Mysterious Stranger. A Romance of England and
Canada. By CHARLES H. THORBURN. Crown 8vo, cloth
extra, price 3s. 6d Postage, 3d.

The Dream that Cheated. By FREDERICK GALES. Crown
8vo, cloth extra, price 3s. 6d. Postage, 3d.

Forreston. By NEWTON TEMPEST. Crown 8vo, cloth extra,
price 3s. 6d. Postage, 3d.

The Redhill Mystery. By KATE WOOD, author of "Lorry
Bell," "A Waif of the Sea," "Winnie's Secret," "Uncle
Reuben's Secret," &c. Crown 8vo, cloth extra, price 3s. 6d.
Postage, 3d.

Laura Montrose. By ADELA MAY. Crown 8vo, cloth extra,
price 3s. 6d.

"The story is well conceived, and is related with much fluency, and not a
little vivacity."—*Public Opinion.*

Ivor; or, Woman's Wiles. By EDITH BENT. Crown 8vo,
cloth extra, price 3s. 6d. Postage, 3d.

"A pretty piece of melodrama."—*Saturday Review*

"The story runs smoothly, and is thoroughly readable."—*Publishers'
Circular*

Novels (*Continued*).

Scenes in the Life of a Sailor. By LAWRENCE CAVE. Crown 8vo, cloth extra, price 2s. 6d.   Postage, 3d.

Waiting for the Dawn. By C. M. KATHERINE PHIPPS, author of "The Sword of de Bardwell," "Who is the Victor?" and "Douglas Archdale". Crown 8vo, cloth extra, price 2s. 6d.   Postage, 3d.

"A pretty graceful little story have we here, full of humane feeling, and impregnated with genuine piety   There are touches in it which reveal a considerable reserve of literary force in the authoress."—*People.*

" A tender little romance of love and parting "—*Literary World.*

Only a Fisher Maiden. By A. MACKNIGHT.   Crown 8vo, cloth extra, price 2s. 6d.   Postage, 3d.

" The author tells the story with commendable delicacy, and there are passages of genuine pathos "—*Manchester Guardian*

"A pretty pathetic story, written in simple language and most readable "—*Dundee Courier.*

A Gipsy Singer. By WARREN TOWNSHEND, author of "The Fantoccini Man". Crown 8vo, cloth extra, price 2s. 6d. Postage, 3d.

Through Sorrow's Fire. By M. MARSH.   Crown 8vo, cloth extra, price 2s. 6d.   Postage, 3d

Sam Saddleworth's Will (Second Edition).   By M. SCOTT-TAYLOR, author of "Boys Together".   Crown 8vo, picture cover, price 1s.   Postage, 2d.

" A brightly-conceived and well-told story.   The opening scene is very happily invented, and the group of the expectant legatees is decidedly well done."—*Manchester Examiner.*

A Woman put to the Test. By PERCY G. EBBUTT, author of "Emigrant Life in Kansas"   Crown 8vo, paper cover, price 1s.   Postage, 2d.

"Gives the world a novel of a highly sensational character.   The plot is excellent in every way."—*St. Stephen's Review.*

In Vain. By EDITH HENDERSON, author of "A Human Spider"   Crown 8vo, paper cover, price 1s.   Postage, 2d.

" The main incidents are ingenious, and we do not remember to have met with their like before.   The story will wile away a passing hour very pleasantly."—*Academy.*

Chiel and I ; or, Our Wedding Tour. By BOTH   Foolscap 8vo, paper cover, price 1s.   Postage, 2d.

"There is a fresh style of writing about the whole of this little book. The clever character sketches of people whom they encounter in their wanderings prove a pleasant variety to the poetical descriptions of scenery and foreign cities "—*Morning Post*

Novels (*Continued*).

Three Christmas Eves (New Edition). By H. HUDDLE-STONE, author of "Under the Black Flag". Foolscap 8vo, paper cover, price 1s. Postage, 2d.

"The tale will be found good reading during the long winter evenings. Interesting, well written, and skilfully worked out."—*People*

A Family Tradition, and other Stories. By Lady MABEL EGERTON. Foolscap 8vo, paper cover, price 1s.; cloth extra, 1s. 6d. Postage, 2d.

"This volume of tales is, from first to last, pleasing. Many of them are marked by genuine feeling and pathos."—*Morning Post*

"Contains a series of short, graceful, and interesting stories, well constructed, and revealing a considerable amount of literary force in the authoress. The book is suitable for both old and young."—*Western Daily Mercury.*

Mrs. Grant's Mysterious Lodger, and other Stories. By GERALD GRAHAM. Foolscap 8vo, paper cover, price 1s. Postage, 2d.

"Mr. Graham has filled his little volume with five good stories."—*Whitehall Review.*

Was Her Marriage a Failure? By RUPERT BROWNLOW. Crown 8vo, paper cover, price 1s. Postage, 2d.

"Written with an animation of style which carries the reader pleasantly through."—*Scotsman*

My Vicars. By a CHURCHWARDEN. Crown 8vo, picture cover, price 1s. Postage, 2d.

For the Good of the Family. By KATE EYRE, author of "A Step in the Dark," "A Fool's Harvest," "To be Given up," &c. Crown 8vo, paper cover, price 1s.

"It is a prettily-written love story."—*Scotsman*

"Far above the average. It is a lively, pleasant, clever story, and worthy of the author of 'A Fool's Harvest'."—*Newcastle Chronicle.*

"A place among entertaining novelettes may be freely accorded to Miss Eyre's 'For the good of the Family'."—*Academy.*

No Way But This. By E. M. MANNING. Crown 8vo, paper cover, price 1s. Postage, 2d.

"The story is told in graphic language, and with a succinctness which is especially commendable in this busy age."—*Dundee Courier.*

"The plot is ingeniously conceived."—*Morning Post.*

"The tale is a creditable production."—*Public Opinion*

Wax. By ALIEL HOPE. Crown 8vo, picture cover, price 1s. Postage, 2d.

"The incidents are original, and the interest never flags."—*Hereford Times*

POETRY AND THE DRAMA.

The Rise and Reign of Chaos. A Scientific Epic By W. J. SPRATLY, author of "Religion; or, God and All Things". Crown 8vo, cloth gilt, bevelled boards, gilt edges, price 7s 6d. Postage, 3d.

A Vision of the Orient. A Poem. By S. R FOREMAN. Crown 8vo, cloth extra, price 4s. 6d. Postage, 3d.

Sonnets and other Poems. By W. G. GRIFFITH. Crown 8vo, cloth extra, price 2s. 6d. Postage, 3d

"Mr Griffith's 'Pegasus' has some pretty paces . One lights on passages of genuine poetic feeling, suggesting that the author has the stuff in him to make a name for himself among England's minor poets."—*People*

Juverna A Romance of the Geraldine, The MacCarthy More, The O'Donohue, &c., in the Annals of Desmond and its Chiefs, in the South of Ireland. By H DEVEREUX SPRATT Crown 8vo, cloth extra, price 2s. 6d. Postage, 3d.

"The metre throughout the poem is stately and dignified, being admirably suited to the subject, and the verses rarely halt, so that Mr Spratt may be congratulated on his poetic effort."—*Cork Examiner.*

"The incidents are told with a great deal of fire."—*Literary World.*

Francesca and other Poems. By WM J NOTLEY. Crown 8vo, cloth extra, price 2s. 6d. Postage, 3d.

"The first is a story of Southern jealousy and murder, told in rather good riding rhyme The 'Epistle to Miranda' is smooth and scholarly 'To My Pipe' is rather clever."—*Graphic.*

"Mr. Notley is endowed with the gift of expressing himself clearly and to the point, and his language is graceful and vigorous"—*Belfast Morning News*

Ruy Blas. Translated from the French of Victor Hugo. By W. D. S. ALEXANDER. Crown 8vo, cloth extra, bevelled boards, price 3s. 6d. Postage, 3d.

"A really fine English version Mr. Alexander's is, we think, the best translation that has yet been done."—*Pictorial World*

"The task of rendering this fine play into English verse has been very efficiently performed."—*Graphic.*

Ocean Echoes from the Lincolnshire Coast. By LISTER WILSON. Demy 16mo, picture cover, price 1s. Postage, 1½d.

"These poetical 'Echoes' from the Lincolnshire Coast will linger—some of them at least—long after the voice which awoke them is hushed. Much of it is pretty and graceful, and it is full of touches which prove the writer to be a genuine lover of nature."—*Western Daily Mercury*

Poetry and the Drama (*Continued*).

Poems. By ARTHUR STANLEY. Crown 8vo, cloth extra, bevelled boards, price 2s. 6d. Postage, 3d.

Poems. By G. A. POWELL. Crown 8vo, cloth extra, price 5s. Postage, 3d.

Religion ; or, God and All Things. An Epic. By W. J. SPRATLY, author of "The Rise and Reign of Chaos". Crown 8vo, cloth gilt, bevelled boards, gilt edges, price 2s. 6d. Postage, 3d. BOOK I. BY WAY OF PROLOGUE

"A striking poem . Full of beauty "—*People.*

"Musical passages . . Well coined phrases. . . . Homeric speeches."—*Scottish Leader.*

"As a repetitionary vowelist, Mr. Spratly is virtuous compared with Milton."—*Glasgow Herald*

Joseph and his Brethren. A Trilogy. By ALEXANDER WINTON BUCHAN, author of "An Evangel of Hope," "The Song of Rest, and Minor Poems," "Poems of Feeling," and "The Vision Stream ; or, Song of Man". Crown 8vo, cloth extra, price 3s. 6d. Postage, 3d

"Tells the familiar Scriptural Story in dramatic form."—*Scotsman*

"A powerful dramatic poem It is something to say of a work of this kind that it compelled a reviewer to read it *through*."—*Literary World*

"Presents Mr. Buchan as a poet in a new and pleasing light."—*Glasgow Herald.*

St. Valentine's Gift. A Poem. By EDWARD A. KEAN. Crown 8vo, cloth extra, price 3s. 6d. Postage, 3d

Poems. By M G. BUDDEN. Crown 8vo, cloth extra, price 1s. 6d. Postage, 2d.

Idonea. A Poem. By E. W. BEWLEY, author of "Dudley Castle," "Perla," &c. Crown 8vo, cloth extra, price 2s. 6d. Postage, 2d.

"A poem showing grace and force "—*News of the World*

"Is wonderfully good. . . . Idonea visits the field of battle as an angel of mercy "—*Perthshire Advertiser*

"It is gracefully written, and the vicissitudes through which King Stephen and Queen Matilda pass are presented in a romantic and readable form."—*Midland Counties Herald.*

The Wrong of Death. A Realistic Poem By L HARLINGFORD NORTH. Demy 16mo, loose parchment, price 2s. 6d. Postage, 1½d.

"A highly finished and beautiful poem displaying both refinement and culture."—*Newcastle Chronicle*

RELIGIOUS.

An Evangel of Hope ; or, Readings in the Spirit. By ALEXANDER WINTON BUCHAN, author of "Joseph and his Brethren," &c., &c. Crown 8vo, cloth extra, price 4s. 6d. Postage, 3d.

"A volume of careful and often fine thoughts on the Gospel, with much in it that commands our agreement."—*Baptist.*

"There is a good deal of suggestive matter in the book."—*Church Bells*

Truth and Trinity : the New Reformation, with Remarks on the Eastward Position (Second Edition). Crown 8vo, cloth extra, price 2s. 6d. Postage, 3d.

The Battle of Death. By the Rev. J EDGAR FOSTER, M.A. (Cantab.), author of "A Fallen Woman, and other Sermons," "The Battle of Life," &c. Crown 8vo, stiff paper cover, price 1s. 6d. Postage, 3d.

Contents :—Life—Beauty—Domestic Life in England—Religion—Poverty—The Battle of Death—The Peasant—Money.

"The addresses are characterised by a strong moral and religious tone They abound in healthy teaching and in good advice. The style is fluent, oratorical, and occasionally grandiloquent."—*Literary World.*

"There is a ring in the style of these lectures "—*Sunday School Chronicle*

"Highly rhetorical in form full of apt illustrative anecdote and quotation that they make pleasant reading."—*Christian Leader.*

Arrows Shot at a Venture ; or, Short Plain Sermons for Country Folk. By the Rev. B. S. BERRINGTON, B.A Crown 8vo, cloth extra, price 3s. 6d. Postage, 3d

"Plain, practical sermons. They are well adapted for village sermons "—*Ecclesiastical Chronicle*

"They are pointed, practical, and often suggestive."—*Christian Commonwealth*

"They are couched in homely but attractive language, and they treat of nearly all the troubles and temptations to which we are all exposed The author's object is not so much to touch the mind as to touch the heart To the heart he appeals, and we believe that the quiet perusal of this little work may bring about that holy, heavenly calm which is the best preparation for guidance to the land of perfect peace "—*Christian Globe.*

Religious (*Continued*).

A Fallen Woman, and other Sermons. By the Rev. J. EDGAR FOSTER, M.A. (Cantab.), author of "The Battle of Death," "The Battle of Life," &c. Crown 8vo, stiff paper cover, price 1s. 6d. Postage, 3d.

"The style of these sermons is crisp, and many of the points are put with clearness and great force."—*Christian Commonwealth.*

"Mr. Foster's sermons have a manly ring about them."—*Literary World.*

"These sermons may be read with profit."—*North British Daily Mail.*

The Life and Times of John Knox. By the Rev R. WILKES GOSSE, B.A. Crown 8vo, cloth extra, price 2s 6d. Postage, 3d.

"The story of the great reformer is told in an interesting narrative presented on well-printed pages."—*Sunday School Chronicle.*

"Mr Gosse has done his work with admirable care, brevity, and accuracy."—*Glasgow Herald.*

"A thoroughly appreciative biographical sketch."—*Aberdeen Daily Free Press.*

"A plainly-written summary of events in the life of the great reformer."—*Scotsman.*

Socialism and Religion ; or, Thoughts after Reading Mr. Carpenter's Ideal England. By an ONLOOKER. Fcap 8vo, stiff paper cover, price 3d. Postage, ½d.

Joy in the Morning. Tracts for the Million. By M. J. CURTIS Price 6d. per doz. Postage, 1d

BOOKS FOR THE YOUNG.

My First School. A Story. By EUSTACE J. C. BAIRD. Crown 8vo, cloth extra, picture cover, price 2s 6d Postage, 3d.

"It is an amusing record of incidents and adventures which were by no means uncommon twenty or thirty years ago   Though the book may suggest some mischievous pranks to youthful readers, it is calculated to do them more good than harm, as the graver faults common among boys, such as selfishness, meanness, deceit, and lying, are exposed in their true colours."—*Morning Post.*

"A capital boy's book; the scenes and incidents are full of fun, but the humour is free from coarseness and vulgarity."—*Newcastle Daily Chronicle.*

The Experiences of Richard Jones. By J. JONES. Crown 8vo, cloth extra, price 6s. Postage, 4½d.

"It is impossible to read much of the book without being persuaded that it is all true, and that some usher did go through experiences which are related in this volume as truthfully as may be."—*Saturday Review.*

"Richard Jones is not exactly a perfect character, but somehow with all his faults he interests the reader."—*Public Opinion*

Books for the Young (*Continued*)

The Cold Heart. Translated from the German of WILHELM HAUFF. By AGNES HENRY. Crown 8vo, cloth extra, price 2s. 6d. Postage, 3d.

"Young people will be delighted with this legend of the Black Forest "— *Pall Mall Gazette*

"The simple, lively way of relating the story so that the reader's interest is kept up to the end of the book is well maintained in the translation. The book, strongly bound and printed in clear type, may be recommended as a suitable present for the young ones "—*Literary World*

"A sound moral which will recommend it to many readers."—*Scotsman*

Ethel Granville. A Story for Girls. By EUPHROSINA. Crown 8vo, cloth extra, price 2s 6d. Postage, 3d.

"Charming story of the lives of two sisters "—*Newcastle Daily Chronicle*

"The heroine is all that is self-sacrificing and devoted in woman "—*Bookseller.*

Desborough Hold ; or, the Secret Chamber. A Story for Boys. By an OLD BOY. Crown 8vo, cloth extra, price 1s. 6d. Postage, 3d.

"Boys will find lively maritime adventures and a fatal secret chamber in 'Desborough Hold' "—*Graphic.*

"The story of Nelson's death is once more retold, and the secret chamber is as mysterious as any boy could well desire Its secret was only explained to the eldest son of the house on his attaining the age of eighteen, and this led to an unfortunate tragedy, a youth locked in there perishing as did the Lady Lovel, through inability to discover the mystery of the spring which could release him "—*Lloyd's Newspaper.*

"A pretty, stirring little story for boys The central incident is almost too sad in its details, but the tone of the book is excellent, and boys will certainly appreciate it "—*Literary World.*

The Knight of the Golden Key, and other Stories. By Mrs. S. D. WILSON Demy 16mo, cloth extra, price 1s. 6d. Postage, 1½d

"We have a very favourable opinion from a competent authority on this book In each of its three stories a useful lesson is taught in the form of a prettily imaginative allegory What 'the Golden Key' is we must leave readers to learn for themselves, only promising that Knight Allcrod's search will be found very interesting "—*Literary World.*

"Is a pretty moral allegory, such as should please young readers The tale of the two fairies, Sunnylocks and Snowdrop, is very prettily told "—*Public Opinion*

Phil: A Story of School Life. By ALFRED HARPER. Crown 8vo, cloth extra, price 3s. 6d Postage, 3d.

TRAVEL.

In Other Lands. By CAROLINE GEAREY, authoress of "French Heroines," and "Daughters of Italy". Crown 8vo, cloth extra, price 3s. 6d. Postage, 3d.

"Is a charming book of travels."—*Morning Post.*

"A pleasantly written book of reminiscences of foreign travel."—*England.*

"Will be heartily welcomed. The authoress writes pleasantly and gives some really clever sketches. We can thoroughly recommend the book."—*John Bull*

"Right pleasant reading is this book of travels."—*People*

"May be read with interest."—*Manchester Guardian.*

"This is a bright little book. Miss Caroline Gearey has a facetious and jaunty style which carries her along in a pleasant and easy manner."—*Lady's Pictorial.*

"Her book is readable throughout, and the introductory chapter on 'The humorous side of travel,' is especially amusing."—*Queen*

"Forms very pleasant reading. It has an easy, gossiping style of narrative, and goes at express speed all the time."—*Scotsman.*

"This is a nice chatty book of travel."—*Freeman's Journal.*

Pen and Ink Sketches, from Naples to the North Cape. By EMILY A. RICHINGS, authoress of "Rambling Rhymes". Crown 8vo, cloth extra, price 2s. 6d. Postage, 3d.

"I congratulate Miss Emily A. Richings on her little book . . . The sketch of the blue grotto of Capri is particularly well written, but the chapters on 'Milan,' 'Pisa,' 'St Peter's at Rome,' 'An Alpine Ascent,' and 'A Picnic in Sweden,' will serve to call up pleasant memories to many, and to others an ambition towards greater enterprise in their holiday jaunts."—*Star*

"This volume of souvenirs of travel will repay reading. Miss Richings is an intelligent observer, and describes what she sees accurately."—*Bookseller.*

"Familiar scenes described in fine language, abundantly seasoned with trite observations."—*Literary World.*

A Holiday Tour in Austria. By the Rev. HENRY PELHAM STOKES, M A, F.R.G.S. Picture cover, price 1s. Postage, 1½d

Romance of a Swiss Tour. By J PROCTER. Crown 8vo, cloth extra, price 2s. 6d. Postage, 3d.

A Transatlantic Voyage. By WILLIAM HAMILTON. Illustrated. Crown 8vo, cloth extra, price 2s. 6d. Postage, 3d.

Sketching Tours; Rambles in the West of England. By a Tourist. Fcap 8vo, paper cover, price 6d. Postage, 1d.

"A chatty little book."—*Western Antiquary*

MISCELLANEOUS.

Chronology and Analysis of International Law.

By WILLIAM PERCY PAIN, LL B (University of London), of the Inner Temple, Barrister-at-Law. (First Class Studentship of the Inns of Court for Jurisprudence and International Law, Hilary Term, 1880.) Crown 8vo, cloth extra, price 3s. 6d. Postage, 3d

"Should be of considerable use to the student of international law."— *Law Times*

"A valuable handbook for the student of international law. The arrangement of the book is admirable Students will find it in all respects a most admirable help to the study of the great subjects to which it relates."—*Scotsman.*

"Mr. Pain's book will be of use even to the general reader in affording him an orderly exposition of the chief rules which govern the intercourse of States."—*Graphic*

"Students are under a debt to Mr Pain for this useful manual . . a book which will be useful not only to the student of international law, but to the student of history."—*Scottish Law Review*

"Mr Pain gives students preparing for examination an ingeniously arranged chronological series of statements which, by means of abbreviations, ranges each event under a category in his analysis of international law, and at the same time gives it a brief description or reference."—*Law Journal.*

Essays on Popular Subjects : Gladstone, Ritualism and Ritual—The Fallacies of Darwinian Evolution—The Modern Strafford and his Policies of Consolidation—Socialism in the North : its Aim and its Fallacies By SAMUEL FOTHERGILL. Crown 8vo, cloth extra, price 2s 6d. Postage, 3d.

"These forcible essays . . . merit unstinted praise . . . telling to the last degree . . author's brilliant criticism of Darwinism Can recommend this volume unreservedly . . well worth reading."—*St. James's Gazette.*

"This is a comprehensive title fully borne out on perusal of the book."— *Lloyd's Weekly Newspaper.*

"The writer's style is clear, and a perusal of the Essays will do good."— *Stamford Mercury*

"Ably and vigorously written."—*Literary World.*

"Mr. Fothergill treats upon matters which have come under popular discussion with a clearness that will be commended Ritual and Ritualism had already been discussed at length, but this author has some sensible words to say about them, and the 'Fallacies of Darwinian Evolution' are successfully exposed in an article devoted to them. 'The Modern Strafford,' and 'Socialism in the North,' will engage many readers' attention."—*News of the World.*

A Child's Solar System. PLANETS, COMETS, METEORS, and FALLING STARS. With numerous Explanatory Diagrams By A. B. OAKDEN. Demy 16mo, limp cloth, price 1s 6d. Postage, 1½d

DIGBY & LONG'S ALBION LIBRARY.

A Popular Series of Shilling Books of Fiction, issued at short Intervals.

VOLUME I.

A Mexican Mystery. By W. GROVE. Crown 8vo, picture cover, price 1s.; cloth extra, 1s. 6d. Postage, 2d. (Tenth Edition.)

The *Saturday Review* says "'A Mexican Mystery' demands attention as a rarity . romance remarkably clever and ingenious . scenes thrilling without being exaggerated A shilling's-worth which nobody will read and yet pretend that he has not had the value of his money."

VOLUME II.

The Wreck of a World. By W. GROVE. Crown 8vo, picture cover, price 1s.; cloth extra, 1s. 6d. Postage, 2d (Sixth Edition)

"Well told. Altogether an interesting book "—*Vanity Fair.*

"Quite as clever as the author's first attempt."—*Newcastle Chronicle*

VOLUME III.

Within an Ace. A STORY OF RUSSIA AND NIHILISM By MARK EASTWOOD. Crown 8vo, picture cover, price 1s.; cloth extra, 1s. 6d Postage, 2d (Fifth Edition.)

"Is one of the best novels we have read for a long time It describes with extraordinary power the execution of a Nihilist at St Petersburg, the imperfect carrying out of the death sentence, the unfortunate or fortunate man's revival in the doctor's dissecting-room, his escape to his comrades, his recovery, flight across the Continent to Germany, and finally his happy marriage. This book is a perfect oasis in the desert of fiction "—*Star*

"The opening is thrilling and startling enough, but when we think the story must necessarily flag it gathers fresh intensity, and, as a sensational novel of Nihilist Russia, it is decidedly a success The style is good and the characters are lifelike "—*Public Opinion*

VOLUME IV.

A Human Spider. By EDITH HENDERSON, author of "In Vain" Crown 8vo, picture cover, price 1s ; cloth extra, 1s 6d Postage, 2d.

A complete Catalogue of Novels, Travels, Biographies, Poems, &c., with a critical or descriptive notice of each, free by post on application.

LONDON·

DIGBY & LONG, PUBLISHERS,

18 BOUVERIE STREET, FLEET STREET, E.C.